Shiny Broken Pieces

A TINY PRETTY THINGS *Novel*

SONA CHARAIPOTRA AND
DHONIELLE CLAYTON

HarperCollins *Children's Books*

First published in the United States of America by HarperCollins Publishers in 2016
First published in Great Britain by HarperCollins *Children's Books* in 2020
HarperCollins *Children's Books* is a division of HarperCollins*Publishers* Ltd,
HarperCollins Publishers
1 London Bridge Street
London SE1 9GF

The HarperCollins website address is:
www.harpercollins.co.uk
1

ISBN 978–0–00–839281–9

Printed and bound in England by CPI Group (UK) Ltd, Croydon CR0 4YY

MIX
Paper from
responsible sources
FSC
www.fsc.org   FSC® C007454

To our girls—Kavya and Riley

Cassie

SOMETIMES YOU WANT SOMETHING SO badly you're willing to do whatever it takes to get it. Your mind stretches your dream out in front of you like putty, folding it into perfect shapes. Your soul whispers anxiously, *You aren't meant to do anything else.* Your heart pumps blood and adrenaline and hope. Each turn, each leap, each role onstage brings you one step closer, reminding you that ballet is one with your heartbeat. Hard-tipped shoes lift your body above everyone else, making you weightless and ethereal.

Because that's what ballerinas are supposed to be. It's what I want to be. Have to be. I'll do anything to get there. Almost.

Two pills stare up at me like eyes, smooth and oblong. Full of promises. They're packed into a vitamin case like pointe shoes in a storage bin, begging to be used. Their glossy coatings gleam in the café's overhead lights. I click my finger along their surface, then taste my fingertips and the acidic bitterness they leave behind. *Just take one to see if it makes a difference.*

The other girls flutter past me. It's the thick of November, and they're talking about things like Thanksgiving break and the latest movie and the boy they think would make the best Nutcracker Prince. All things familiar and mundane, but since I moved back from London, it all feels so foreign. Here, the bodies are smaller, lighter, a little more delicate than mine. I can't quite blend in like I did there. They hate me for it. That's what it feels like, anyway.

"Are those your little secret? The reason you're so good?" Bette slides into the seat beside me. She scoots close, so close I can smell the hair spray she uses. We are the same shade of blond. Or we were. Now mine is tinted purple because someone put hair color in my conditioner.

"No, they're just vitamins." I scan the café for Alec. RAs staple paper turkeys up on the café bulletin boards, and the lunch ladies set out low-fat pumpkin yogurt as a treat. When I look back at my tray, Bette's staring me down. I'm still not used to being around her alone. I should feel grateful that she sits with me when the others won't. It's like her presence at the table creates a protective bubble around me. It's safe, secure, and impenetrable, except that now I'm trapped in here with her. "I don't do pills." I try to keep my voice from having a judgey tone.

Bette's hand goes to her collarbone, her fingers following the little chain down to her locket. She wears it everywhere, like it's a glittering ruby she wants us to look at, instead of just a dull and faded thing, the size of a half dollar. "Then what's in the case? What were those?"

I want to ask her why she cares so much. But here at the American Ballet Conservatory, no one asks her those types of questions.

"Vitamins. For extra energy," I lie, looking down at the little diet pills. The food in this café is different from that at the Royal Ballet School, and even though I've only been here two full months, all the adjustments make me feel like I've lost my center in a pirouette. I'm up three pounds from where I want to be. My eyes volley between the *petit rats* stacking their lunch trays on the conveyor belt and tables full of Level 7 and 8 dancers stressing over what to eat before ballet class. But I can't dodge Bette's strong glare.

Her eyebrow lifts. "Just two vitamins?" She takes the case from me before I can close it. She peers at the pills, like she's trying to decipher some code, then hands it back to me, done with her little detective game.

"My daily dose. I take them with food." I snap the case shut and slip it into my dance bag, hoping it ends this conversation. Eleanor walks toward the table, clearly planning to sit with us. I almost sigh with relief. But Bette flicks her hand like she's shooing away a fly zooming too close to the water she sips. Eleanor slips away, just like that. "She could've sat with—"

"It's fine," Bette says. "I'm not really in the mood to deal with her today." She drums her nails on the table, scans it for my case. "You know, you don't have to keep things from me." Her blue gaze sinks into mine. "You're new, so I want you to have a friend here. We're practically family now. I told Alec I'd look out for you. He thinks it's a good idea."

I want it to be a good idea. I want to have a confidante here. I miss my friends from Royal Ballet. She inches even closer. Her shoulder rubs against mine and we slip farther into the bubble. She looks left and right, then unclasps her necklace, taking it from around her neck. Laying it down on the table in front of us, she opens the locket delicately. A perfect circle sits in the tiny space, a blue outer layer of pills surrounding a smaller white one. The white ones look identical to mine. It makes me wonder how they can all share similar shapes and sizes but promise different things.

"I don't really do pills, either," she says. "Only when I really need them. That extra boost to get through Morkie's corrections. Even my sister and others in the company take these. It's not a big deal." She pats my leg in just the right way. Café noises underscore her words. "A little advice—don't ever run out of energy. The Russians will take things away as quickly as they give them."

"I know," I say, thinking about how I was cast in *La Sylphide* with the Level 8 girls. Mr. K says I'm one of the most gifted dancers he's seen at my age. But I'm not sure if I should've left Royal Ballet to come here. She slides her locket closer to me. "What are they?"

"Adderall. Gives you energy." Her eyes grow larger as she studies mine, looking for a response.

"Side effects?"

"Seriously? Your loss." She snaps the locket shut and puts it back around her neck. She snatches her offer away as quickly as she'd given it, but manages a smile to soften it, like she's doing me a favor. "Just trying to help."

"Thanks, but—"

Alec and his dad, my uncle Dom, walk into the café and straight to my table. Uncle Dom sweeps me up into a hug, and Alec slips into my empty seat.

"How are things, Cass?" Uncle Dom's worried tone brings tears to my eyes, but I rub them away before he sees them. His eyes are the same as my mom's. He touches my hair. "The purple's almost gone. I kind of liked it."

He's trying to make me laugh, but I struggle to smile.

It's one of the many pranks the girls have pulled on me in my two months here, along with the vinegar-soaked pointe shoes, shredded tights, and stolen mail—the love letters from my boy-friend, Henri, in Paris. Just thinking about that makes the tears come again, but I can't cry. Not here. Not now.

"I'm okay," I say, wanting it to be true. He kisses my forehead and smiles at my brave face. "The beginning is always rough, right?"

"Hang in there, Cass." Uncle Dom gives me one more hug, then turns and leaves the café. I miss him instantly.

Alec stands, too, looking at his phone. "Ready to go?" He's asking both of us, but looking at Bette.

Ballerinas shuffle out of the café, headed to stretch before class. I turn back to the table. Bette is holding my vitamin case in her hands. "Don't forget these. They slipped out of your bag." She sets them on the table, then sidles past me. "See you in there." Alec wraps his arm around her neck, gives me a goofy grin, and they leave the café.

I guzzle water from the fountain, but still have trouble swallowing the pills down. I think of them dissolving in my stomach, helping me be the best I can be.

In the studio, I find a space tucked away near the back, far from the others—especially Bette. I pull out my ballet slippers. I sprawl along the studio floor and start a long, deep stretch, my legs in a wide V, my arms up and over my head, then extended down to my toes. We warm up for twenty minutes, then Madame Genkin claps her hands, calling us to attention.

We work at the barre, completing exercise after exercise to warm up our legs and feet and core. Madame Genkin smiles at me as she inspects my *tendus*. "Your line's perfect, Cassandra. Everything in place."

I flush with warmth and feel like today might be a great one.

She moves back to the center of the room, and the mirrors on either side make it look like there are a thousand of her. "Time to work in the center. Change into pointe shoes."

We scramble to our bags, tape our toes, pad them, slip on our pointe shoes, and lace the pale pink ribbons around our ankles. We leap up and down, warming up the shoes. The thumping and thwacking of pointe shoes fill the room. Madame Genkin gives Viktor piano chord instructions.

"Girls, we will do a short combination that ends with four turns. Two times each before the next pair begins from the corner. I need to examine your spotting."

There are low groans.

"Cassie and Bette first, followed by June and Sei-Jin."

We both come to center and stare at each other through the mirror. We echo: pale blond hair, ice-blue eyes, and even our builds are similar.

Madame Genkin shows us the combination—a series of *piqué* turns from the corner to the center, a jump left and a jump right, three pirouettes into a *balancé*. Bette drops into a deep *plié*. She flutters her arms out. I mimic her.

The music starts. She's quick and balanced, her rhythm falling in line with the music effortlessly, like she's done this a million times. I extend my leg forward into another turn, and I absorb the music. My mind quiets: the worries, the criticisms, the faces in the studio windows, everything drifts away. I catch myself in the mirror as I do each turn—the long, lean lines; the twirl of pink and black and cream, like a prima ballerina. Like the ballerina I was born to be.

The lines get fuzzier with each turn. My limbs feel heavy and thick. I can't get them to lift as quickly as I want them to. I spin faster, pushing myself to spot. Madame Genkin claps along the beat. I'm too slow. In the mirror I see Bette, the hot-pink bow of her mouth as it purses. A wave of heat trickles over me, and I feel like I've lost my strength, floundering as I do another turn.

My eyelids flutter. I fight with their heaviness. The need to sleep overwhelms every part of me.

I drown under the spell of the music. Bette catches me, smiling as she whispers, "It's okay," when my body slumps toward her, heavy and cumbersome. Like she was expecting this. Like she knew it would happen all along.

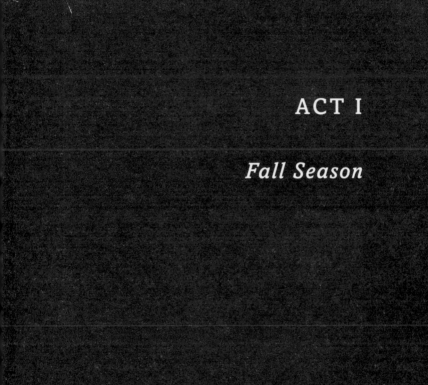

ACT I

Fall Season

1.

Bette

I'M BACK TO THE BASICS: fifth position in front of
the mirror. The Russian teacher my mother hired—Yuliya
Lobanova—rotates my left hip forward and backward with
small wrinkled hands. It pinches and burns, and I relish the heat
of the pain. It reminds me that underneath all this pale pink, my
muscles are strong and trained for ballet.

Yuli's gray-streaked hair is swept into a bun, still obeying
the elegant, upward pull. Bright green eyes stare back at me in
the wall of mirrors in my home studio. "You keep sitting in this
hip, *lapochka*." She used to be one of the stars of the Maryinsky
Theater. I had her picture on my bedroom wall, young and bold
and startlingly beautiful. "Turn out, turn out."

I push harder to please her and myself. To be strong again.
To be *me* again.

"Lift! Higher, higher."

Practicing five hours a day, seven days a week keeps me

from having to think about everything that happened last year. The pranks, the drama, Gigi's accident, and my suspension are replaced with pirouettes, *fouettés,* and *port de bras.*

"Show me you're ready," she says, happy with my new and improved ultra deep turnout.

I step toward the mirror and lengthen my spine as long as it can go. I am still the ballerina in the music box. I am still an ABC student. I am still me.

My mother keeps paying my tuition, and she's on the phone with Mr. K and Mr. Lucas every night battling to get me back into school. "Bette did not push that girl. She's completely innocent. And you have no substantial proof that my daughter was the only one *teasing* Miss Stewart." She'd said the word *teasing* like I'd called Gigi fat. "Still, we've settled with the Stewarts. They've been well compensated. So Bette should be back in school as soon as classes start. The school can't afford any more scandal. The Abney endowment has always been generous to the American Ballet Conservatory and the company. The new company building is proof of that. I mean, it's called Rose Abney Plaza, for god's sake!" She never even paused to let whoever was on the other line get a word in.

"Now, turn for Yuli." My ballet mistress doesn't care about rumors and truths. She's focused on practicalities, the here and now.

I take a deep breath and exhale as she starts to clap. The smell of my hair spray—powdery and sweet—fills my nose and the room. For a second, I'm back in Studio A for the very first time, the sun pushing through the glass walls while I swing my leg into a turn.

I'm a new Bette.

A different Bette.

A changed Bette.

Last year is a blur of images that I don't want to deal with. If I let my brain drift away from focusing on my ballet lessons, the memories squeeze in like a vise: losing two soloist roles, losing Alec, losing the attention of my ballet teachers, being accused of pushing Gigi in front of a car, being suspended from school.

"Faster!" Yuli hollers. Her claps and shouts fold into my movement. "Out of that hip. Don't lose your center."

I can't afford to lose anything else. My mother won't tell me how much it cost her to settle with Gigi's family or how much Mr. K's been charging to keep my slot open. But I know it's more money than Adele cost in all her years of intensives, private lessons, and special-order dancewear. I'm the expensive one now. But it's for all the wrong reasons.

"Now, opposite direction."

I hold my spot in the mirror, whipping my head around and around. Sweat drips down my back. I feel like a tornado. If I had my way, I'd be returning to ABC, ready to take down everyone and everything in my path.

In a week, everyone moves into the dorms. Eleanor will settle into our room. *My* room. I should be there.

Not here, in a basement studio that might as well be a prison.

Level 8 is the year that matters. This is the year we finally get to do it all—choreograph our own ballets, travel the country (and the world) for audition season, explore other companies. But the main thing, the most important thing, is that American

Ballet Company's new artistic director, Damien Leger, will be visiting ballet classes and figuring out who his new apprentices will be. Only two boys and two girls will make the cut. I *need* to be there for that.

After my last pirouette, Yuli jostles my shoulder. "You ready to go back . . ." It's half a question and half a statement.

"Yes," I say, breathless. "I am ready."

"Madame Lobanova." My mother's voice travels down the staircase and bounces off the mirrors in the studio. The slur beneath the words makes me cringe. "No more today. Bette has company."

"Yes, of course, Mrs. Abney." Yuli gathers her things and kisses my sweaty cheek. I want to reach out, touch her shoulder, tell her not to leave. But she slips away before I can say anything.

"Bette, freshen up," my mother says once I reach the top of the stairs. She's perched over the kitchen island and halfway through a glass of red wine. She points it up in the air, directing me to my room.

I go upstairs and take off my leotard and tights. I gaze out the window and look down on Sixty-ninth Street to see if there's a car parked out front that I might recognize. Nothing. I take a two-second shower, change into a dress, then ease down the front staircase. Justina squeezes through the French doors in the living room.

"Who is it?" I whisper.

"Man from your school, I think. And a lady." She pulls my hair away from my shoulders, smoothing it. Her fingers are warm, her touch light. "Be my good girl in there, okay?"

14

I peek through the French doors before committing to opening them. The back of Mr. Lucas's blond head stares back at me. I nearly choke.

"Oh, there you are." My mother waves me in.

I take a deep breath and exhale, like I'm standing in the wings, preparing to take my place center stage. I step into the room and sit across from him.

A man like Mr. Lucas doesn't just show up at your house unannounced. He's with a woman who isn't his wife. She's got one of those haircuts meant to make her look older, more sophisticated, less hot in a beach-babe way. She probably wants to get people to pay attention to more than just her very blond hair and the fact that her shirt is a tad too tight, showing off her large breasts.

"Hello, Bette." Ballerinas are mostly flat-chested, so I'm lucky not to have her problem.

"Hi, Mr. Lucas." I dig my nail into one of the curved rosewood armrests, leaving a half-moon shape behind. One evening, not long from now, my mother will settle into this high-backed chair in front of the fire and ask Justina for her nightly glass of wine. She will run shaky, wine-drunk fingers across the indentations and yell about it.

"This is my new assistant, Rachel." He motions at the young woman. She gives me a slight smile. He unfolds a thick bundle of papers and flashes them at me. "Your mother showed me this." He's holding the settlement agreement. All the things I supposedly did to Gigi are spelled out in black and white. The little typed script makes them look sicker, more disgusting and official than they actually were.

"You know, I still don't understand how any of this happened." His brow crinkles in the same way Alec's does when he's confused.

"I'm sorry," I blurt out because that's what the Abney family therapist told me to lead with. I flash him a half smile. I try to show him I'm a different Bette. That I've learned whatever lesson they've been trying to teach me. That I'm ready to go back to normal now.

"Do you know what you're sorry for?"

"Messing with Gigi."

My mother steps in. "Dominic, we don't need to go back through this entire incident. That can't be why you came here."

"It's okay, Mom. I'm taking responsibility for my part."

"Things have been settled, and you didn't—"

"Mom, it's fine." It feels good to clip off her words the way she's done to mine so many times. She takes hurried sips from her wineglass and motions Justina over with the bottle. Mr. Lucas's assistant shifts uncomfortably in her seat and tugs at her shirt. Mr. Lucas refuses a glass of wine or any of the expensive cheese my mother goads Justina into offering.

"You're lucky it wasn't tragic," he says in the gentlest way possible. The words hurt even more when they hit me softly. The sting burns long into the silence in the room.

"Can I come back to school?" I ask.

"No," he says, and his assistant looks at me like I'm this fragile thing that might break at any moment. "We've deliberated long and hard, and we still can't let you return. Not at this point."

"But—" My mother rises out of her chair.

"What would it take?" My eyes bore into his. I hold my body perfectly still but my heartbeat hammers in my ears. I lift my rib cage and drop my shoulders like I'm ready to jump off this chair into the most beautiful firebird leap he's ever seen.

"This"—he shakes the papers—"doesn't fix it. Not all of it. Not by a long shot. I don't understand you girls. The boys don't behave this way."

He's right. But I want to remind him of how different it is to be a female dancer, treated like we're completely replaceable by choreographers, while the boys are praised for their unique genius, their dedication to being a male ballet dancer when the world might think it's unmasculine. He rubs a hand over his face and passes the settlement papers back to my mother.

"I didn't push Gigi." My words echo in the room. They feel heavy, like they're my very last words.

"If you're innocent, prove it."

I can. I will.

2.

Gigi

STUDIO D BUZZES LIKE DRAGONFLIES swarming in the September sunshine. Everyone's chatting about summer intensives, their new roommates, and their ballet mistresses. The parents are comparing ballet season tickets or grumbling about the rise in school tuition this year. New *petit rats* storm the treat tables, and other little ones steal glances, cupping their hands over their mouths. I hear my name whispered in small voices. None of the other Level 8 girls are here.

Just me.

I should be upstairs, unpacking with the rest of the girls on my floor. I should be breaking in new ballet shoes to prepare for class. I should be getting ready for the most important year of my life.

Mama's hand reaches for mine. "Gigi, please be an active participant in this discussion." I'm back to reality, where Mama has Mr. K pinned in the studio corner. He looks pained. "Mr. K, what have you put in place so that Gigi is safe?"

"Mrs. Stewart, why don't you set up an appointment? We can go into more detail than we did in our last phone call."

Mama throws her hands up in the air. "Our last conversation was all of ten minutes. Your phone calls have been—how can I put it? Lackluster. You wanted her back here. She wanted to be back here. You told me she'd be safe. I am still unconvinced."

Her complaints have been following me around like a storm cloud. *Why would you ever want to go back to that place? The school is rife with bullying! Ballet isn't worth all this heartache.*

A younger dancer walks past me and she whispers to her friend, "She doesn't look hurt."

I look at my profile in one of the studio mirrors. I trace my finger along the scar that peeks out from the edge of my shorts. It's almost a perfect line down my left leg, a bright pink streak through the brown.

A reminder.

Mama thinks the scar might never go away completely, even though she bought cases of vitamin E oil and cocoa butter cream made for brown skin. I don't want it to go away. I want to remember what happened to me. Sometimes if I close my eyes too long or run my finger down the scar's raised crease, I'm right back on those cobblestoned streets, hearing the metal-crunching sounds when the taxi hit me, the faint blare of sirens, or the steady beep of the hospital monitors when I woke up.

I flush with rage, hot and simmering just under my skin.

I will figure out who did this to me. I will hurt the person who pushed me. I will make them feel what I went through.

Mama touches my shoulder. "Gigi, participate in this conversation."

I watch her anger grow.

"She's still in the hall with all those girls." Mama's tone is pointed.

"Each student lives on a floor with the others in their level. The Level 8 hall has been traditionally the most sought after of them all," Mr. K says in that soothing voice he uses with benefactors and board members. "We wouldn't want to isolate her."

"She is already isolated by virtue of what she looks like and what happened to her."

"Mama, it's fine. It's where I need to—" She shushes me.

Parents turn their attention to us. In this room, Mama sticks out like a wildflower in a vase of tulips, in her flowy white dhoti pants, tunic, and Birkenstocks. They all take in Mama's exasperated hand gestures and facial expressions, and how calm Mr. K remains under all her pressure. He even smiles at her, placing a gentle hand on her shoulder, like he's inviting her into a *pas de deux*.

"I assure you that we're doing everything we can to make sure she is safe. She even has her own room this year—"

"Yes, and that is much appreciated, but what else? Will there be a schoolwide program initiated to address bullying? Will teachers be more mindful in addressing incidents? Will security cameras monitor—"

"Aside from Gigi having her own personal guard, we will do as much as we're able to," he says.

She jumps like his words are an explosion and shakes her

head, her billowy afro moving. "Do you hear that, Giselle? They don't care. Is ballet really worth all this trouble?"

I touch her arm. "Mama, just stop. We've had this conversation a million times." A flush of embarrassment heats every part of my body. "Please trust me. I have to be here."

No one moves. Mama's eyes wash over me. I chew on the inside of my cheek, afraid that she'll change her mind and take me back to California. I want to tell her that she doesn't understand what ballet means to me. I want to remind her that I almost lost the ability to dance. I want to tell her that I can't let Bette and the others win. I want to tell her that I'm stronger than before, and that those girls will pay for what they did. I have been thinking about it since the day I left the hospital. Nothing like what happened last year will happen to me again. I won't let it.

Mr. K winks at me and moves to stand beside me. He places a very warm hand on my shoulder. "She's *moya korichnevaya*. She's strong. I need her here. She was missed during summer intensives."

His words fill up the empty bits of me. The tiny broken parts that needed a summer of healing, the ones that needed to know I am important here. I am supposed to be dancing. I am supposed to be one of the great ballerinas.

It took all summer to heal from a bruised rib, fractured leg, and the small tear in my liver. I stayed in Brooklyn with Aunt Leah and Mama, dealing with countless X-rays and doctor visits, weekly CAT scans and concussion meds, physical therapy twice a day after getting out of my cast. And, of course, counseling to talk about my feelings about the accident.

I worked too hard to get back to this building.

Mama touches the side of my face. "Fine, fine." She pivots to face Mr. K. "I want weekly check-ins with you. You will have to make yourself available." He walks Mama to the beverage table. She's smiling a little. It's a tiny victory.

Warm hands find my waist. I whip around. Alec's grinning back at me. I practically leap into his arms. He smells a little like sunscreen.

"They're calling you the comeback kid, but can I just call you my girlfriend?"

I laugh at his terrible attempt at a joke. Young dancers look up from combing through their colorful orientation folders, full of papers that list their current ballet levels, new uniform requirements, and dorm room assignments. I grab him and push my tongue deep into his mouth, giving them something to stare at.

I didn't get to see Alec a lot this summer. Dance intensives kept him too busy. Phone calls and video chatting and texting took the place of hanging out. I almost forgot what he tasted like, felt like, smelled like.

He pulls back from kissing me. "I've been texting you."

"My mom's been interrogating Mr. K." I point behind me. Mama and Mr. K are still talking.

He groans. "Wouldn't want to be him."

"Nope."

"You all right?"

"I'm great." I stand a little taller.

"Nervous about being back?"

"No," I say, louder than I mean to.

He touches my cheek. My heart thuds. The monitor around my wrist hums.

"I've missed you." He takes my hands in his and turns me like we're starting a *grand pas*. He lifts me a little, so I'm on my toes. My Converse sneakers let me spin like I'm on pointe. It feels good to partner and dance, even if it's just playing around. Being hurt made me miss dancing every single day.

Everyone clears away, giving us some space. Enthralled, they watch us.

We do the *grand pas* from *The Nutcracker*. Our bodies know every step, turn, and lift without the music. I can hear it in the rhythm of his feet and how he reaches for me. Invisible beats guide our hands, arms, and legs. The music plays inside me. He sweeps me into a fish dive.

"You're even better than you were before," Alec whispers as he brings me back down, his mouth close to my ear.

His words sink deep into my skin, making it feel like it's on fire. The room claps for us. Mr. K beams. Mama smiles.

No one will take this away from me ever again.

3.

June

IT'S LATE BY THE TIME Jayhe and I finally get to school. Jayhe double-parks his dad's delivery van and hops out to unload my stuff. Usually my mother drops me off, and we suffer the whole hour trek in from Queens in an uneasy silence, her disapproval seeping into every nook and cranny of her silver car and my brain.

But this year, everything is different.

I have a boyfriend. Now that I know about Mr. Lucas, my mother doesn't have the power to control me anymore. My hard work is finally paying off. Summer intensives went well, and I'm ready to be on top this year. It's finally my time. I plan to enjoy it.

I look up at the towering buildings that surround Lincoln Center. The conservatory sits nestled in the northwest corner of the complex, in the shadow of the most beloved performance space in the most important city in the world. Sometimes I still have to pinch myself to believe this is actually my life—that at this time next year, I'll be one of two apprentices at the American Ballet Company. Well, if all goes according to plan, anyway.

Which it will.

"Hey, you going to help?" He rushes around to the front of the building with the first batch of stuff. His too-long hair falls into his eyes and his forearms flex as he lifts the heaviest boxes first.

"In a second." I breathe in the scents of dogwood trees, the fountains, and even the pretzels sold at the food truck on the corner, so familiar, so comfortable, like a second skin. Jayhe pauses all his hauling and pulls me into a deep kiss. It makes me want to leave those boxes on the stairs and get back into the van, to let him drive us off somewhere. It erases the world around me until I'm forced to take a breath.

As I open my eyes and see the school buildings rising behind his head, part of me aches for the daily tedium of school, like muscle memory. I crave the countless ballet classes, the endless rehearsals, the control that comes with calorie-counted cafeteria meals, and even Nurse Connie's scales.

I stay with the van as he finishes unloading. I spot other girls—ones with moms and dads—lugging boxes inside. A father teases his daughter about the rocks he claims she filled the boxes with. "Dad!" She giggles, her eyes lighting up with love and laughter. The word *dad* thuds inside me like an anchor, and I think of Mr. Lucas, even though I shouldn't associate that word with him. My dad. A flush of embarrassment zips through me when I think of the email I sent him this summer and the voice mails I left on his phone that went unanswered. I won't make that mistake again. I can't even remember why I tried to talk to him.

I hear a giggle again and see one of the younger Korean girls point in my direction. I stare right back at her until she walks up the school stairs. I look left and right for Jayhe, but he's still MIA. I wonder if Sei-Jin's here already, if her aunt dropped her off early like she usually does. Her texts popped up on Jayhe's phone this summer, and I know he didn't respond. I checked. I feel bad for a second, but I have to look out for myself, even with him.

I'm afraid to ask him about the exact details of their breakup. What did he tell her? How did she react? How did they leave it? He probably let her down easy, with his usual diplomatic touch. But did he mention my name? Deep down, I don't really want the answers to those questions. I shouldn't want to know. I shouldn't care. It doesn't matter. But it does.

His cheeks are rosy when he comes back down, and there's a bit of light sweat running down the side of his face. The old June would think it's gross, but I kind of think it's sexy. Everything about him is sexy—the depths of his eyes, the charcoal on his calloused fingers from his hours of drawing, the way he says my name—especially when he's annoyed.

"There's only a small box left." Jayhe sets it on the curb. "You got it?"

"Yeah." I want to be in two places at the same time: here on this curb with him and upstairs in my new single, unpacking.

Jayhe's phone rings and for a tiny second, the paranoid place in my heart and brain thinks it's Sei-Jin. He speaks in a flurry of Korean, but I hear the words *restaurant, grandmother,* and *busy.* I've learned more Korean from hanging out with him these past few months than my mom taught me in all of my sixteen years. He would cup his hand under my chin and make me speak the words back to him—wouldn't kiss me till I got them just right. I always had to ask him in Korean—*kiss-jwo.* No Korean, no kissing. The thought makes me smile.

He hangs up. "I left your stuff in the foyer," he says. "They wouldn't let me upstairs. Something about no boys on the girls' dorm floor even on move-in day." The irritation must show on my face, because he touches my cheek and grins. "Parent volunteers are taking it up." His hands wander to my waist. "I'm really glad you got a single this year."

"Me, too," I whisper, suddenly feeling embarrassed. Gigi got a single this year because of her injuries, and that means I get one, too, by default. It'll finally give me and Jayhe some space. Part of me thrills at the idea of sneaking him past the RAs and anyone else who's watching, at the chance of getting caught, at the possibility of people knowing that a boy wants me. That Jayhe wants me.

I grab the last box, the one with my teakettle, and my rolling bag. I give him one more kiss and head around to the front of the building.

Ten minutes later, keys in hand from the front desk, I'm ready to make myself at home. I take the elevator up to my new floor—twelve—where only the senior girls live. But when I finally get up to my room, the door is wide open—and someone else's stuff is sprawled all over it. Well, most of it. A pink frilly comforter covers one of the beds, ballerina posters hang on the wall, and postcards from Paris are already lined up on the bulletin board above the pair of desks. When I look across to the other side, there, entangled on the bare mattress, are Cassie and Henri, sweaty and giggly and flushed like little pink pigs.

Henri nods, acknowledging my presence, and tries to get back to nuzzling Cassie's neck. But she shuts him down cold, sitting up straight and readjusting her deep V-neck sweater.

"About time you got here," she says, perfectly content and casual, as if she was expecting me. I was most definitely *not* expecting her. "Nurse Connie came looking for you. You missed dinner. Apparently she thinks I'm your keeper." Her voice is as cold as those ice-blue eyes.

"What are you doing in here?" I ask.

"I was supposed to have the single, but I gave it up, you know, because of Gigi's situation. I don't want to make things harder on the poor girl." She frowns at me.

"But—"

"Look, I'm not happy about it either. But it's not like you're entitled to a single." Her words are clipped, sharp, with a hint of a British accent popping up now and again. "Anyway, it's too late to do anything about now, right, E-Jun?" She stretches out my name like it's a heavy, foreign thing she has to carry. A burden.

"Everyone calls me June," I say, which she should know because we're not strangers.

"Cute," she replies flatly. It makes me feel like I've said my American name is Star or Poppy or Rainbow.

Then she lumbers off my bed, as if it just occurred to her. When she catches me frowning, she shrugs. "He knows I hate messing up my covers."

Henri smirks. "Among other things," he adds, then winks in my direction. Gross. He gives her a deep, grabby good-bye kiss before he slinks off. I shudder at the thought of him. Something about that boy has always been off to me, and I hate the idea of him being here, in my space. Well, *our* space, I guess.

I seethe in silence as I start unpacking slowly, mentally willing away Cassie and all her stuff. There's just so much of it. The closet is two-thirds full already, and she's got stacks of books— Machiavelli, Marx, and other political things, along with all the major ballet books—lining her shelf. In the corner, a small cube is filled with dance gear—dead toe shoes, leotards, ribbons, warm-ups. My side of the room—what's left of it—is stark in comparison.

When Cassie started at the conservatory in tenth grade, she'd take half her ballet classes with us in Level 6 and the other half in Level 7 with the junior girls. No one really knew her. No one really wanted to know a girl who was *too* good of a dancer. She was Alec's cousin—my cousin, I realize with a start—and everyone knew that she'd been specifically recruited from the Royal Ballet School. She was that good. But then, after what Bette and the girls did to her—the hair, the shoes, and especially the lift accident with Will—she disappeared. Now here she is, completely invading my space.

I unpack the box marked "tea" and plug in the electric kettle, filling it with bottled water, hoping it will relax me. I open up my new glass-lidded tea box—a gift from Jayhe—and pull out a small satchel of chamomile and lavender that he prepped for me. "It'll help you chill," he always tells me. As if anything could really help with that tonight.

"Careful with the kettle," Cassie announces. "Fire hazard and all."

"I've had it for years and nothing so far."

I don't realize I've said it aloud until she whips around and comes right up in my face. "I don't want any attitude from you." She stares down at me, her skin pulled taut over her skull, like Charlie, our bio class skeleton. I wasn't exactly nice to her when she first came to ABC. When I flinch, she laughs. "Mr. K pretty much promised me the Sugar Plum Fairy, and that basically guarantees one of the apprentice spots. So you better not mess with me."

My heart sinks into the depths of my stomach, where it's sloshing along with the bits of grilled chicken I ate off my sandwich. It all threatens to come up again, right then and there. I rush to our private bathroom, locking the door behind me.

Cassie's put down a bubblegum-pink mat that's enough to get me nauseated. I run the tap, waiting until I hear the room door close with a thud. She's gone. Thank God.

There's a scale in the corner. The last time I checked my weight was during summer session. Mom doesn't keep scales around the house. I try to focus on breathing and my face in the mirror. But I can see it out of the corner of my eye.

I can't resist. I need to know. The numbers quickly shift from 0 to 80 to 90 to 100 and then 110, 112, 115. I shift my weight a little and they scramble again, settling, finally, at 108. That's heavier than I've ever been. By far.

I swallow down the sob that's rising in my throat. I hear Cassie's nasty words in my head again. Seconds later, I'm cradling the toilet, the tile floor cold and hard under my hands and knees, the familiar scent of lemon disinfectant triggering that same response instantly. With it comes relief, a sense of control. I tell myself it's just the bile and burning that's causing the tears. No matter what Cassie says, I'll be the Sugar Plum Fairy when that cast list goes up, just like I'm supposed to be. My performance in *Giselle* last year made that happen.

This is my year. This is my turn. I'll be the lead soloist. I'll be chosen for the company. I'll do whatever it takes.

4.

Bette

I'M SITTING ACROSS FROM MY father in his favorite steak house downtown. The restaurant, with its high ceilings and marble floor, echoes with snippets of stuffy conversations and the clink of wineglasses being set on white-clothed tables. Ours overlooks the Hudson, and while he chews, I watch a boat sail up the edge of Manhattan, headed north. You can forget this place is an island when you live close to the large expanse of Central Park cutting right through the middle.

He's grown his beard in. White hairs poke through the blond. He lives about eight blocks from our house on the Upper East Side, but I haven't seen him in months. My mother insisted on having it that way, ever since I was twelve and he bailed on Adele and me for a Christmas brunch, jetting off to the Turks and Caicos with his latest assistant girlfriend instead. But before that, he was around, sometimes, randomly, cooking breakfast in the kitchen on a Sunday morning or spending the afternoon reading the *Times*.

The *Times Magazine* pokes out of his bag under the table. I peep at it, wondering if it's a sign that things will go back to normal. I used to love reading it with him while Adele was busy in the basement, getting in extra rehearsals with the latest Russian expat ballet mistress my mother had hired. He'd tell me about the state of the world, explain it to me like I was a grown-up, like it should all make sense. And it did, the way he said things. I would fish those old magazines out of the trash to save in stacks under my bed.

Blood seeps out of his rare steak, and I watch it ooze out into the fluffy mounds of mashed potatoes. I push my salad around my plate, my appetite disappearing.

"I guess Adele isn't coming," he says after finishing his bite. Even though we've been sharing this awkward silence for forty minutes. Even though we both already knew that and ordered without her. Even though he's halfway through his steak. Even though she hasn't spoken to him in years. She won't even talk to me about it.

"She has rehearsals," I lie, not sure what she has planned this evening.

"What role is she dancing? What ballet are they performing again?"

He doesn't even realize that casting hasn't happened for the winter season yet.

"I don't want to talk about ballet." Our gazes finally meet, and it's like looking into my own eyes. Ice-blue and cold. Adele says I crinkle my nose like he does when I'm upset or I've said something rude.

"What do you want to talk about?" He motions for the waiter to bring him another Scotch and soda. I want to give him a list of off-limits topics: my mother, Adele, ballet, school, what I plan to do with my life, what actually happened last year, the reasons he's been away so long, why he left us, his latest girlfriend. Which means that we really can't talk about anything aside from the weather, which is relatively cold for a Sunday in the middle of September.

"Your tutor? How's that going?" There he goes again, with the interrogation. "The private ballet lessons? Your friends? Have you seen any of them?"

I don't answer. What is there to say? Nothing's changed, least of all him.

"The point of having dinner is to talk to each other," he says. "How's Alec?"

"I don't want to talk about that either." I fill my mouth with slimy lettuce tossed with too much low-fat salad dressing. I wish that I didn't still eat like a ballerina. I'm in the real world and not in the third-floor café at the American Ballet Conservatory. I could eat like a normal person—whatever that is—if I wanted to. But I have to stay in shape for when I get back to school.

My dad raised an eyebrow when I ordered salad—just salad—for dinner. He hasn't gotten used to the difference, still. We haven't had that many meals together since he left, and he still expects the little Bette that would order a kiddie burger or chicken nuggets when he'd pick me up from the conservatory for a visit.

Plates come and go before us, even a palate cleanser of mint leaves. I escape to the bathroom and open up my locket. I swallow a pill and I wait for some kind of focused calm to emerge after it hits my system. I wait for the warm flicker of relaxation. But it doesn't come. I want to wretch or scream or call Adele and cry, which would be the worst thing of all. I dread the *I-told-you-so* on the other end of that call.

She warned me about going to dinner with him. She told me I would end up disappointed. But she's always been my mother's girl, and I was always sort of his, until he left.

When I return to the table it's been cleared.

"Are we ordering dessert? They have a panna cotta I was thinking about trying." He thumbs the dessert menu.

"I shouldn't eat dessert, Robert." I test out using his first name to see how it will land on him. "I'm a ballerina."

"Robert? I'm your father." He waits for the accusations—"then act like it"—but I won't give him the satisfaction. He sets down the menu. The woman at the adjacent table hears the deep pinch in his voice and looks over at us. He clears his throat and leans forward. "Are we getting dessert tonight?"

"I'm a ballerina."

"Are you going to still be a ballerina?" he asks, his words clipped. I've clearly hit a nerve. "Your mother told me about the school's decision, Bette."

"Don't you think I know that?" Head high and eyes straight ahead, I make sure not to look away. He taught me that. "You all of a sudden care now what happens to me?"

"I've always cared."

"Then where have you been?"

His wide shoulders seem to jump with what I can only assume is surprised humiliation. I think about saying something to smooth over the anger, but my mind fills with other mean things to say instead. Since he left, our relationship has been a series of missed dinners and empty apologies and bank deposits.

"Your mother can make things quite difficult." He puts a hand under his chin, like the words coming out of him are too heavy for even his firm mouth to handle.

"Mom is difficult. No, she's terrible. And you left us there with her." I clutch the locket around my neck. It was his grandmother's. He gave it to me for my thirteenth birthday. My hands are shaky. The buzz of the pill is finally settling in and I am hyperfocused on the way he looks at me, the fact that he opens and closes his mouth more times than words actually come out.

A flicker of guilt flutters in my chest as I think about what it must've been like to be married to my mother. But I won't feel sorry for him. I can't. He *chose* to marry her. He left us with her. We didn't get a choice. So, no, he won't get any pity from me. Not now, not ever. "Have your panna cotta," I tell him. "I'll see you next time. Whenever that is."

The maître d', used to scenes like this, I guess, already has my slim red peacoat waiting for me and slips it over my shoulders as I walk out, my stride strong, not revealing the shakiness inside.

But once I'm out the door, my shoulders drop and my pace slows. It's exhausting pretending to have it together. I wait a few seconds, thinking he'll run after me and beg me to come back to the table. I had hoped—stupidly, I guess—that maybe, just maybe, today I'd find in my father an ally. Like the way we used to be. But no one comes outside. And now more than ever, I know that I'm in this on my own.

On Monday morning, after my mother goes off to the spa for her usual weekend recovery appointment, I call the lawyers' office. I pretend to be her—slurred, angry voice—and demand that the files from the settlement with the Stewart family be sent over for her review. They arrive within an hour.

I have the courier set the lawyers' boxes on the dining room table. In the dark, they are shadowy tombs. I turn the light up, pull open the drapes, and the boxes become less scary in a haunted-house way but more intimidating in a real-life way. My whole life is in these boxes, filed away forever, everything in them shouting that I was bad.

I riffle through the files. The first one has pictures of each person in my class, their names scrawled along the bottom in black marker. I set them out on the table like I'm a ballet master placing dancers into a piece of choreography.

Giselle Stewart

E-Jun Kim

Eleanor Alexander

William O'Reilly

Henri Dubois

Sei-Jin Kwon

Alec Lucas

I run my fingers across Alec's face, missing him. He hasn't called. Not once. I haven't exactly reached out to him. I couldn't bear the idea of calling him and being clicked to voice mail or sending a text and having it go unanswered.

I comb through the boxes and lay out all the evidence that led to the settlement with Gigi's family:

1) A copy of Henri's statement saying that he saw me push Gigi in front of that taxi.

2) Pictures of the crime scene: the street outside the club, the curb where we stood, the hood of the taxi bent with an indentation from Gigi's body.

3) The police report from that night.

4) A copy of Will's statement about past pranks I've pulled on other girls. Though there's no mention of the role he played in any of those pranks, of course.

Reading these just confirms what I know: I am the most hated person at American Ballet Conservatory. Maybe I deserve to be, according to the quotes from Will, Henri, and half a dozen other dancers, some of whom I've never even talked to.

"Bette is toxic."

"Bette has it out for anyone who is better than her."

"Bette's jealousy turns to madness."

"Bette terrorizes people."

I'm not supposed to be going through these files. The Abney family therapist said I shouldn't fixate on things that I don't have the power to change at this moment. But she should know by now that I don't listen, and I don't follow directions well unless they're doled out by Madame Morkovina. I wonder what Morkie thinks of me now. I feel a hot pinch in my stomach. One I can't ignore.

I look at a lawyer's crude drawing of the scene. They've used basic, almost stick figures to draw where I said everyone was standing that night. I'm on the curb next to Alec, Gigi, and Eleanor. Henri is off to the left or maybe it was the right. This summer my memories of the night skewed each time I was asked to replay them out loud for the lawyers. Sometimes Henri was on the right. Other times he was behind me. Sometimes Will lingered behind Gigi.

I bend the edges of Gigi's picture. The audition photo she took before getting accepted to the conservatory smiles up at me. Bright white teeth, happy eyes, and perfect sun-baked skin. I look at my own picture. My mother had a famous fashion photographer take it. I don't think I've ever been as happy as Gigi is in that single photo. I remember her first ballet class with us. She stuck out. It made me realize, for the first time ever, just how white the ballet world is. Even the Asian girls sort of blend in at initial glance, with their pale little arms and tiny frames and quiet personalities.

But not Gigi. She barreled into the room, her hair a burst of wild curls, pins between her teeth as she wrestled it into a bun, and she wore a hideous, multicolored leotard, totally ignoring the very specific ballet class uniform instructions in the conservatory packet we all received. I remember thinking she was gorgeous, despite it all. Her skin glowed like she'd just run three miles.

I close my eyes and can see her dancing. I see how loud it was. How riveted everyone was. How much fire she had in her movements. A hot and angry knot forms in my stomach. I throw her picture back in the cardboard box and slam the lid on it. I may hate her but I *didn't* push her. I didn't hurt her in that way.

I take my phone from my pocket and dial Eleanor. Voice mail. I hang up and dial again, and again. She still doesn't answer. I leave her several messages, telling her I need to talk to her, that I miss her and she's my best friend. My only one.

I build up my courage and dial Alec just once. I leave the smallest, vaguest message ever: "Call me. Need to tell you something." I'll regret it in an hour, but the adrenaline of it all pushes me. If he calls me back, I need to figure out what that *something* is.

I pace around the room for what feels like hours. That night floods back to me—dressing up June to come with us to the club, the cab down to SoHo, seeing Gigi dance with Alec. I remember trying to be nice to her and buying her a drink, making a truce, and owning up to some of the petty things I did. I think through every step I took that night after we left the gala, like it's a diffi-cult variation I have to learn. In slow motion, I try to recall every detail again: the slur in Gigi's laugh as she and Alec were tripping on cobblestones in front of us. The spring mistiness in the May air. Alec's hand resting on the small of Gigi's back as we walked toward the street. The look on Will's face as he caught that same moment. It must have mirrored mine.

And then, the light shifting from red to green as Gigi stum-bled forward, traffic taking her with it. I shudder at the memory, so vivid in my mind.

"Who hates me?" I say out into the room.

A voice inside answers: *Everyone.*

Tears prick my eyes. I shake my head. This is not the time to

fall apart. My mother would say Abney women never fall apart.
I pull my hair out of my face, sweep it up into an easy knot. It
is trained to behave even without the bobby pins and hair spray
and water.

I pore through the papers again, trying to figure out who
could have done this. The obvious choice: Cassie. But Cassie
wasn't there that night. Henri made his intent to destroy me clear
last year, with Cassie as his impetus for the whole thing. And I
can't remember where he was standing. The feeling that I'm right
is overwhelming as it bubbles up inside me, ready to erupt.

All the evidence I really need is inside the dorms because
everyone is there.

I have to find a way back.

5.

Gigi

A MAGIC SORT OF FEELING zips through me as I change for ballet class. The sounds of slippered feet and laughter push through the thin walls of my room. Doors open and close. The ping of the elevator echoes. I can feel the excitement of the girls getting ready for afternoon ballet class.

I pull on tights and try to figure out if you can see my scar through the pink. Just a little. I pack my dance bag, which is now outfitted with one of Mama's ugly suitcase locks. I sew the key into the lining of my leotard so that it's close. It makes me wonder whatever happened to the little rose charm Alec gave me last year for luck. It's long gone.

I put on my heart monitor. Everyone knows about it now. I don't care anymore. I text Alec that I'll see him downstairs and receive a smiley face back. I filter through all my social media feeds. First-day-of-ballet-class posts fill the screen. Good luck messages and pictures of pointe shoes flash. I check various students' feeds: Eleanor, June, Will, Alec, new girl Isabela, even Bette. I let my guard down last year, and it nearly killed me. This year, I plan to know exactly what everyone's up to.

I skip going to the café for lunch and head straight down to the first-floor studios instead. I can't eat anyway. My stomach is a tangle of nerves.

The lobby is thick with bodies. Moms and dads drop off their *petit rats* for afternoon ballet. Little dancers zip around in a chaos of white, red, yellow, and green leotards, looking for their ballet class locations. Parents position themselves outside the glass walls of the studios, hoping for a prime watching spot. For a small moment, I wish Mama was still here, fussing with my hair, slicking down the edges so they won't frizz. She used to love to watch me dance, and she'd bring me to the studio early and stretch alongside me. Then she'd peer through the glass, ignoring the other watching mothers who tried to chat with her, focusing on me. She'd always ask me how it felt to move like that. She used to like ballet then.

One of the moms stares at me. She nudges the woman beside her. They cup their hands over their mouths, exchange looks, and whisper. A few others have now spotted me. Some of their faces bear weak half smiles or pitying grimaces. I want to elongate my arm and break out into the deepest arabesque *penchée* they've ever seen. A full 180-degree standing split right above their heads. They'll know nothing's wrong with me after that.

The elevator opens. I just see the blondness—a familiar golden halo—and it feels like I'm seeing a ghost.

I step back. A knot twists in my stomach. My heart beats

faster. The little monitor on my wrist vibrates.

I tell myself, *You are not afraid of Bette. She should be afraid of you.*

But it isn't Bette. It's Cassie.

"Hey," she says.

Their resemblance is unnerving.

"Hey," I finally manage. We've never spoken before.

"I'm Cassie. You must be Gigi." She grins, and in that moment I can see the difference between her and Bette. "I've heard we have a lot in common. I mean, *besides* my awesome cousin Alec, of course."

"We do."

Her eyebrows lift in a telling way. Dancers stare at us from their stretching spots as we walk down the corridor toward Studio B. When we pass the front office, Madame Yelena Dorokhova—one of the company directors—steps out. She's dressed in dancewear and is tapping away at the tablet in her hands. Instantly, every girl in the hall sinks into a deep *révérence*, bowing her head in respect. The teachers command a presidential authority here. I'm in awe of her. After all, she is a former principal at ABC and danced fifteen years as one. I can't help but smile. She smiles back. She's beautiful—dark hair, dark eyes, pale white skin. She nods, and we all disperse, like we've been unpaused by a remote.

Cassie and I scurry toward Studio B. We drop our stuff in the hall and plop down. She fingers the suitcase lock on my bag. "Smart. I should do that, too."

"Yeah." I look at her profile as she sinks into a deep stretch and realize that she's the only other person in this building, in this entire city, in the entire world, who knows the exact shape my life took last year. "I guess I was the new you."

"You're not kidding." She faces me. "Did you find out who did all those things to you?"

"Yes. And you?" A strange web of energy grows around us. We're complete opposites, and yet we're exactly the same—the hurt, the fear, the anger connects us.

"Yes."

Neither of us says her name.

"I had my boyfriend, Henri, investigate a little. You know, to confirm everything. I was so naïve when I first got here. I didn't realize how far people would go just to dance."

I nod and think of Henri, that weird intensity in his eyes and the surprising softness in his touch. It makes me shiver.

She helps me stretch forward. "We should keep each other *informed.*" The word lands in my bun. I nod, then inhale and exhale. I lift up and pull her forward toward me. Her hands are soft yet strong, and she smells like hair spray and baby powder and resin. Like Bette. But she's not, I remind myself. She's not.

"Henri told me you were always so nice," Cassie says. We open our legs into a stretch, touching our feet together. I wonder if he told her that he kissed me. Just my cheek, but still. I wonder if that was part of his *investigating.* "How's your foot? He told me what happened with the toe shoes. Also, the whole ballet school online world."

"Brand-new." I flex my foot. Aside from a tiny scar, you'd never know shards of glass had pierced the skin and muscle.

"Henri told me that Sei-Jin's the one who did that."

I drop her arms. She sits up. Her face is calm despite the hugeness of what she's just said to me. "What did you say?"

"That Henri overheard Sei-Jin bragging about the glass in your shoe." She doesn't break eye contact with me.

"How could he just hear something like that?" I've never done anything to Sei-Jin. I've barely even spoken to her.

"He's good like that. People pretty much ignored him last year. Didn't realize he was even around, let alone listening." She lets her arms glide over her head and down to her ankles. "I just thought you should know, in the interest of us, you know, being in the same situation."

Girls shuffle down the hall as ballet classes begin. Cassie and I stand up and walk into Studio B. She rests a hand on my shoulder before we enter. "I know exactly how you feel."

I follow her into the studio. The space is just as I remember it. Clear glass walls, smooth floor, sunshine streaking through, the scent of tights and ballet shoes and a little bit of morning sweat. Chairs hug the front mirror. Viktor sits at his piano, tinkling the keys to warm up. Next to him, perched on a chair, is Madame Dorokhova—already making notes about us. A little flutter bursts in my chest. Why is a company director here on the first day of class?

The other girls cluster along the walls, stretching their muscles, hydrating, and sewing ribbons and elastics onto new pointe shoes.

I scan the room. I make eye contact with Eleanor. She smiles but quickly drops her gaze. Her face looks the same—round, rosy, with impossibly bright and hopeful eyes. I don't smile back at anyone. I want them to know I'm not the same girl anymore.

I want them to be afraid of what I might do.

There are new girls: another brownish girl named Isabela from Brazil, and a new Japanese girl, Riho, who seems to have been adopted by the other Asian girls. Maybe if they had taken me in, I'd have a group. I look for June, but she's not with them, of course. She never was. I see Sei-Jin. She smiles. Cassie's words echo inside me. Anger simmers.

I turn away.

"Hey, Gigi. Welcome back," a few voices say. I don't return their warmth. I ignore them. I find a spot to plop down and get a final stretch in. I feel eyes on me, but focus my attention on loosening my hamstrings and making sure my hips are open.

A foot touches my leg and I look up. It's June. She's smiling down at me. No, beaming. It catches me off guard—the smile is gracious and real, like it's coming from deep down inside. I get up and we just stand there, staring at each other for what feels like a long moment. Then she wraps her arms around me and the hug feels so out of place. I don't know what to do with my arms and head. I try to sink into it, to find a place to rest my worries, and finally she just pulls me closer and tucks me in, as if she knows. She feels softer than before. More comfortable.

"How are you?" Her words rub against the nook of my neck.

"Okay."

She pulls back and opens her mouth several times, the words stuck in her throat.

"It's good to see you," I say, so that she will stop wrestling with whatever she's trying to tell me and just be. "How was your summer?"

"Good. You look a lot better," she says, tentative. "Stronger."

"I'm great." I can feel the others listening in. "Brand-new."

"I'm—" she starts, but a round of claps cut her off. Mr. K strides into the studio. Our female teachers trail behind him, Morkie first, then Pavlovich. Madame Dorokhova hugs Mr. K briefly, then she settles into her seat again.

The rest of us stand, smoothing our buns, and shuffle into the middle of the studio, ready to listen, ready to dance. I remember why I love this so much—the routine, the discipline, the elegance.

"Welcome to the most important year of your life," Mr. K says with a flourish of his hands. We all clap and bow. "You all are reaching the pinnacle of your career as students entering Level 8. And this year, some of you will transition into the realm of professional dancers." He paces around the front of the studio, rubbing his goatee. "You must love it. That's the only way through the rigors you will face this coming year. *Love*."

The group starts to part as he enters our flock. I feel his strong gaze on my face. He's towering over me again, and I flash back to the first casting last year, the moment that started me on this difficult path.

"And speaking of it, let's welcome back *moya korichnevaya*, Giselle," he says.

Brown butterfly.

I think of my own fluttering butterflies, slaughtered and sacrificed and pinned to my room wall, and I can't stop the shudder that shoots through me. He kisses both my cheeks, takes my hand like we're preparing to do a *pas* onstage. I wonder if he notices that it's shaking. He leads me to the front of the studio.

He turns me. "You are resilient," he almost shouts, then faces everyone. "That's what ballet is all about."

I do a deep curtsy down to the floor before he reaches for me again. Morkie squeezes my hand and kisses me.

"You are better," she says, shaking my hand. "You look good and strong." I want her words to sink into my skin and down into my muscles and bones, which still feel so fragile and out of practice.

Mr. K goes back into the group and pulls out Cassie. "Another one has returned to us." He presents her. She does a spin. "Cassandra Lucas. I'd thought I'd lost this butterfly long ago." He lifts her by the waist and twirls her. She winks in my direction. Everyone claps again before he leaves to go next door to the boys' studio.

We start class at the barre with Morkie hovering around us. Right away I can feel the difference—my *tendus* are not as smooth, my *relevés* are not as high on my left foot. I've been working all summer, but I have a long way to go. As much as I tell myself that nothing's changed, my confidence plummets. I can feel Madame Dorokhova's eyes on me, curious, judging.

Morkie doesn't say a word. She notes every little fault in the other dancers, but she skips right over me, not mentioning even my stumble as we make *piqué* turns across the floor. She's trying to make me feel better about all this, but it's just making me feel worse.

After class I wait for June, thinking we can go to the café and fill each other in on our summers. But she rushes out without a word. In the hall, I see Jayhe. He kisses her, lacing his fingers through hers, and they head for the lobby. When did that become official? Was I just not paying attention? I think back to the end of last year, and my head starts to hurt. I remember Jayhe's face at the club after the gala. I remember seeing them together and Sei-Jin being upset. I remember wondering if June actually liked him or if it was just a ploy to make Sei-Jin angry. I remember Alec walking in front of me, and trying to catch up.

I stop in the middle of the crowd of dancers. The noise of their feet and chattering voices, the pings of the elevators, piano chords escaping other studios, it all drains away and the faces blur around me. I can feel my feet slipping out from under me, feel myself plunging forward into the darkness, all of me shattering, just like on that night. The night when everything changed. I back into the nearest wall, desperate to cling on to something.

A hand on my shoulder pulls me back into this building, into this hallway, into this space. It's Cassie again.

"Just breathe, Gigi, breathe." She's looking deep into my eyes, making me focus on hers. "Better, faster, stronger, payback," she says with a smile.

"Yes." That's what I have to be. That's what I have to do.

I lean in close, so the others can't overhear. "What you said about Sei-Jin—"

"Every word was true."

I don't have to say the rest. My eyes tell her everything. Sei-Jin's going to pay. They all are.

"The new Gigi is going to be mean," Cassie says, grinning.

I let myself sink into that tiny four-letter word. *Mean.* Yes. It's about time.

6.

June

THE SUN POURS IN ON me from the studio's wall of glass windows, warming the back of my shoulders. I sip my *omija* tea from my thermos and wonder why Mr. K is calling us all together so early in the year for a meeting. It feels like fall casting, but it's not even October yet.

The room is filled with hushed chatter, all butterflies and anxious expressions. It's just Level 8s in the room, except for a few random students, like the Brazilian chick, Isabela, and the new girl hanging with Sei-Jin's crew. They are both from Level 6. They're giggling and gushing, admiring Sei-Jin's new pink leather dance bag—a Korean import, no doubt.

Surrounded by everyone, I've never felt lonelier.

I watch Gigi and feel that same strange pang in my stomach. She's sitting beside Cassie and powdering her face with makeup. When did she start wearing it? Maybe she's different now. Maybe everything's different now. She was my roommate and sort of my friend. Part of me hopes that she'll never find out what I did last year. That I can still consider her someone who actually likes me.

She laughs with Cassie. Everyone turns to look. They're hysterical, falling all over each other. When did they become close friends? It's only been a few days since school started.

My heart sinks down to the depths of my empty stomach. I feel like I can't breathe in this place anymore—not even in my room now.

The boys trample in. Alec sits with Gigi, then Henri follows, tucking himself against the wall next to Cassie. Will lingers near the door. Cassie watches him for a second, and then her ice-blue eyes flitter in my direction, cutting right through me, her face serious and smug, her body confident. She leans close to Gigi and whispers something, and the movement sends a tremor through me. More whispers, and Gigi throws her head back with that old tinkling, hiccupping laugh, like she'll die if she stops, bringing all eyes back to her again. It's all coming together, the beginning of the end. Cassie is the new Bette, and Gigi is her Eleanor.

Gigi catches me staring at them, and she sort of waves for a second, but Cassie says something funny again, and they all erupt into laughter.

I look away.

As if echoing my loneliness, Eleanor walks in solo. She's carrying with her a gaping hole in the shape of Bette. She sits close to me, but we've never really talked, so the thought of starting now feels weird. I focus on the lint on my tights.

Snippets of conversation envelop me. The biggest worry: *Why are we having a morning meeting?* The second: *Why is Mr. K late?*

Mr. K is a stickler for punctuality, in himself and his dancers—and his assistant is waiting with a frozen, panicked smile pasted on her face as she tries to keep us at bay.

Mr. Lucas walks into the room then. A deep heat rushes through me, like I've just touched a hot stove. He takes a seat in one of the chairs along the front mirror. I try not to stare, but I can't help but compare the planes of his face, his long fingers, the shape of his nose to my own and to Alec's. He must feel me staring. I let my eyes burn into him like a laser. But he doesn't even glance my way. He acts like he doesn't even see me.

"He's coming," someone says. An instant hush falls over the room when Mr. K finally makes his way into the studio, his shoes clacking across the floor. But this time, the reverence isn't reserved just for him. With him is Damien Leger, the dark-haired former principal of the American Ballet Company, who was recently announced as the new director. If Mr. K is the moon or the sun in this world, then Damien is the sky—endless and all encompassing.

There's a silent shift in the energy of the crowd, a collective sway toward the front of the studio where Mr. K and Damien stand side by side. I try to stand taller, hoping my energy is brighter, willing a glance my way, willing them to notice me. Their faces are expressionless as their eyes scan the crowd, giving nothing away.

"I've called you all together because things will be different this fall," Mr. K begins, waving his hands in his signature flourishes. "Usually, by next month, we would be doing auditions and casting for the yearly production of *The Nutcracker*. But this year, the winter show will be danced by the underclassmen in Level 6 and below."

I'm so shocked that I can't look away from his mouth, afraid I might miss something. He pauses and taps a pointed finger to his lips. "Last year's tragedy has left a stain on the American Ballet Conservatory and the company itself. What you all don't realize is that our beautiful ballet world is very small, and what happens here"—he motions all around him—"ripples out. That scandal has affected even other notable ballet schools and companies. We need to do something—something big—to rescue the school and the company."

He pauses to let that sink in. "This means boosting enrollment numbers, increasing ticket sales, revitalizing the school and company's image—making ABC a force once again in the dance world. Revamping the way you all interact with one another—creating a real community here. What dancer wants to come to a place where she feels under attack?" He looks pointedly toward Gigi and then Cassie. "How will American Ballet Conservatory put a legion of talent into its own company, and those around the world, if people don't want to come here? If people are afraid?" He gestures toward his assistant and the papers she's holding. "To that end, we have started a new initiative—a mentorship program. Some of you will be paired with the newer students in order to guide them as they adjust to life at ABC. Make them feel welcome and integral."

He holds out his arm. "I've also asked Gigi and Cassie to speak a few words about how the bullying affected them."

Gigi stands first and walks over to Mr. K. He puts a hand on her shoulder. She takes a deep breath. "Everyone basically knows what happened to me." Her voice quavers.

My heart races. I grip my thermos tight, the heat of it almost burning my fingers.

"It all started as little things. Nasty looks, whispers, and messages. Glass in my shoes. Even—" Her voice breaks and I know what's next.

The word *butterflies*. It thuds in my chest and I can't help but remember the worst thing I did last year. The worst thing I've ever done.

Everybody says butterflies are beautiful. In Korean they're called *nabi*. My grandmother used to send me cards every spring back when she and my mom still spoke. She told me to look for pretty yellow butterflies out my window because they signaled good fortune.

Maybe some are lucky and pretty. Gigi's were not. They were a dull orange, with black stains streaking across their backs, and large, menacing dark eyes that stared at me when I reached into Gigi's window terrarium, that trusted my delicate and graceful hands coming toward them. Eyes that still haunt me now. But in that moment, it felt good to push needles into them and finally still that endless, frenetic flapping that bothered my sleep for months.

My *halmeoni* would say that I gave up all my good fortune that day.

The memory causes me to shake. I will myself to forget about it. I tell myself I'm not the same girl who did that. I can make it up to Gigi. Mr. K claps and I startle out of it. Cassie and Gigi hold each other's hands before sitting down again.

Mr. K motions at Damien. He steps forward. "Thank you, Anton. I'm not going to sugarcoat anything. Honesty is part of what makes us all artists. I've heard much about you—some of it good, a lot of it not so good. The press calls you a morally flawed lot of dancers. Last year's Level 8s were a disappointment, too. Their talent and technique subpar, and not ready for the ballet world. You all have the talent, but your choices have had a tremendous effect on the company itself. Along with not dancing *The Nutcracker*, you also won't be choreographing senior workshop pieces at the end of the year."

The gasp is an audible, deep, collected breath. The weight of it, of hearing this news aloud, is staggering. We knew this could be a possibility. All of us knew, deep down inside, that our actions could deem us unworthy—after all, we nearly killed a girl. But surely Gigi should get to dance? I'm staring at her—we all are, I realize—and her face has gone pale, the way it does when her heart gets out of control.

"This year, under a close collaboration between Mr. K and myself, we will be performing *Swan Lake* in the spring for the fiftieth anniversary of the company. The company will dance opening night, and you will dance the second. The principal positions—in particular Odette and Odile—will be danced by two different dancers. I will choose my apprentices from that performance." He takes a moment to breathe, sipping lemon water from a glass. "However, the dancers cast in the principal roles are not guaranteed to be my apprentices."

"Damien will choose two girls and two boys. And maybe

fewer, if you don't rise to this grand opportunity," Mr. K adds. "He chose no one from last year's class."

Shoulders slump a little. Some are already accepting defeat. I refuse. I know that I was born to do this, that I *will* do it. Mr. K rounds this out with his serious, signature three claps, refocusing our attention. "Mr. Leger and Madame Dorokhova will stop by frequently to observe you all, which means you must be your best in every ballet class, every rehearsal."

The applause starts slowly but spreads through the room, and soon I find myself clapping, too. It's hard to not want to please these men, to show them you're ready for this challenge. But so many of us want this, and so few will get it.

I will be one of the few, I tell myself. And I'll do it the right way, by simply dancing my best. The best.

I will.

7.

Bette

I WAIT UNTIL THE LIGHT snores waft from my mother's bedroom before calling her car service. I hide outside near the holly bush my mother sets out in the little front patio every fall.

I spot the car lights as he turns on to Sixty-ninth Street. I'm on the curb before he can call up to the house to confirm a pickup.

"Sixty-fifth and Broadway," I say, like I'm an adult and he shouldn't for one second question where my parents are. It's only 8:56 p.m, but at school, most of the students will be heading back to the dorm for curfew. At least those who are following the rules will be. But Eleanor posted a picture of a fresh latte five minutes ago. She's at the coffee shop a block away, probably with her head in some book, instead of being out on a Friday night like normal people. The way we would both be if we still lived together.

"Lincoln Center?" he asks.

"Yeah."

The driver cuts through Central Park. It's pouring and the wind whips fat raindrops across the windows. Dark trees have already lost their leaves. Fall is coming too soon. As the weeks slip by, so, too, does any chance of my ever really coming back to school.

He zips down the winding street until we exit the park and we're on the West Side of Manhattan, where it's all bars and restaurants and late-evening chatter. Green subway lamps leave a glow along the sidewalks. The driver makes a left to head downtown toward the school, following the bustle of Broadway.

My heart bangs against my rib cage like I've just rushed offstage. "Get it together," I tell myself. They're just kids, like me. They can't actually do anything to me. Besides, it's not like I'll really be on school property. I can't risk turning my suspension into an expulsion.

The driver makes the final turn and the great glass windows of the American Ballet Conservatory glitter in the streetlights. It's still just as beautiful as it was the first time my mother brought me here to watch Adele dance.

I get out of the car. I don't march up to the front doors and stomp past the guard like I wish I could. I casually walk past the building, heading south. The coffee shop windows glow with warmth.

I linger at the edge of the window and steal glances inside. I recognize a few girls from Level 7, but nobody I know too well, thankfully. I'd blend right in here. I'm dressed like a ballerina who has spent the day dancing. Big, cozy sweater thrown over the lean lines of dancewear, leg warmers tucked into sheepskin boots.

In the far corner next to the coffee shop's small fireplace, Eleanor sits at a table by herself. I pull up my hood.

Before walking in, I listen, like I'm counting the beats of music before I have to go onstage. There's a flutter in my chest. The door opens and someone leaves. I catch it before the bell jingles and slip inside. I hear Eleanor's humming as I take the smallest steps in her direction. She sounds very pleased with herself. She has earbuds in and dips carrots into a tub of hummus. She gazes between her phone and a set of math problems, half-solved.

She hits a high note in whatever terrible song she's singing along to, and as much as I hate to admit it, I wouldn't even mind having to deal with her pitchy voice again every night. Because then my life would be back to normal.

I steel myself, drop my shoulders, and walk up to the table. She seems skinnier, happier. I tap her shoulder. She lifts her head and yanks the earbuds from her ears.

"You look good, El." Quiet, direct, for the most dramatic effect.

She drops the earbuds on the table.

"What are you doing here?" Her eyes bulge so big that they're no longer bright and beautiful. She looks like a bug.

I wait for her to stand up and hug me. She doesn't move. I slip into the seat in front of her. "Happy to see me? I called you a million times."

"Bette, you shouldn't be here."

"I need to talk to you."

"You—"

"I already know I'm not supposed to be here, but I don't care right now."

She retreats to her chair. A long, cold moment stretches between us, one that the fire can't even begin to thaw.

I press on. "How are things?" The air is thick with the scent of coffee and pastries and things that need to be said, but that's all I can manage for now.

"Fine." She puts her phone in her lap. "Bette—"

"Just be normal."

"What is that?"

I shove the lump down in my throat. We spent so many nights here at this very coffee shop—dissecting all the crap that went down in ballet class, with Will, with Alec. She spent countless days with me in hell on family vacations to the Cape or in the Hamptons, witnessing my mother's drunken dramas firsthand. We danced every class and performance together, whispering *merde* to each other for good luck, ever since we were six. She's not getting off that easy. "I need us to be *us*. Just tell me what's going on at school, like we're in our old room again and about to go to bed."

She sighs, not looking up. She picks up her phone, texting, like I'm not even there.

"Why can't you just talk to me?"

"So much has changed." Her eyes finally meet mine. They aren't scared or begging for my approval like they used to. They're different now. Her pupils are dilated, drowning out the golden sunflowers that usually rim them. They glitter with newfound confidence or self-assurance. Something she didn't have last year. Something she hasn't had in the whole time I've known her. I want to like her new strength, but it might mean she doesn't need me anymore.

I move my chair closer to her, so close to her I can smell the rose-scented shampoo she's using now. "Please, Eleanor. I miss you." I drape my arms around her and don't let go until I feel her hands finally land on my shoulder, the stiffness slowly softening. I can feel her breathing, that old hiccupy rhythm. I wish I'd been nicer to her all these years, treated her better.

"I miss you, too," she whispers.

"I'm going to fix everything. I didn't do it. I swear to you."

She doesn't tell me she believes me. I just feel her hand stroke down my back.

"We'll be roommates again and everything will go back to normal."

She pulls away a little. "The accident has caused problems here. Serious ones. The company has lost major sponsors and donors. Mr. K is being crazy. Enrollment is down. My scholarship could go. Families are pulling their kids out. Especially, the *petit rats*. There's been bad press about the school—"

"I've seen the papers."

"Level 8 isn't even allowed to dance in *The Nutcracker* this year."

"How is that—"

She railroads through my question. "Be quiet for a sec, so I can tell you."

The words keep bubbling up and pushing out and I've lost all sense of how you're supposed to talk to people in the real world. I used to be great with words. Mean ones.

"They're doing a performance of *Swan Lake* for the fiftieth anniversary. Opening night is the company, then the next night is us. The new director, Damien Leger, will be casting us along with Mr. K. He'll decide from there who gets spots at ABC. If any of us do."

I try to absorb it all. Damien Leger? That means I actually may have a shot at the company. If I can prove myself innocent. If I can get back to school. I open my mouth to tell Eleanor all this, but she's packing up her things.

"It's late, Bette," she says, sounding more tired than I've ever heard her. "I've got character class in the morning."

I nod, zipping up my sweatshirt and pulling the hood up. "Will you help me?"

"With what?"

"I need everyone to know I didn't do it."

"But didn't you settle? Everyone's saying—"

"My family settled with hers, but that doesn't mean that I pushed her. I didn't. We just wanted it to all go away." I feel the desperation slip into my voice and try to erase it. "I need help finding out who did this. Nobody believes me. But you do, don't you? You will?"

"I don't know what you're asking me." She stands.

Her phone lights up in her hand, and it's like she's gone already. I wonder if I made her feel that way—unwanted, unimportant—all those countless times. I wonder if this is how it felt.

"I've got to go." Grabbing her bag, she pushes past me and

out the coffee shop door. The bell chimes.

Someone recognizes me and snickers. A table of younger ballerinas point in my direction. A year ago, they'd be cowering in my presence or hoping I'd join them. They'd be coveting what I had: the looks, the roles, Alec. All of it. And now I stand here, the tears stinging my eyes, wanting what they have: nothing more than a group of friends who secretly hate each other. This is what it's come to.

I slip back outside into the cold. The streetlamps glare down at me. I walk quickly toward Broadway, then pause, pondering calling the car service. Instead I decide to walk. Going through the park at night is a risk I wouldn't usually take, but right now, in this moment, I've got nothing to lose.

8.

Gigi

"I NEED YOUR HELP." I grab Will's arm and drag him down the hallway outside Studio E. People zip by, dropping off their bags for afternoon ballet classes, and heading up to the café for lunch or off to find a corner to stretch in.

He wrestles his arm away from me. "Oh, so you have time for me now?" He pets the newly shaved lines in the left side of his scalp, and fusses with the perfect topknot he's put in his red hair.

"I meant to text you back." We haven't hung out since the start of school, and every time I've invited him to hang out with Alec and me, he's refused.

"Sure you did," he says.

"I invited you to come for dinner last night."

"I don't want to hang out with Alec. I want to hang out with you." His tone shifts from shattered to mock annoyed. Tears shimmer across his green eyes.

"Okay, come hang out with me now. I need you." I poke at

his side until he laughs. "Forgive me?"

"Fine. Since you're begging."

We laugh.

"I really missed you this summer, so you know I need my time with you," he says, squeezing my hand.

"I saw you every weekend." He showed up at Aunt Leah's every Friday without fail. More than Alec even. He'd come with frozen yogurt and ballet movies. Aunt Leah's boyfriend got so tired of seeing him that I had to make up fake Friday plans or pretend to be sick sometimes.

"But still"—he rubs my arm—"isn't it so much better now that we can see each other every day?"

I nod, just to get that sappy, pitiful look off his face. He's been weirdly clingy lately. But I should feel grateful for his friendship. I can only trust three people in this building: him, Alec, and Cassie.

"So what is it?"

"Cassie told me something," I whisper.

"You two are friends now?" The way he recoils at her name, it worries me for a second. But I tell myself he's just being sensitive.

"Um, not really. She's been nice." He starts to say something about Cassie, but I interrupt. "Sei-Jin is the one who put the glass in my shoe."

His hand covers his mouth. "But—"

"I want to get back at her." A cold tingle shoots up my spine.

"Why would you just believe Cassie like that?"

"Why wouldn't I? What does she gain from lying to me?"

His eyes get all big. "She's just—"

"What? The same stuff happened to the both of us. She's looking out for me."

"The Cassie I knew, she was just—different. So I wouldn't—"

"Well, so am I this year. I've changed, too. Are you going to help me or what?"

"But I love the old Gigi."

"The old Gigi was weak, and too nice." I jostle his arm and try to get him to laugh. "Come up to the café with me. I need to see if Sei-Jin's there. And I need vinegar." I drag him into the elevator and up to the third floor. The room bursts with laughter and chatter and moving bodies.

"She's over there." Will nods his head to the right while he pretends to look over the makeshift fruit stand they've set up for us.

I look and see Sei-Jin and the rest of the Asian girls at a table.

I put a hand on Will's shoulder. "Perfect. I'll be right back. Watch her." I walk to the doors that lead to the café's kitchen. I ask one of the workers for vinegar to add to a foot soak. He gives me a small bottle. I thank him, tuck it under my ballet warm-ups, and rejoin Will. "Do you think she'll be in here a while?"

"She just got her food."

I smile. We go to Studio B, where our ballet class will start at two p.m. The studio is empty aside from Viktor warming up on the piano. He doesn't look up. I scan the bags, looking for Sei-Jin's. They're all official conservatory bags embroidered with the school's logo and our names. Except for hers. It's bubblegum pink and covered in K-pop stickers and buttons. I drape the bag over my shoulder like it's my own. We slip out of the studio and into the unisex staff bathroom near the elevator banks. Will locks the door behind us.

"What are you going to do?" He drums his navy-blue-painted fingernails on the sink.

I smile at him and unzip Sei-Jin's bag. It's a jumble of pointe shoes, seaweed packs, makeup, leotards, and tights. I fish out three pairs of pointe shoes—one brand-new and the other two worn in. "Pull the stopper up to close the sink drain."

Will does it. His smile fills up the small bathroom. I place Sei-Jin's shoes in the sink. I uncap the bottle of vinegar and pour the sour-smelling liquid all over them. The pale pink darkens as the vinegar seeps in, like a withering rose. The pungent scent mingles with the sweaty, stale odor of the older pointe shoes and erases the clean, promise-filled smell of the brand-new pair.

Will covers his nose and I try not to vomit. I toss the empty bottle in the trash bin, covering it with paper towels and bits of toilet paper.

"She's going to be so mad." Will examines the shoes. "Those were perfectly broken in. She'll have nothing for class."

"I hope she's pissed. This isn't nearly as bad as what she did to me."

"And she'll never see it coming!"

I smile to myself, ignoring the tiny pinch of guilt that rushes through me. A tiny voice inside me whispers: *You're not a mean girl.*

"Yes, I am," I say.

"Yes, what?" Will asks.

"Oh, nothing."

"I should do something like this, too," Will says as we wait for the vinegar to completely soak into the satin so it doesn't drip.

"To who?"

He flushes pink. "Remember, I told you, last year that I had a sort of boyfriend?"

"What's a sort of boyfriend?" I want to ask *who*, but can sense that would be the wrong question right now.

"I dunno." He shrugs. "I thought I was with someone, and then it all disappeared. He won't return my texts. Won't talk to me here at school."

"Well, did you all have the talk?"

"The talk?"

"Yeah, where you decide if you're together or not."

"It didn't really work that way. It was more casual than that." He fusses with his hair, avoiding eye contact.

"Then what was it like?" I lift one pointe shoe up and shake it a little.

"We'd hang out. He'd flirt with me hard-core. Find ways to touch me playfully. We'd stretch together."

I don't want to tell him that this doesn't sound like a relationship.

He continues: "We did stuff for each other. A lot of stuff. Like I'd write his English papers for him 'cause he was bad at it. And I—I'm so mad he just dropped me."

I put the vinegar-soaked pointe shoes back into Sei-Jin's bag, and I can already see the wetness seeping into everything else. "Well, I'll help you think of something. Let's go. Almost time for class."

Will eases out of the bathroom first. I count to twenty and follow. No one notices as I zip through the lobby and back to the studio. I drop Sei-Jin's bag right where it was before. As I watch the others shuffle in—Sei-Jin among them—I fill with satisfaction.

Of course Alec's house has a cherry-red door. I stand marveling at it and running my fingers over the smooth surface. The Lucas home looks like something out of a movie, with little candles in each window and wrought-iron bars arched into beautiful shapes. We're here for his kid sister Sophie's birthday, and I'm nervous. It's my first time visiting, even though Alec and I have been together almost a year now.

"C'mon," he says, pulling me inside.

It's probably the most expensive home I've ever been in. The entire block feels so different from the one I live on in San Francisco. Mama used to tell me that our house was made of blue-frosted gingerbread, with its pale yellow panes and sky-colored trim and little red staircase.

"Welcome to our home, Gigi." Mr. Lucas greets us in the foyer. A sparkling chandelier casts shadows on the hardwood floors and there's a huge flower arrangement on a table. Tasteful black-and-white family portraits line the wallpapered hall, and shelves hold trinkets and knickknacks that remind me of a museum. I cross my arms over my chest so I don't accidentally knock anything over.

Alec unwraps my arms and slips his hand in mine. He gives me a quick tour of the main floor—the living room, den, his father's home office, and the kitchen. Mama would say just breathing would track dirt into this house. She'd hate it.

His room is on the third floor. It's clean and lavender scented, with white sheets and white walls and even a white wood desk. It doesn't feel like Alec—at least not like the Alec I know. I feel completely out of place here.

"I have something for you." He presses me into the wall and kisses me. His dad could walk in the room at any second. But I kiss him even longer, just to feel the tiny beat of excitement. He pulls away, reaching for a wrapped box on his desk. "A little welcome-back gift I've been saving."

"Origami?"

"Look and see."

I unwrap it slowly, instead of tearing into it like I want to. The wrapping paper is the expensive kind, glossy and thick with cutting lines and instructions on its underside. Mama doesn't believe in spending money on such things, so she always wrapped everything in newspaper, then painted her own patterns over stories about wars and broken traffic lights. I always saved the wrapping, decorating the inside of my closet with her newspaper Picassos.

Under the paper is a cardboard box poked with holes. It holds a glass orb filled with soil, rocks, sand, and strange bright plants in purples and greens. Some are freckled, with thick, fleshy stems. Others are spiky and ridged. There's even a cute little three-fingered cactus. The terrarium fits in my hands like a cantaloupe.

"They're suc-succulents." He stumbles over the term, and I

fill it in for him. "I don't really know what that means, but I bought them at the farmers' market near the Museum of Natural History. I built it for you. I thought, you know, these could replace—" I put my finger to his mouth. I don't want to talk about my butterflies. I don't ever want to think about what happened to them again.

"It's beautiful. Thank you." The words fall out lopsided and tangled with one another, like I've never received a gift before. I try to keep my voice steady.

"I know it all must be hard." He plays with my hair, tucking and untucking that section near my ear. "Coming back to the conservatory to dance."

"I just like being here with you." I kiss him again until someone calls his name from the hall.

We go back down another set of stairs. "Your home is beautiful," I say to him.

"It never used to look this way," he whispers close to my ear. "My stepmother changed everything. Renovated it for two years, and it feels more like a hotel than a real home." He opens the doors to the dining room, and there she is with an unamused expression on her face, like she heard what he said.

"Hello, Giselle." She takes my hands and kisses both of my cheeks. "So happy you could join us tonight." Her lips are cold.

The table is decked out with candles, flowers, and ribbons. Sophie wears a crown of flowers, and she's laughing with three other girls I've seen at the conservatory. They swallow their laughter after seeing me. I wonder if I should print out a sign that says Did Not Break and tape it to my chest and back, like an audition number. Then all the questions people are thinking when I'm not around might go away.

I've only said a handful of words to Sophie. She watched our Level 7 classes last year, and if our eyes met, she would smile and I would smile back, but it's never been more than just that.

"Happy birthday, Soph," Alec shouts out and rushes over to kiss her cheek. She squirms away from him.

"Lay off," she says, but she's smiling.

"You know Gigi, right?"

"Of course, everybody does." Her friends parrot her and nod their heads. Their eyes volley around the room from me to each other and back again.

"Happy birthday," I say.

When Sophie looks at me, I see Alec's blue eyes and how the corners of hers crinkle up just like his when she smiles.

"Please sit." His stepmother motions at two empty seats at the table. Her nails are painted cream and a diamond bracelet rings her thin wrist. She's so put together she looks more like a portrait than a person. I know she isn't Alec's mother, who went back to England after the divorce, but she has the same blond hair, bright blue eyes, and pale white skin. Like Mr. Lucas buys them from the same factory every time. Mr. Lucas kisses Sophie on the top of the head before he takes his seat at the head of the table.

"I can't believe Alec's never brought you over for dinner before," Mrs. Lucas says.

"Yes, why is that?" I tease him.

"We've always been too busy." He reaches for a roll that seems to have appeared out of nowhere. I look around and catch the back of a woman dressed in a maid's uniform. It reminds me of a Halloween costume from one of those tacky stores, except unsexy. I try to imagine Mama and Daddy at this birthday party. Mama likes messy food, she calls it—family-style dishes that litter even her nicest tablecloths with remnants of her cooking—and lots of laughter and singing until the neighbors call and tell them the music on her old record player is too loud.

The dining room door swings open. "Sorry I'm late." Cassie's voice rings through the room like a bell.

Mr. Lucas stands up to hug her, and he kisses both her cheeks. Cassie makes her rounds—tickles Sophie's neck, acknowledges each of Sophie's little *petit rat* friends, thumps Alec's ear, and kisses her stepaunt on the cheek. She winks at me and takes her place to the left of Sophie. I'm actually happy to see her.

The server returns with a porcelain bowl. No one says thank you as she ladles the thick, rich potato leek soup into our bowls, but I whisper it.

Her smile is faint and brief as she moves on to Alec's bowl.

"How's Level 6 with Armeiskaya?" I ask Sophie.

"She's always pushing— 'Swing, swing! Your legs are too heavy. Lift from the top of the head! Turn faster!'" one of the girls mimics.

The soup disappears before I can finish. It's replaced with a perfect portion of salmon and green beans.

Mrs. Lucas waves her hand in the air. "No ballet talk please. It sets you all on a rampage. I need one ballet-free night."

A deep blush settles on my cheeks and I chew several green beans in succession. I stab my fork too hard on the plate and the sound it makes brings everyone's eyes back on me.

"Everything okay, Giselle?" Mrs. Lucas asks, her perfectly plucked eyebrow lifting with concern.

"Yes. Great. Everything is delicious."

"I see that you enjoy green beans. I'll have Marietta serve you more." Mrs. Lucas motions at the woman who stands off to the side awaiting anyone's wants or needs.

"Oh, I really shouldn't have any more," I say.

"I insist. You barely touched the salmon."

"I have a slight fish allergy," I say.

"Oh, my apologies," she says. "I called Alec several times to go over the menu with him."

Alec's jaw clenches.

"I could never quite get him on the phone." She waves at the servant. "Please serve Giselle something else. That's so funny. Bette was allergic to fish, too."

The woman approaches with green beans, piling them on my plate. The room freezes. Alec lets his fork hit the table and sighs. Bette's name feels like a pinch.

"What would you like? I can have something else made for you."

"No, it's fine, Mrs. Lucas. I'm pretty full from the soup, the green beans, and salad."

"Name it. Marietta, here, is a fine cook. What about some steak? We have a few nice fillets in the fridge. Or farfalle carbonara? That only takes a second."

"Mrs. Lucas, it's okay."

"Don't be silly. What would your parents think? You must—"

"Back off, Colette," Alec says.

"Aunt Colette, I think she's fine," Cassie adds.

"Honey, it's okay." Mr. Lucas pats her hand.

"Yes, Mrs. Lucas, everything has been delicious. Wonderful. I am full. I promise."

Her forehead creases. "I was just—"

Alec gets up from the table and cuts her off. "Let's go."

"Now just wait a minute." Mr. Lucas stands, but Alec is already halfway to the door.

"No, we have to get back to the dorms." Alec storms out of the room.

Cassie motions at me, and she gets up to exit, too. She kisses her uncle, then Sophie again. Alec's stepmother is biting back tears now, her eyes all bloodshot and red. She bites down on her lip to, no doubt, keep it from quivering.

"Thank you so much for dinner, Mr. and Mrs. Lucas," I say. "It was great. Really."

Alec's stepmother doesn't say anything. It's like she can't get a word out.

"You are most welcome," Mr. Lucas says, walking me out. "Anytime. I'm sorry we didn't know about your fish allergy."

"It's fine, really," I say. "And happy birthday, Sophie." She doesn't look up from picking at the pink, fleshy bits of salmon on her plate. The dining room is completely silent now. All the air sucked out of it, the little girls focusing on pushing the food around on their plates. I scoot to the front door.

Mr. Lucas closes the door behind me. Alec already has a cab waiting. He's staring out the window when I slide in. Cassie sandwiches me in the middle.

I put my hand in Alec's. He resists at first, then loosens his hand to let mine in.

"It was okay, you know?" I whisper.

"No, it wasn't," he says without looking at me. "You don't force food on people. She's always trying to control everyone and everything around me. I refuse to let her do that to me or anyone I bring over."

"It was just food. Not a big deal. She was trying to be nice. A little pushy, but nice."

"My mother would've never done that. 'Those who are hungry—'"

"'Will eat.'" Cassie finishes Alec's sentence. "I miss Aunt Gemma, too."

Alec puts my hand to his mouth and kisses it. "She would've loved you."

He slumps in his seat, settling in for the ride, his head resting on my shoulder, his hand still tightly wrapped around mine.

Somehow, I had it in my head that today's visit to Alec's would bring him and me even closer. But instead, I feel like I really don't know him well at all. I can't help but think that maybe it was Bette who belonged there, at that long, carved mahogany table, not me. She'd know exactly what to do, what to say, right now. That thought, it kills me, just a little.

9.

June

IN THE LAST WEEK, I'VE gained a second shadow. One that's threatening to eclipse me completely, despite her small stature. Mr. K wasn't joking about this whole mentor thing. I was assigned a new kid, and of course she's Asian. Riho Nakamura. She's Japanese, which is a totally different country, but Mr. K doesn't think about things like that. She's a Level 6, so she has morning ballet. But she's taking afternoon classes with us, too, which means Mr. K thinks she's really good. So I guess it makes sense to keep an eye on her anyway.

I've taken her to lunch in the café once, and tried to tell her things I'd thought would be useful—like how Morkie likes quiet feet on the dance floor and big, bold arms or how Pavlovich will nitpick your fingers—but she didn't say a word the whole time. She just bowed her head a little in a Japanese way and followed me silently through the halls without making a peep.

"Did you study the Vaganova style of ballet in Japan?" We're waiting outside Studio B for afternoon ballet class to start.

She stares up at me with blinking eyes and I wonder if she understands at all. I could probably tell her anything: That I have never been to Korea, and that fact embarrasses me. That I stole Jayhe to get back at Sei-Jin, but now I might really love him. That I murdered Gigi's butterflies. She wouldn't understand a word of it.

She's been hanging with Sei-Jin and her group, which means they've probably already filled her head with all kinds of crap about me. I wonder what they call me now: boyfriend stealer, bitch, pathetic.

"Sei-Jin isn't a nice person, you know."

She nods her head in that fake way, when someone is agreeing with you but they don't know exactly what you're saying. She doesn't say anything.

"She's evil. Really." *You'll see.*

I scramble to my feet as girls enter the studio and ballet class starts. Morkie calls the class to attention in her megaphone voice. Morkie's in a mood, so we work extra time at the barre. We start with a series of deep *pliés* to open up our hips and rapid *tendus* to warm up our feet. Then it's forty-five-degree *ronds de jambe en l'air*. My legs burn and sweat already soaks my leotard. Gigi stands tall in front of me, and little Riho is behind me. As we work, Riho echoes my movements, her arms lifting in tandem with mine, her legs swishing in the same exact manner, but better. I can't stop watching her in the mirror. She's precise, controlled, but still fluid.

"Higher, June," Morkie snaps, catching my leg and lifting

it as I sweep it behind me. "Focus. You need to be here. You're drifting. I do not like it."

The reprimand stings. I center my mind and try to make every motion flawless, the most outstanding in the bunch. When we're warmed up, Morkie calls us to the center. "The adagio will be tough today. No one is working hard enough," she says. The positions she rattles off in French hit me one after another. She quickly shows us the combination with a half flourish of her arms, legs, and hands.

The door opens. Damien Leger walks in, and his presence drowns the whole space. He nods toward Morkie before taking a seat near the mirrors.

"All together first, then trios," Morkie says. We stretch out into rows and try the combination twice. Morkie complains and shows us again. "Now, clear out of center. Three at a time. Two in the front and one in the back. Riho and June up front first."

I swear Riho flashes me a grin as we head to the center. Level 6 dancer Isabela is placed behind us.

"Clean adagio, girls," Morkie reminds. The point of the adagio is to show your strength, your fluidity without the barre as an anchor. It's what people think of when they think ballet. We've been perfecting our strength in the center since we were *petit rats* in Level 1.

The combination that Morkie has us doing today is challenging. Viktor presses the piano keys, and the chords ring out long, smooth, and heavy. I feel wobbly and rushed. I needed to see others go before me, so I could have a little time to think through the movements.

I thought no one could make me stress like Mr. K, but my muscles spasm under the pressure of having to perform in front of Damien. He is a clean slate—for me, for all of us. He's the man who decides if I have a future in his company.

As we start the movements, we are mirrors—I see myself reflected in Riho's dark eyes, in her somber expression. Delicate arms gliding overhead—fifth position down to first and out to second. Our legs sweep high in arabesque, toes extended, strong. I can feel my body reaching, working, and hitting every step, catching every note.

I have this. I worked hard for it.

But in the mirror, my shadow, Riho, reflects the same. While you can see the work, the thought, I've put into the variation, Riho has given herself over to it completely, her eyes soft, her face serene, her smile effortless. I'm perfect, but she's magic. Angelic. Effortless.

I put all my focus back into the dance, back into myself, and then, just as we're wrapping up, Morkie shouts again: "Add three *piqué* turns to finish."

I spin and spin and spin across the floor in a diagonal, and Riho bursts out in the other direction—her turns a tiny bit crisper and quicker. In opposite corners, we each take our bow.

"Brava," Morkie shouts cheerfully, nodding her appreciation. "Riho, flawless."

Damien's face betrays no emotion, no pleasure or critique. He's stone, unyielding.

Morkie steps right in front of me. She pats my cheek. "June, your technique is very nice." I bask in the praise. "Relax a little, like Riho. Look like you're enjoying it. I need to see passion. The *danseur russe*." She stamps her foot and bells out her arms in a signature *danseur russe* movement. "We have to *want* to watch you."

I deflate. Energy shoots out of my arms, legs, feet, and heart. I turn to face the wall so no one can see my face or the tears welling in my eyes. *I'm fine. I can do this. I do have passion.*

We scurry back to the corner, where the rest of the girls wait, as Gigi and Cassie and Eleanor take the center. Riho immediately is enveloped by Sei-Jin's group, and I can already hear them giggling and twittering in Korean. How does Riho even begin to understand what they're saying? Maybe she just doesn't care.

"Oh, too bad," comes Sei-Jin's voice, a low whisper so Morkie won't hear—but loud enough so I do. "Poor June, never quite good enough, huh? So sad."

I try my best to ignore her, focusing on Gigi and Cassie, and the contrast between them, but Sei-Jin gets right up in my space, not two inches away, her warm breath on my neck as she continues. "Maybe it's time to give it up," she says in my ear. "Why not quit? Bow out gracefully."

I can feel my cheeks burn. I can't let her get to me. Not now. Not anymore. I grab my dance bag and take out my phone. I type up a text to Jayhe right where she can see it.

I can't wait to see you this weekend!

"You're such a bitch," Sei-Jin says—a little too loud. "He's using you. Just wait."

I turn around to face her, nearly knocking her over. "Oh,

82

Jayhe loves me—he told me so himself. Maybe he used you."

That's when I notice that the music has stopped, and Gigi, Cassie, and Eleanor are paused—Gigi angry, Cassie amused, Eleanor confused—as Morkie storms over to us. Damien stands near the piano, looking irritated.

"Girls!" Morkie shouts, her eyes flashing to Damien and then back to us. "Have you lost it? This is *not* how we behave in ballet class. Go to your rooms. I will talk to Mr. K."

Sei-Jin and I don't speak as we make our way to the elevators, and ride in silence up to the twelfth floor. When the doors open, she gets off, but I let them shut again in front of me.

"Where do you think you're going?" she shouts. I like seeing the doors close and erase her face and voice. I press the button for the first floor and ride down again, the anger slowly building up inside me, threatening to burst. How can Morkie treat me like that? Would they if they only knew who I really am? Or maybe they all know Mr. Lucas is my dad, and they don't care, because after all, he doesn't claim me.

I storm through the hall, past Studio B where my ballet class is still going, past Mr. K's office, until I finally get to where I want to be. I don't knock. I just barge in.

There he is, the man I've always known as Mr. Lucas, cold and distant. He's startled out of reading some stupid report by my bold entrance, distress spreading across his face, widening his pale blue eyes, eyes just like Alec's. Not like mine.

"Shut the door behind you," is all he has to say to me. "Take a seat."

He puts down the papers, an indication that I have his full

attention. It's laughable. "What can I help you with?"

I don't sit. I lean forward on his desk, looking him straight in the eyes. "What can you help me with?" I say, in a low, guttural voice that even I don't recognize. "You can tell everyone here that you are my dad. That I'm a legacy, just as valid as Alec or Sophie or Cassie. That I belong here. That I was born to dance. That they can't treat me badly. That I am important."

He looks shocked. He opens his mouth to speak, but I collapse into the chair, the tears overcoming me. They rush down my cheeks, hot and furious. He stands and walks over to me. But instead of embracing me, comforting me, he puts a cold hand on my shoulder and whispers, "June, pull it together, for your sake and mine. This simply cannot be. No one's to blame here—it's just the way things are. The way things have to be."

"But why?" A sob breaks my voice. "I don't understand. Why weren't you there?" I lay my head down on his desk, let its polished solidness share my burden. I wonder what it's like to have a real father. The dads that pick up their *petit rats*, hug them, and ask them how their ballet classes went. I wish that just once, he'd ask me about my life and I could know what it feels like.

He doesn't say a word. He hovers awkwardly, like he really is just a school administrator and not the man whose thin nose sits on my face, whose long slim fingers are mine, too.

He removes his hand from my shoulder, and walks back around to the other side of the desk, settling back into his chair. "Listen, June, and understand." His tone is serious, as if he was simply talking to a student in trouble. Which, in his eyes, I guess he is. "Before you were even born, your mother and I signed a contract. She told me you've read the document. You know what it says. Your education—both here and at the college level—is completely paid for. Your mother was able to start a very successful business. And with her wise investments, you could never work and you'd be okay. She made the decision before you were born. We have no choice but to honor it."

I sit openmouthed across from him, trying not to let his words sink in. "No choice?"

He stands and opens the door. "You should get back to class." He looks at his watch. "Quickly, before it ends."

He returns to his seat as I slowly rise. It takes every ounce of my energy to get out of the chair, to walk back down the hall and to the elevator, which, thankfully, is still empty.

I make my way down the Level 8 dorm hall, open the door to my room, and throw myself onto my bed. But instead of the soft embrace of the comforter, I feel the distinct crunch of paper—a lot of paper. I pick up a piece and realize it's a photo from today's ballet class—about a hundred copies of the same one: Riho, graceful and elegant in a turn, while I look awkward and rigid beside her. On each one, the same distinct taunt, no doubt from Sei-Jin: "Stiff competition!"

My phone starts to buzz. Alerts race down the screen for the same pictures. They are tagged with both Riho and me.

For a second, I wish I had really hurt Sei-Jin when I pushed her down those stairs last year. But I think about how differently I wanted this year to go. I have to be bigger than this. My mom was a dancer. My nonfather was a dancer. I am meant to be one.

I just have to prove it, again. To all of them. To myself.

I skip dinner, even though I know Nurse Connie will harass me about it. I can't even deal with the charade of eating tonight. And I don't want to see Sei-Jin and the others. I thought I'd have the room to myself, but Cassie has been in here doing homework the whole time.

I'm in bed, the boring book I have to read for Lit class on my lap, the blankets piled high on my legs to keep my feet cozy. Jayhe's texting drawings for his art class—the ballerina series he's doing based on me—and joy flushes through me like too much sugar, leaving me giddy and off-balance. I almost turn to show it to Cassie, who's at her desk, listening to the Odile sequence on repeat. But then I remember it's her, and not Gigi, and I feel that familiar pang again, missing Gigi despite myself.

Cassie's hunched over her laptop, her back to me as she plucks pieces of dried apricot from a bowl by her side. The chewing is incessant—the swish, swish, swish of it. I kind of want to throw something at her. Or throw up. But I can't, not with her here. So I just glare until she says, "You know, you could take a picture. It'll last longer."

The blush takes over before I can even respond. "Those aren't allowed." I stand up, suppressing the urge to grab the bowl and dump it. "The sugar attracts bugs. You're supposed to leave that stuff in the kitchen area."

"Oh, poor me. I'm so scared of little E-Jun ratting me out." Her voice is so frigid that it makes me shiver.

I can feel her coldness deep inside. Most people just see those bright blue eyes and straight white teeth when she flashes that pageant grin. Most people remember how well she danced. Most people remember what all of us did to her when she was here before. They don't realize that maybe she deserved it. So I just grit my teeth and try to focus. But that's hard to do, given the commotion in the hall. I hear knocks on the doors in quick succession.

An RA check. What perfect timing! I watch her face, the panic quickly spreading over it.

"What's that?" Cassie scrambles up, knocking the bowl over on her desk. She should be scooping up the apricots, getting them out of sight, but instead she opens the drawer and grabs something from it—a small white box—and shoves it into the pocket of her robe.

I calmly answer the knock at our door, making sure to flash Cassie a smile. It's one of the RAs. "Room check," she announces in that bad cop voice she always uses. "Up and out!"

She barges in and starts rummaging through the room, running her hand over our beds, combing through drawers, looking in the closet, checking the cleanliness of the bathroom. She spies Cassie's fruit on the table and dumps it in the trash bag she's carrying. Cassie opens her mouth to object, but the RA cuts her off. "These are not allowed in your room. Give me an attitude, and I'll write you up."

I offer up a demure nod and smile. As the RA turns to leave, I reach out. "Wait—" And I swear, in that moment, Cassie's pale skin goes translucent, the blue veins on her face a map that could lead someone right to the truths she's hiding. Instead, I pick up a fallen fruit from the hardwood and hand it to the RA. "You missed a piece." I flash my sweetest smile.

Cassie glares, but I refuse to cower. This time, I win.

As the RA disappears around the corner, I let my eyes drop, following Cassie's pale arm down. Her fist is clenched tight around the pillbox she's put in her pocket. I can't stop the smug smile that pops on my face.

10.

Bette

IT'S HALLOWEEN, A NIGHT OF costumes and secret identities, and I let myself sink into a role as I sneak into the ABC lobby. The school's all decked out—cobwebs stretch over the benches in the plaza named after my great-grandmother, glowing pumpkins sit on every step leading up to the front door, and spooky cutouts plaster the studio's glass walls. Ghosts, ghouls, and tombstones freckle the glass. Costumed bodies move in and out of the various studios. The conservatory's cheesy Halloween party is in full swing.

I'm a court jester, with a sparkling green-and-purple mini-romper, my hair tucked under a green velvet cap, green stilettos sky-high, and most important, a clever Venetian-style mask that covers the top half of my face. Three years ago, Eleanor and I went to this lame party together as Peter Pan and Tinker Bell. Back then we actually thought it was fun to be around everyone, drinking warm pumpkin cider and bobbing for apples and playing all the games the RAs set up for us. Everyone had told us how cute our outfits were. I'd dressed up Eleanor in feathery wings and a silver leotard and enough makeup to put a room full of glamorous drag queens to shame. We'd laughed the whole time about secrets and boys and ballet class as we played dress-up, danced, got a little crazy, and pranced around the Halloween party like we owned the place. The desire to be back in that space and time is so strong it's drowning me.

But I need to focus. I've got a plan tonight.

I slip right into the costumed pack of ballerinas. The front desk guard doesn't look at me twice or ask me for my ID. I belong here. It's imprinted on me.

The whole school is spread out among the four studios on the ground floor. Every muscle in my body squeezes as I step into Studio B, where the upper students are. I spot Alec easily costumed as a pirate. Gigi is at his side, dressed as a damsel. Couple's costumes, how cute. And boring.

I hear Gigi say, "Arrgghh, shiver me timbers." Then she lifts a long, lean leg, all sexy. It doesn't even sound like her. It sounds like something flirtatious and perfect. Something that I might say.

The room vibrates a little, a deep bass line thumping through from the records the DJ's spinning in the far corner. My heart flutters when Alec walks close by me—and I catch a whiff of that warm, soapy scent, so familiar and comforting—as he heads toward a table boasting orange-tinted treats. I feel his eyes drift over me, but he doesn't stop. I wonder if he can smell me, too. If he remembers my scent like I do his.

The room is streamered with black and orange decorations.

Old wooden trees from the *Giselle* set were taken out and positioned in the studio corners and draped with more cobwebs. The mirror is caked with fake dust, probably makeup. Lightbulbs swing overhead, making a shifting menagerie of shadows dance on the walls. And then there is an intangible thing, a terrible energy from all that's happened in the school in the past year, the strange echo of the things I've done. Things I've started.

I will my hands to stop shaking, taking care to stay away from the mirror where I wrote Gigi that message. There are too many terrible memories packed into such a tiny space, now also brimming with underdressed, underfed bodies. Everyone is taking Halloween too seriously. Or maybe I've just forgotten what it's like to have fun and be around people who know and love ballet as much as I do. That was the best part of this whole place.

I scan the crowd for Eleanor, but she's nowhere to be found. Or maybe she's costumed beyond recognition.

A girl I don't know waves at me. She's obviously a cat, with a leotard and ears and very little else on. She's tiny, or maybe my eyes are used to real-world bodies now that I don't live here anymore. Her kneecaps are strange and bulbous on her twiggy legs, and even the tiniest suede skirt threatens to fall from her hips. Whatever butt she might've had is nonexistent, her thighs meet her hip bones in what looks like a painful arrow. I can practically hear the bones grinding against each other as she walks toward me.

"Don't talk to me, don't talk to me," I mumble under my breath. But I'm not that lucky.

"Is that you, Megan?"

"No, I'm a new commuter student." I don't know who Megan is, and I don't care. I need this girl away from me as soon as possible. "Susie." I pick a name I hate.

"Level 6 with Ivanov? I've never seen you in class."

"Level 5." I try to soften my voice and act like I'm fourteen and in ninth grade. She pets my shoulder like I'm a charity case and starts telling me the ins and outs of the conservatory. Her name's Piper. Figures. Another stupid name. She's one of those people who talks too much and tells too much of their personal business because she never learned the rule that no one really cares.

I step away from Piper midsentence, tired of playing nice.

I hear *her* laugh before I can see her.

Cassie.

I look to the left. An unlit cigarette hangs from Henri's lip and he drapes an arm around her shoulder. She's Ariel from *The Little Mermaid*, complete with the coconut bra. She shouts out for Gigi, and then Gigi drags Alec over. Alec has an arm wrapped around Gigi, and for a strange instant, they seem like they're all on a double date. Alec leans forward and yanks the cigarette out of Henri's mouth and I wonder when they became friends. If Cassie forced them to get along now that she's back. The very sight of Henri sends shivers through me, and I remember the cold, merciless look in his eyes that night Gigi nearly died. Now, here she is, laughing at his jokes. If I didn't hate her so much in this instant, I would warn her. She should know. Alec should know, too. I wonder what he'd think of his new friend if he knew the way Henri touched me last year, the things he manipulated me into doing.

But instead Alec's hanging on his words, laughing as they mock fight, basking as he watches Gigi share a knowing look with Cassie. Sweet Cassie. Of course they're friends. They're meant to be BFFs, both sappy idiots who ooze charisma, who steal the show without even trying, who were "victims." They deserve each other. As good as Cassie looks, Gigi's the standout in that little foursome, with her skin aglow—from the lights, from inside, whatever—and the tinkle of that head-thrown-back laugh. From the way she leans, casual, comfortable, against Alec, from the way she kicks up those endless legs, you'd never know anything happened to her at all. She's flawless. It's infuriating.

"Who's drinking?" Alec calls out, and Gigi gives him a dreamy look: sleepy eyes, blinking lashes, her lips soft and ready. I want all that back.

Alec pulls out a few water bottles that must be filled with liquor, handing them out, trying not to trip over the sword to his costume, which dangles awkwardly off his belt. Level 6 sophomores pass by, leaving a trail of girly giggles in their wake, no doubt in love with them both, Alec and Henri.

That's when I notice Will. He hangs near the very edge of the little foursome, talking to some girl dressed as a sexy maid, and staring over her head into their conversation. He seems desperate to be included, but relegated to the outside. I try to keep from smiling and fail.

Alec looks around for the RAs, then takes a big gulp of his drink, as if to show everyone how it should be done. I want to march over there and reveal myself, tell them I'm coming back, that I was wrongly accused. I'll have proof soon. I want to shove my hand in Alec's and feel the calluses on his palm from lifting tiny ballerinas. I want to feel the steadiness that he brings, the reminders of when everything was right.

I take a step in their direction. Clever phrases play in my head. I freeze as more girls cut in front of me. The hairs on my arms lift with a little fear, a little excitement, a little anticipation.

Gigi's body is wrapped around Alec's. But up close he is stiff, upright, and not grabbing her back, in spite of what I assume is a good amount of vodka in his system. He pokes Henri in his chest with his water bottle and slurs out, "I used to think you loooooved Gigi."

Cassie leans forward and her lips purse. She never was good at hiding her emotions. Henri stops laughing. Gigi tries to say something, but drunk Alec keeps talking. "The way you used to look at her. That's why I didn't like you at first."

Henri stiffens even more, tightening the few muscles that weren't already flexed. Alec's accusing him of something dangerous, and I don't really know why. Maybe it is the Halloween spirits, if you believe in such things, making him crueler, turning them all into troublemakers, bringing out emotions.

"You looked at Bette like that, too," he slurs out, which makes me blush. He does think of me. Deep down he still cares.

"Why would you bring her up? You're too drunk, Alec," Gigi says, grabbing the water bottle from his hands. And I agree with her, because that is what alcohol does: erases that pause between thoughts and words said aloud.

"What are you talking about, Alec?" Cassie's eyes turn to

SONA CHARAIPOTRA & DHONIELLE CLAYTON

slits, lost in eyeliner and glitter, the blue of them no longer visible. She's in his face now, searching for answers about how her doting boyfriend behaved while she was cooped up recovering. Was he not a perfect angel?

The DJ lets the room know that this will be the last song, so I turn to leave and do what I came here to. I slip out of the room and into the dimly lit hall.

In the office corridor on my way to the elevators, I hear familiar laughter. Eleanor's.

I want to reveal myself, to show her how clever I am. I want her to remember all the fun things we did together.

Then there's more laughter. I follow her voice toward the stair doors. There she is, dressed as Little Red Riding Hood in a tight bodice, flowing skirt, and hooded cape, the deep red making her look as pale as snow. Her skin is luminescent with shimmer, a glow so soft and deep and inviting, you want to touch her. And someone is. A tall, masked figure leans in close, whispering in her ear, serving as the cause of that ringing laughter. I can't see his face.

They hear me scuffle as I tumble forward, a bit wobbly in these heels. Then they disappear into the stairwell, and Eleanor's gone.

Who was she with? If this were last year, I would've known everything about that mystery boy before she'd built up the nerves to talk to him. I'd know what he liked to eat for dinner and how many siblings he had, and every nauseating detail about the way he danced. There's a squeeze in my chest and I feel like I've missed so much by being at home. That the space I used to occupy in this building, in this world, in her life, is disappearing.

I go up to the twelfth floor. The RAs have decorated the bulletin boards and doors with spiders, witches, and ghosts; and little pumpkins sit outside every girl's room. I wiggle all the handles of the rooms on the right side of the hall. My side, if I were here. They all turn easily and it seems the open-door tradition of the school is still in effect, regardless of what happened last year. I get to Gigi's room. Maybe it's just the magic of the night, but her door opens, too.

When I flip the lights, Gigi's room comes alive. Her butterflies are gone, but a large glass terrarium full of strange-looking plants sits on the windowsill. Halloween cutouts of ghosts and witches are taped up around the room, and a bowl of orange-wrapped chocolate pumpkins sits in a candy dish. She's got some physical therapy stuff stashed in front of the closet in the corner, and a few of Alec's old sweatshirts are tossed on the spare bed. A ballet barre crowds the middle of the space.

I find a spot for a tiny video camera in between a bunch of books lined up along the desk shelf, tucking it securely between her copy of Shakespeare's tragedies and the latest teen romance. I open the app on my phone that's connected to the feed and make sure it works properly. There's a pinch in my stomach. I shouldn't be in here, doing this, invading her space like this. What if she finds it?

But I have to. She invaded my space, took everything—and everyone—from me. I wasn't the one who hurt her. So I will watch her. Whoever wanted to hurt her will try again.

I hear voices in the hall and quickly step out of her room.

There's too much movement and laughter for anyone to really pay attention to me. I get bumped several times. I used to walk into a hallway and girls would move out of my way. They'd hold their breath or try to talk to me. They're all so spindly and narrow I can push right through them. The weakest ones look like haunted little skeletons that will never make it because they think they can just starve themselves and that will be enough. They forget about strength, that crucial component of ballet.

The elevator door opens and more girls pour out. It's Gigi and Cassie and a few others I don't recognize in their costumes, or maybe because I never got to know them. Then there's Eleanor. I get into the elevator, standing right next to her. We don't say anything to each other. I wonder if she recognizes me, if she can smell my perfume, if she can tell that it's me. She gets off on the next floor and looks back. Her eyes find mine and I see a flicker of recognition. I blow her a kiss as the elevator doors close. Her mouth drops open in a surprised O.

As the elevator descends, tears wet my mask and become so furious that it can't catch them all. Not angry or bitter ones. Little girl tears. Sad tears. Unexpected tears.

11.

Gigi

THE SOUNDS OF A FIGHT drift through my bedroom walls from the stairwell. Angry shouts and the noise of clomping footsteps and slamming doors seep through. It's almost midnight. I slip out of bed, step over bits and pieces of my Halloween costume that should've made it to the hamper, and creak open the door. The hallway is dark now that the RAs have turned down the lights postcurfew.

It's Sei-Jin, dressed as a black cat, which makes her blend a bit too well into the darkness of the stairwell.

I freeze and press myself against the wall, so I can see Sei-Jin, but she can't see me.

"You tell so many lies, E-Jun, I don't know how anyone believes you."

June.

"Someone went through my room," Sei-Jin says. "My stuff was everywhere."

"Well, it wasn't me," June yells back. "I'm not the only one who hates you here."

"You messed my pointe shoes up, too. All this feels just like something you'd do."

"I didn't do anything to your shoes." June's voice echoes out of the stairwell and into the hall. "And you left those pictures of Riho in my room."

Shoes? The vinegar. She thinks June did it. That feels like such a long time ago. I remember Sei-Jin's embarrassed face, pink from crying and her sitting out of ballet class after discovering the ruined pointe shoes.

My heart accelerates and I don't need my wrist monitor to tell me it's beating too fast. A hot pinch of guilt twists in my stomach. I liked seeing Sei-Jin upset in ballet class, but part of me still felt terrible.

"I know you did," Sei-Jin says. June's stuck in the stairwell— probably trying to sneak in past curfew. She looks panicked. Sei-Jin won't let June pass her and come out onto the floor. "You've always wanted what I had. And you've always been willing to do whatever it takes to get it. You're pathetic. You're disgusting."

"You didn't always think I was that way. Or did you forget?" June lunges forward, in Sei-Jin's face. She's so close that Sei-Jin turns her head in the opposite direction, her arms flailing as she tries to shove her away. "You remember kissing me? You're the liar."

I take a step back, unsure about what I've just heard. Sei-Jin and June kissing. I hold my breath and keep listening, even though I know I shouldn't.

I think about the things June told me about Sei-Jin. How they used to room together in ninth grade and spend all their time at Sei-Jin's aunt's house. How they used to share clothes and Sei-Jin tried to make her learn Korean by introducing her to K-pop. How Sei-Jin was dating Jayhe, a boy June had known since she was in diapers. I remember the wistfulness when she told me that, the pain underneath, like it was an old scar that still felt sore to the touch sometimes.

Sei-Jin's voice breaks. "I don't know what you're talking about."

"Oh, yes you do." June tries to shove past her again, but Sei-Jin blocks her. "Do you want to kiss me again? Just come out to your parents. Tell them you like girls *and* boys. I'm sure they'll be thrilled."

"You shut up. Just shut your mouth," Sei-Jin says through her teeth. "Stop with your lies and messing with my things."

"I didn't touch your shoes, and I didn't tear up your room."

"If you mess with me again, I'm going to tell everyone the truth about you."

"Oh, that old lesbian rumor. Dating Jayhe has erased that."

Sei-Jin smiles. "No, E-Jun. I know something so much worse. Something no one would ever forgive you for."

"You don't know anything about me. I'm not afraid of you."

"I'll tell them that you killed Gigi's butterflies."

June's face looks terrified, like she's seen a ghost.

My breath catches in my throat. I feel like I've been punched in the chest. I press into my door. The knob jams into my back.

"You're sick, E-Jun," Sei-Jin says, as June sways, like she's been socked in the stomach. "Really messed up. Mental case."

"I didn't—" June pushes forward. "Let me out of the stairwell."

Sei-Jin puts a hand on her shoulder, and I can see her bare white teeth despite the dark. I can hear her angry growling. "I saw you sneak out of rehearsal early that day, when you thought no one was watching. Then, magically, you were back in rehearsal to collect tutus. I bet if someone checked the security cameras that day, they'd see you going up to your room."

"I don't—"

"Your needles gave you away. You're the only one that coats the middle with nail polish to grip them." Sei-Jin pokes a finger in June's chest. "I saw them. Clear-nail-polish-coated needles."

Silence stretches between them. I hold my breath, waiting for June to say that Sei-Jin is lying again. I wait for her to deny it all. I wait for her to storm straight through Sei-Jin.

"Fine, I did it. Is that what you wanted to hear?" she snaps. "Is that going to get you to move? Or should I start screaming for the RAs?"

Tears roll down my cheeks, unstoppable. How could she do that to me?

Doors start to open. Girls step into the hallway. The RA comes out of her room. A chorus of confusion starts.

"What happened?"

"June, are you okay?"

June starts to cry now. Her sobs echo, wet, snotty, and hysterical.

"Sei-Jin, let her out of the stairwell," the RA says. "Why is everybody still up?"

I walk backward one soft footstep at a time and slip back into my room. I stand in the middle and put a hand on the practice barre. I close my eyes. I remember my butterflies' dark, dead eyes and frail wings. I remember the needles piercing their bodies, pinning them in place. I remember how my heart beat like a drum in my chest, threatening to burst. I remember how I screamed so hard that my throat went raw.

A knot hardens inside me. I think of all the times I wanted to be June's friend, brought her little gifts and asked her to hang out with me, trying to forge some sort of friendship. I think about how I'd catch her admiring my butterflies on the windowsill sometimes, how we'd talked about how they are the ballerinas of the insect world. I think about all the times Alec said mean things about her cold personality or weird behavior. How much I stuck up for her.

My hands squeeze the wood barre. I bite down on my lip, trying to hold in the scream building in my chest. Anger flickers inside me like a live wire. The pain lingers right behind it.

I think of things I could do to June: tell the RAs about her eating disorder, tell Jayhe about the butterflies, tell everyone about the kiss between her and Sei-Jin. But no. I want it to be something that hurts, something that makes her feel like she's lost a thing that she needs, something that embarrasses her, something she will always remember.

More tears race down my cheeks as I sit at my desk. I pull a mirror in front of me. The scarf covering my head has slid down, and some of the pin curls I put in my hair before bed have escaped. I sniff and wipe my face, then wrap pieces of my hair around my finger and pin them to my scalp with bobby pins. I retie my scarf and take a few soft breaths.

I stand before my barre and do the nightly physical therapy exercises to strengthen and lengthen the muscles in my left leg.

An idea creeps into my head like a whisper. A dark one. I know exactly what to do to June. I know how to really hurt her.

The only thing more beautiful about New York than California is the changing leaves. They are everywhere today, blowing past the glass windows and making me want to be outside in Central Park instead of in Studio C, doing my physical therapy exercises on a Sunday morning. I've done two hours of stretches and movements already, but I'm shaky today—my pirouettes a mess, my *grand jetés* not quite as grand as they once were. The anger, it's rippling through me, throwing everything off-balance.

Sore and exhausted, I sit myself in the center of the room, my reflection staring back at me from all the mirrors. I close my eyes, blocking it out, and I meditate, just like Mama and some of her holistic doctors have urged me to. I hate it usually, because each time I close my eyes I can feel the accident again. Now I'm only thinking about my butterflies, June, and how much I want her to hurt.

I turn my phone off. I've been obsessively looking at June's online feed. Sei-Jin has filled it with hundreds of pictures of butterflies. They're all tagged with her name. Even Bette has chimed in on how harsh that prank was.

I try breathing deeply, counting backward, hanging on to a single word or sound, like *om*, until everything fades away. But it never does, not really.

I let my hands rest on my knees. I find the biggest tree that

I can see through the windows. I don't know if it's technically "right," but I let my eyes focus on the branches and watch the colors blur together and make my mind go still. Red, orange, and yellow crowd out all the other colors of the city, overwhelming the brownstones across the street and the silvery gray of the high-rises.

I'm about fifteen minutes into what should be a half-hour meditation session (if I'm going to be honest when I report back home to Mama tonight), when I feel someone standing over me. I don't know how many times she's had to say my name, because when I do hear her, there's a distinct edge.

"*Gigi*," Eleanor says, the sound of my name cutting through the quiet of the studio and my own orange-and-red Zen moment.

"Oh! Hey!" I shake my head a little to reenter the world of the conservatory.

"How's it going?" she says.

"Fine." There's a strange pause between us, a thing that can't be filled, so we just listen to the wind outside the window and the light scratching the leaves make when they brush against the glass. Seeing her makes me think of Bette. We've exchanged more words right now than we have since the school year started. I try not to remember the last real conversation we had—the one when she told me she sent that disgusting heart-shaped cookie to me covered in dead roaches.

She presses her hands against the glass and stares out at the trees. "I was going to go to Central Park today."

"Good for you."

Her eyes bulge. "Okay."

"Why are you talking to me?"

"I just saw you in here and thought I'd say, you know, hi, or whatever."

"Lonely now that Bette's not here?" Mean words won't stop pouring from my mouth. I flush with heat. I've never said anything like this in my entire life. It feels good to see her face twist, her mouth purse, her cheeks turn red. Her body tenses up, like it's ready for a fight.

"I'm not friends with Bette anymore. And I'm sorry for my part in all that stuff last year."

"That *stuff* nearly killed me."

"I know," she whispers.

"I've got to focus." I turn away from her and start to stretch.

"I can help you figure out who did it if you want." She digs in her dance bag and takes out a tub of hummus and little baggies of sliced veggies and carrots. She waves them at me. "You want some?"

I grimace. "I hate hummus, and I don't need your help."

"Well, I could just—" She hands me a packet of carrots. She smiles a little, but it doesn't hide her worries. "I mean, things just feel different this year, like a fresh start, right?" She dips another carrot, and a small dollop of hummus lands on my tights. I flinch, but she doesn't notice. Then I flick it off and onto the studio floor. "I'm excited about all these new opportunities. But it is lonely sometimes, you know?"

She looks up at me, eyes brimming a bit, waiting for me to agree, to sympathize. But I don't have that to give her. Not anymore. I shrug. "Not really. I'm busy all the time." I wonder what she does with all her time now that Bette is gone. "Like right now."

The extra Sunday Preparatory 4 class lets out. Parents trickle through the hall with their *petit rats*. The little ones wave at us through the glass. They're a blur of hunter-green leotards and pink tights, wide grins, bright teeth, and innocent eyes. We wave back. I hear them say my name so loudly it sounds like a thwack against the glass. Parents grin at us.

"They really love you." Eleanor looks wistful, disappointed, like she's just realized something big. "You've got something special. More than charisma. It's—"

Cassie walks in then, and Eleanor leaps up and away, like a kid caught stealing a cookie.

"You ready?" Cassie says to me as Eleanor gathers her stuff, that panicked expression still exaggerating her soft features. "I got us a table at ten." She turns to Eleanor, her face stone cold. "Still snacking instead of squeezing in those morning workouts, huh, El? Guess you can't teach an old dog—"

I jump up. "Let's go," I say, grabbing Cassie by the arm and leading her out. I don't need to look back to see that Eleanor's still standing there, frozen, devastated.

"I was just getting rid of her when you came in."

"That's exactly what she deserves. I should've said even more." She's walking so fast and furious, I race to keep up. "You've got to stop letting her fool you with those crybaby antics. She's not nearly as innocent as she looks."

"Oh, I know."

Cassie stops short. "No, after everything you've been through, you still don't get it. She's always been a sidekick, a lapdog. With Bette gone, this is her big chance. You better believe she's going to take it."

I fill in the blanks. "And she's learned from the best."

Cassie nods solemnly. "Exactly. So no hanging with the enemy." Then she adds with a smirk, "Unless, of course, you plan to set a trap."

12.

June

"A PICNIC?" I ASK, LAUGHING. "In November?"

I feel shaky as I sit with Jayhe, and not just from the cold. A part of me panics, wondering if he can see the scars Sei-Jin's words left on me last night. After that fight, I had to see him, had to reassure myself that this is what's real, not those dead butterflies that will haunt me for the rest of my life.

"Chicken wings. Dumplings, too." He gestures from one dish to the next, all spread out on a red-checked blanket in the park. He unwraps a pristine white box and sets it in the center of the blanket. "And coconut cake for dessert."

"Ballerinas don't eat dessert." I try to make it into a joke. He doesn't laugh.

"I'll eat it myself." He's got a doofy grin on his face, like he's just realized his mistake. "You can enjoy the show." He starts pulling out napkins and boxes of food and bottles of the calorie-free fizzy water we had on a beach day in Brooklyn last summer. He holds one out to me, and I realize it's watermelon—which they no longer make. "Your favorite."

I grin, taking the bottle from him and popping it open. I take a few sips, letting the fruity bubbles settle the anxiety that's filling me up. I pull my peacoat tighter around my shoulders, wishing I'd brought a heavier jacket.

"I know it's cold," he says, wrapping me up in a bear hug. I try to let the warmth envelop me. It's only the beginning of November, but you can already tell that this winter will be brutal, the chill settling into you like an anchor. "I brought us layers."

We both sink down onto the blanket, and pull another checked wool one on top of our laps. He starts piling food on to a plate, careful that each thing gets its own space, no touching, just the way I like it. Then he makes a plate for himself, everything smushed all together, and drizzles it all with chili sauce. He tucks himself in next to me and digs in.

I inhale the salty pork and chives of the dumplings, made by hand in his dad's restaurant. I can't bring myself to take a bite. My stomach churns with bile and anxiety. Instead, I lean into Jayhe and listen to him talk between bites—about his little cousin, whose first birthday is coming up, and how different she'll look a year from now. He lifts my plate up, noticing that it's still full. "Try the chicken," he says. "It's delicious. My dad started adding a touch of honey to the sauce to make it less hot." He holds up a piece. "The white people love it."

I take the piece and chomp down, trying to drown my worries in grease and home cooking. "It's yummy," I say, then reach for the chili sauce. "But I like it hot." I don't eat all of it. Just enough to get him to stop focusing on food.

I can feel him watching my mouth, and then our eyes lock like magnets. He smiles and there's a gleam in his eyes, and before I know it, we're both sprawled out on the blanket, food tossed aside. It's all play at first, a roll onto the grass, me giggling, a button flying off my peacoat as he tries to pull it open. I feel his hot, calloused hands climbing under my sweater and up my back, wandering in places we've left unexplored. His tongue goes farther into my mouth, and I push back, wanting to erase last night. The goose bumps spread wherever his touch goes, the cold and the hot conflicting, strange and familiar. It's like the odd pleasure and pain a new pair of toe shoes brings.

I don't know how long we lie there, frozen in time, letting the world fall away, but a shrill whistle knocks us out of our daydream and scrambling back into our coats. A group of kids zoom by, their teacher—blowing her orange plastic emergency whistle—trying to get them to line up and hold hands. "Everyone find your partners," she keeps shouting, and I blush, thinking maybe I finally found mine.

He watches my face and then grins, reaching for the dumplings. He eats one and then a second, offering me some, too. They're cold and congealed now, and I can feel that familiar bile rising in my throat. I tell him I'm full. He frowns but lets it go.

"Just one more month until the new Brooklyn restaurant opens." He dips another into that salty soy-chili-scallion sauce his dad is famous for. "I think my dad will want me to take over that one." His voice is low, as if someone might overhear. But aside from the kids, the park is really quiet for a Sunday afternoon, probably because of the chill. I'm so absorbed in my own worries that it takes me a minute to realize what he means.

"It's a lot," I say, ever the supportive girlfriend. "Can you handle that along with your classes?"

He starts talking about the college-level figure drawing class he's been taking on Thursday nights. "We're two months in, and she still hasn't even approved my sketch." He reaches into his backpack and pulls out one of those familiar black sketchbooks. He opens it up to the middle, and there's one of the first drawings he did of me as I pirouette in the center of the studio, with echoes of me reflected in the mirrors. He keeps talking about the color and the shading. To me it just looks beautiful, so I say so. But he sort of shrugs it off.

I guess that's the thing—it's not me he needs to hear it from. It's the same with me and ballet. To Jayhe, what I do is beautiful and perfect. He doesn't see the flaws in my pirouettes or that my leaps are not quite high enough.

"I asked Professor Tadeka for a recommendation for RISD. The Rhode Island School of Design. She went there, so she might have some pull."

"That sounds great. Is it a good school?"

"One of the best. I don't know if I'll get in, but it's like you always say, I have to try." He's lost in thought for a minute, then finally says it. "But I've been thinking. Rhode Island is five hours away, you know. We hardly see each other now, and we're forty-five minutes apart. So . . ."

"I'll miss you." I reach across, putting a cold hand on his warm cheek. "I miss you now."

He puts his hand on mine, then moves them both away from his face. In that moment, he's not the same, sleepy-eyed boy I've always known. His seriousness leaves lines across his forehead, down his cheeks. He looks older. Weary. "I was just thinking. You always seem so miserable there." I know what he's about to say, and I'm already shaking my head. But he plows forward. "This summer, you were doing so well. The intensive was less stressful. You were eating a little more, you were going to that therapist, you were learning Korean, you were hanging with family—even your mom. And now, you're—"

"I'm what?" I can't listen to all this. Not now. Not when I've worked this hard and come this far. "You know I can't give up dancing. I've got a real shot—"

"Really?" He's completely pulled away now—there are only a few inches between us, but they might as well be miles already. "It just seems like you're unhappy whenever you go back there. So I thought maybe you could come with me. Or we could both go somewhere closer. Together."

It feels like I misheard him for a minute.

"There are a lot of universities nearby. You could study almost anything. Can you imagine it? Taking classes together, hanging out."

I think about the picture he's created for us: college, dancing, being with him on weekends. It would be so easy. Like a normal girl.

I could have everything I've ever dreamed of.

Except professional ballet. Sure, there's the Boston Ballet and the New England Ballet. But there's nothing like dancing in

New York at the American Ballet Company.

He waits for an answer. I try to calm myself down before I speak. I want this—I want him—more than I've wanted almost anything. But he makes it seem too easy.

"I can't do that." I don't let my voice waver. "You don't get it. You don't have to. But if you love me, you'll accept the fact that I need to dance. To do that, I need to be in New York."

He smiles. "Okay, I thought you'd say that, so I've looked into a few places in New York, too. Could you do the same?"

He reaches down into his backpack and pulls out pamphlets for schools in Boston and New York and everywhere in between. For a minute, just a minute, I can't be mad. He's really trying to make this work. It feels so strange because my life looks so different from the way it was last year, facing this type of decision, having someone who wants me to factor him in. Right now, it seems like I'll have to choose one or the other, Jayhe or ballet.

"Okay," I say. "I'll think about it, I will."

But I can't make any promises.

I'm standing at the barre between Gigi and one of the new girls, in perfect formation. My arms are up, my leg extended, my right foot swishing back and forth, in unison with the others. I'm invisible and yet perfectly in tune, exactly how it should be. But I'm not thinking about the music, or the perfect line my leg makes when I lift it straight up to my head. Jayhe's words absorb my thoughts, every moment. Knowing that it might have to be over, that I can't give up ballet or New York.

Morkie's shadow drapes over me, and I remember her lecture about focus from last week, so I straighten up even more.

"Legs in *grand battement*. Hold." She stands beside me, waiting. I lift my leg to the side, trying to ensure a solid turnout. Her bony fingers stretch out and touch the inner part of my thigh. Her fingers pinch at the tights until they grab part of my skin, burning through the thin material, sharp and mean, with a firm grasp. Tears prick at my eyes, but I swallow hard, determined to hold them back.

"Too much," she says.

I'm drowning in shame, the heat of it threatening to melt me as she continues to pinch that excess flesh.

"Now it's time to be long and lean. It's almost audition time." Morkie pauses for effect. "Because this will not do."

Everyone freezes. No one breathes at all. But in my ears, I can hear the snickers, the laughter they're saving for later. She moves on to Riho. "Extend, extend." She's shouting now, and Riho kind of ducks, as if she's about to get hit. Morkie pulls her out of the line and lifts an arm, indicating that Riho should kick to the side, into *grand battement*. When Riho does, Morkie lifts her leg even higher, and the girl lets out a little yelp of pain. For a moment, I feel bad for Riho. She's too young, too small, for such harsh treatment. Then again, we all were once.

When class is over, I wait until the hallway outside the studio is clear. Then I head straight down to the physical therapy room, where the PT therapist will contort my body in a dozen directions, pulling me apart and putting me back together again.

Pretty much all of us go to PT, but some need it more than others.

I lie facedown on the therapy table, my head supported by the headrest, a towel covering me even though I'm wearing a tank top and shorts. The shooting pains I've been having in my shins could mean the beginnings of a stress fracture. I don't tell her that. She'll tell Nurse Connie and Morkie, and I'll be out of ballet class for at least a week.

I inhale the scent of her rubber gloves, melding with the nutty scent of almond oil as she rubs my scalp. She stretches out my limbs and massages the tension out of them.

"You're all set," she says in her chirpy tone. "You can stay for another few minutes. Try to relax." She always says that. She puts a hot, wet towel on my back, the warmth of it seeping into my sore muscles. I hear her rubber soles squeak as she leaves the room.

My brain is a tangle of stressors: Jayhe, Morkie, Cassie, ballet class, food, and Gigi. But eventually I drift off to sleep.

I wake up, pull the towel off my back, and slide off the PT table. My bare feet feel soft furlike piles beneath my toes. I fumble around in the dimly lit room. Clumps of black hair make a trail between the treatment table and the door. My heart thuds. My hands find their way to my head—the once long strands now end abruptly by my ears.

I start to scream, the rasping, gasping sounds scraping their way up and out of my throat. Tears stream down my face like fat raindrops, ominous and endless. I cry out of confusion, out of anger, out of pain. The hair is all over the floor and the PT table.

The therapist's sneakers make their signature squeak as she

skids back into the room. "June, June! What's wrong?" She turns the lights all the way up. "Oh, no. Your hair. How did this happen?"

I know exactly how it did. I watched it all happen to Gigi and didn't say a word. Now it's my turn.

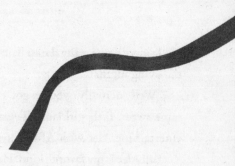

13.

Bette

AFTER A SESSION WITH MADAME Yuli, I'm standing at the bottom of the basement stairs, working up the energy to go back upstairs.

"Bette," Justina calls down, "your mother—"

"Coming." I steel myself, then I climb the stairs. I walk through the kitchen and into the foyer. The space is lit up and warm, and there's laughter. It makes me think, just for a second, that I've walked up into the wrong house.

But the laugh—bright and deep and rough—is Alec's.

It takes all my strength not to run into the living room. Instead, I compose myself at the foyer's wall mirror, wiping the sweat from my brow and pulling my ballet sweater down a little on my shoulders. I make a few settling noises so they know I'm out here.

When Adele finally calls out, "Is that you, Bette? We've got company!"

I smooth down my damp hair and finally poke my head into the living room.

"Well, actually, you've got company." Adele giggles, the same sweet, little girl laugh I've always wanted. "I've just been entertaining Alec with ARC horror stories while he waited."

Fall Alec is my favorite kind. He always wears fancy, grown-up pants and cozy, oversize sweaters that are always roomy enough for me to climb right into, not an inch between us, his long arms wrapped around me like a scarf. The craving for him is so sharp, so elemental, tears prick my eyes.

"Hey." I try to keep my smile in check and fail.

Alec stands immediately. I can tell he's happy to see me from the way his ears go pink.

Adele rises, taking her teacup. "Well, I guess I'll let you guys catch up. I'm headed back to my apartment."

I smile gratefully, and she points to another cup on the table. "Chamomile, Bette."

"Thanks," I say, then she leaves.

I sit across the coffee table from Alec, who's still grinning and blushing, although he probably doesn't realize it. I'm a safe distance, so I can trust myself not to let my hands roam over those familiar shoulders, that buzzed hair. From here I can absorb him without scaring him off.

"How have you been?" he asks, taking a sip, which clearly scalds. He doesn't drink a lot of tea. "You, uh, you look great."

Now I'm blushing, which is silly, and makes me feel like we haven't had a million moments like this. It's Alec. I've known him my whole life. "Thanks. Private ballet lessons. You know how it goes."

"Yeah, I do." He looks at me. "So is it okay being back here with—" He nods his head up toward the ceiling where my mother's bedroom is.

The way he looks at me then, that mix of worry and pity—and maybe, just maybe, still a touch of love—unravels me.

Just like that, I'm crying. All the things I've been holding in—the hurt, the loneliness, the stress, the struggle to prove myself innocent, the need to be back at school, the fear that I have no ballet career to start—all of it comes gushing out in a cascade of sobs. He's only really seen me cry a handful of times. I don't like showing him this tiny broken piece of me.

He immediately crosses the small space between us and wraps his arms around me.

I inhale his familiar scent and let him just hold me for a few minutes, the tears soaking his new sweater, although he doesn't complain. He rests his head on top of mine, the weight of it comforting. I could tilt my head up right now and be kissing him in a minute. He tightens his arms around me more. I take it as the answer to my unspoken question. He misses me.

"I was worried about you," he whispers, so soft, the words landing in my hair. I want to close my eyes and fall asleep there in his arms.

"I missed you." I sit up.

"So." He shrugs. "Gigi told me you all settled it."

The sound of her name stings. "Yeah, it's over."

"Does that mean you—"

I stand and move closer to the fireplace. "I didn't push her, Alec. And I don't think you'd be here if you really thought I had. I admit to doing some awful things," I tell him, trying to stop the bleeding before it starts. "Like the lipstick and the naked pictures of us. I wanted to scare her, to psych her out. Honestly, if I thought she deserved to be there—"

His face flashes with emotion—anger, sadness, frustration.

I take a deep breath, trying to find the right words. The words that will make him believe me. Because he has to believe me. "Honestly, I never meant to hurt anyone—not Gigi, and definitely not you."

He just stares down at the floor, and I can sense I'm quickly losing whatever goodwill he'd managed to build up for me.

"Then why did you do it? And why'd you have Will drop Cassie?"

The question heats me up more than the fireplace at my back. Over the summer, the lawyers asked me this same question a thousand times, and I snapped back with quick answers about how they were just pranks and I didn't mean anything serious by them. But coming from Alec, it finally has weight.

"I—I—" I stutter, like the words are stuck on the roof of my mouth and I can't quite scrape them out. The word *jealous* bubbles up from my stomach, but I'm too proud to say it.

"Why did you do any of it?" He starts to repeat more slowly, like I'm not processing what he's saying.

I sit back down in the chair next to him. I pull my knees up onto the seat, trying to get comfortable. How do I explain everything to him in a way that might make sense—inside my head and out? I smooth the hair along the sides of my bun, even though no hair is ever out of place.

It's just Alec. But that's the problem. It's Alec.

"I got caught up in it all. I got nervous that I wasn't good enough anymore. Not in contrast to Gigi or Cassie." The words sound disgusting out in the air between us.

"So you messed with her, instead of working harder. You—"

He starts to stand up, and I grab his arm—catching a handful of that too-large sweater. He doesn't pull away, but he doesn't sit down again either. "Alec, you know me. Do you really think I'm capable of hurting her? I didn't push Gigi—you know I didn't. With Cassie, I asked Will to just mess up the lift a little. Not to drop her so hard that she needed surgery. I might not be perfect. But I wouldn't do something like that. I wouldn't try to permanently injure someone, and I certainly wouldn't try to kill them." I jump up.

"I came over here for answers." He seems torn—between the lies and the truth, between me and Gigi.

"Alec," I whisper up to his ear, on my tippy toes. "I'm sorry." I repeat it until the words become only a rhythm of breaths. I want him to know that I'm still the same Bette and he's the same Alec.

He shushes me. "Things haven't been the same at school."

I pretend he's said that things haven't been the same *without me*.

"It's all a mess," he says. "We're all a mess."

I can hear the pain in his voice, see the cracks beneath the brave face he's put on. He pulls away from me, a bit of a blush still warming his cheeks, and sits on the sofa across the way. He looks down at his hands, the ones he just had wrapped around me. "It feels off that you're not there, Bette. You've always been there."

I walk toward him. Before I can touch him again, though, he gets up and walks straight out of the room. The front door slams a little behind him.

In the hall, my mother's grandfather clock strikes midnight. I grab my laptop and open my bedroom door. Moonlight pours through the large window across from my mother's door. I know it's locked. She'd always made sure neither my sister nor I could get in, not even when lightning rang out or thunderclaps shook our windows, and we wanted to climb into her sprawling king-size bed.

I go into the dining room and turn the lights up just a little. I turn on my laptop and pull up the camera app site, but Gigi's room is empty and dark. I scroll through the backfeed quickly to see if there's anything relevant, but it's just her and Will giggling, or her and Alec kissing—and I don't want to torture myself with that.

Closing the tab, I open another and search online, typing in the key words—ballerina, ballet, ABC, Gigi Stewart, taxi, accident, SoHo.

Several dozen of those trashy articles pop up—"Ballet School Scandal," "Killer Competition," "Bullying Ballerinas Shock ABC Sponsors." I make sure my eyes don't zone in on any that could mention my name. Girls from other ballet schools have created get-well memes and pictures for Gigi. A knot hardens in my chest. People love her, now more than ever.

I click on videos, and scroll. Some of them are past ballet productions, secret snippets of the conservatory's auditions, or more love outpourings for an injured Gigi. But one on the bottom is called "Girl Gets Hit by Car." I click it and while the little circle shows the video content is buffering, I read the video description: *Worst thing I've ever caught on film.* The date is Friday, May 16.

My heart starts to pound as the video plays. I see the club exit. Girls parade in front of the camera. I see myself. The person filming taunts us about our skintight dresses and too-high heels. Then I think I see someone who looks like Henri slip out of the club. He runs his hands through his shaggy hair and steps behind me.

The things I've been keeping calm start to rebel: I can't stop my hands from shaking or from sweat dripping down my back.

I wait for the push. I wait to see Henri shove her. I wait for the relief of all this to be over.

The video feed cuts off and an error box appears. I almost scream before clicking a thousand times, and restarting my computer. But every time I reopen the video, it cuts out in the exact same spot. I keep clicking, over and over again, until it's no use.

A sob looms large in my chest. I try to hold it in. Thoughts scream in my head. The impossibility of this, the gigantic shift it has caused in the shape of my life, the desire to have this all over with.

But I can't let myself give in to it. I have to do something.

I leave a message for the videographer with my phone number and email, even though he hasn't posted anything since that date. I wonder if the account is still active. I bookmark the page and make a plan to find out who posted this. I have a deep headache now from too much concentration, one too many Adderalls, and staying up too late. But I know I'm close. I just have to find that last piece.

14.

Gigi

ALEC'S LEGS HANG OFF THE edge of my bed. His lanky frame swallows up the whole thing. I can barely see the swirly pattern on the comforter Mama bought me. He keeps reaching for me to come lie on the bed with him. With all the new rules and more RAs on staff, we've been trying to be careful. Neither of us can afford to get in trouble. But even as I remind myself of this, I still like being with him in my room and the scent his skin leaves behind on my blankets and sheets.

"So what do you think? About the magazine?" I asked Alec if he'd want to do a couples story for *People* magazine, but he's been blowing it off. "We have to let them know this week. The publicist has been calling me and my parents."

He shrugs, lying back down. "I dunno." He's frowning, staring up at the ceiling. "I mean, isn't it a tabloid? Serious people who love dance don't read that stuff."

We've already argued about this twice already. "It's a media opportunity. It's exactly what we need to lock our apprentice spots in the company—they love that stuff. The school needs good press. And the magazine has done all the big names."

I know what he's thinking. It's what *I* need. He's a legacy, and clearly the best male dancer the conservatory's trained in years. He's definitely getting a contract at ABC at the end of the year. I don't have that certainty. I should plan to audition for the Hamburg Ballet and the Dutch National Ballet when ABC hosts their US auditions in January. I should plan to tour the country auditioning so I can have a backup plan.

"Why don't *you* do the story?"

"They don't want me, they want us."

"Then they suck." He rests an arm over his eyes, and I know he's done talking about this.

"You just need to focus on ballet class. Show them your technique is still strong. Better even."

His phone buzzes. I crane to see the screen. I spot Bette's name, plus smiley faces and hearts.

I flush with heat and frustration.

"You should come lie down." He strokes and pats the spot beside him on my bed. "Be little spoon." He turns on his side, carving out a sliver of space for me to curl into. My heart does a little flutter—in a good way. He begs a little more, and I finally sit down beside him. "We'll go back downstairs soon. We will have to go sign in at the café, eventually."

I nibble at the inside of my cheek, trying to find the right words. He lifts my hair and kisses my neck. I try to shake out the tiny trembles in my hands as I rub them over his buzzed blond head. A twinge of guilt flickers through me. I think of June's hair, and what I did to her. If I'd cut it any shorter, she would've had to buzz it all off like his. What would Alec think if he knew what I did? Would Alec understand? Would he like the new me?

He kisses me. I try to sink into it, but all I can hear is the ping and vibrate noise his phone makes. I kiss him harder, so it'll erase whatever strange feeling is spreading inside me.

"I missed you," he murmurs into my neck between deep kisses and tugs on my newly straightened hair. "I feel like we barely get to see each other."

The phone vibrations get louder.

I lift my shoulder and push his face away. "I need to ask you something."

"I told you I don't want to—"

I put my finger to his lips. "Just shut up for a second."

He props up on one of my pillows, looking at my face. "Okay."

"Have you been talking to Bette?" I grab my phone, tighten my grip around it, ready to show him the pictures of Bette that he liked on social media. Maybe I'm making too much of this. But I can't stop thinking about it.

He frowns. "No, not really. Why?"

"Is it a no or a yes?"

His fingers graze my leg, but I dodge his touch. "What's going on?"

"I just saw—" I turn over my phone. Bette's grinning face stares up at us. She's documented every bit of her quarantine at home, like she's on some glamorous vacation. "You liked her photos. I—"

"Are you serious?"

"Yes." I click the phone off. "And I just saw her name flash on your phone. It's weird. If you aren't friends anymore, and you aren't together 'cause you're with me, then why would you like them?"

"They're just photos."

"It's confusing. Makes me think you don't really like me."

"You know what's confusing?" He sits all the way up and moves away from me. "You stalking Bette's social media and going through her likes."

"But—"

"You know what else? It's weird you spend so much time with Will. That you let him talk you into this magazine stuff. I know this was all his idea. It sounds just like him. The old Gigi wouldn't—"

I stand up now. "He's your friend. Or he was. And now he's my friend, too."

"He and I haven't really been close since the end of last year. You know that. It's been weird. He's been weird. I just—he's just changed a lot. So have you."

"What's that supposed to mean?"

"That you're different." He shrugs. "I didn't mean it in a bad way. I don't want to talk about this anymore."

We didn't really talk about this at all. "Okay."

He plays with my hair again. It's a habit I used to find charming, but now it's annoying.

"I'd rather be kissing you," Alec says, leading me back to my bed, pulling my legs on top of his, rubbing his hands up and down them. He finds the nook of my neck again and kisses it. I want to fall into it all, but my mind buzzes with more questions and worries.

"But what does it mean?"

Alec untangles our bodies. "I'm not going to have this pointless argument with you about nothing. I liked her picture on social media. So what? I've known her forever. Does it have to *mean* something? I'm here with you. I'm with you."

"I don't want to fight."

"Then let's drop it."

"Fine," I say.

"We should probably go to the café now." He's halfway out the door. "You coming?"

"Not hungry. I'll meet you after ballet class."

"Okay." That four-letter word stretches out long and hard. He rushes out the door, leaving it wide open.

I just sit there, stunned by the weirdness of our half argument. Minutes go by.

"You all right?" Cassie stands in the doorway.

"Yeah. Alec and I had an argument."

She closes the door behind her. She walks around my room and grazes her hand over the barre I have set up. "I wish I had one of these in my room. Well, I wish I had a single. You lived with June last year, right?"

I jump at the sound of June's name. "Yeah, I did." I offer her something to drink so she'll stop asking questions about June. I go to my minifridge and open it. "Do you want—hmmm." There isn't much in here. "Fizzy lemonade?"

"No, I'm good. That has a ton of calories in it."

I set the tiny bottles back inside and make a mental note to tell Mama to stop sending them. "Okay."

"Alec can be a bit of a pretty little princess sometimes."

I nearly choke on my laughter.

"He used to throw a tantrum when his nanny wouldn't cut his carrots into shoestrings and his PB&J into triangles."

I think about what he might have been like as a child, how much they know about each other. I wonder if I should ask her about Alec and Bette, about him liking her photos, about whether I'm being paranoid. But I'm afraid she might tell me I am, so I don't say anything.

"There must be something going around because June just threw a tantrum when trying to put her hair up in a bun for class." She squeezes her eyes shut the way June does when she's upset. She pretends to work with her hair. "What a terrible haircut."

I let out a nervous laugh. "Oh, I didn't notice." But of course I did. June got it done professionally after the incident, but it still looks awful, like a kiddie bowl cut gone awry.

"Um, that's a lie." Cassie makes the sour face June does when she's upset. I burst out laughing. "Everyone's saying it was a prank. I asked her, but she denies it. Says it was just a slip of the scissors during a haircut. But now she cries herself to sleep at night." She mimics the sniffling and low crying.

The desire to see June suffer overwhelms my body. I think about the tearstains on her silk pillowcase and how she looks like a three-year-old now with her bowl cut, flat chest, and frowning face. I push down any feelings of remorse. She deserved it. She killed something so valuable to me. Her hair will grow back, but my butterflies won't come back to life. "She deserves it." I don't realize I've muttered those words until I look at Cassie's face.

"You did it."

I open my mouth to tell a lie.

"I had a feeling—" Her mouth curves into a little smile.

"I didn't."

"Ha! That's awesome! It's about time. By the way, the streaks in that new girl Isabela's hair? That was me."

"Really? She's telling people she went to the salon."

"Ha, such a liar." She nods proudly. "Isabela thought she was going to talk shit about me, try to ruin my reputation with Morkie, and think it didn't have consequences. I told myself I wouldn't be a victim this year. I refuse to be one."

"Me neither." I hold her gaze for a long time. "Yeah, I did it. I cut June's hair." It feels good to say it out loud, to have someone smile back at me like I've won for once, like this is ballet class and I've just finished a million perfectly clean pirouettes and Morkie is beaming at me. It feels good that Cassie's smile erases a little of my guilt.

"What did June do to you? I need to watch my back."

I take a deep breath, my eyes drift over to my window where my butterfly terrarium used to be. The succulents Alec gave me sit in little clusters inside the glass terrarium. "I had butterflies. She killed them."

Cassie looks genuinely shocked. "She's super messed up. That's like killing someone's cat." Her lips purse together. "When

I was first here, they tortured me."

"What did they do to you?"

"What didn't happen?" She sighs. "They slipped purple hair dye in my shampoo. Put up terrible pictures of me in the Light closet. Hacked my private emails from Henri, and printed them. Spread rumors about me. Cut up my performance tights. They wrote shitty things on my pointe shoes—"

"They wrote things about me on the studio mirror."

"Lipstick?"

"Yep."

"Bette!" She clenches her teeth. "And June was part of it, too."

"Yep." I want to ask Cassie how she hurt her hip, but I know I shouldn't. I can't even find the words to form that question.

"We're going to get back at each and every one of them. It's time to stop being victims. This is our year." The way she says *our* feels empowering and sweet. She goes to the door where her bag sits, and she riffles through it. "I need you to do something for me." She returns with a tub of hummus, fire-roasted red peppers and garlic.

"I hate hummus." I examine the labels. "Reminds me of a facial mask."

"It's not for you. It's for Eleanor. I need you to get her to eat it."

I quickly hand it back to her, like there's poison seeping out of the plastic. "What's in it?"

She pushes it back into my hands. "It's her favorite. I just added a little bit of peanuts to it. Makes her lips get all puffy and gives her a small rash."

"Peanut allergies are dangerous."

"Hers isn't. When I was here, I remember her gorging on peanut brittle that Bette's grandmother would send from Boston." She bats her eyes at me, like I'm so kind for being concerned about poor Eleanor and her slight allergy. "You know she used to do things for Bette all the time. She was her little minion, the one who put the hair dye in my shampoo and printed out the emails I got from Henri."

"She sent me a moldy old cookie last year. Complete with dead roaches."

"See?" She taps the lid. "She deserves it."

"Then why don't you do it?"

"Because she knows I don't like her. She still thinks you're her friend."

"I don't think she'd call us friends."

"But you talked to her for more than five minutes, so she probably knows you don't completely hate her."

I think about that for a second. Eleanor and I haven't hung out since that day in the studio. But she doesn't realize how much I really know about her and about Bette. About all the things they did. I'm the only way she'll fall for it.

"Okay," I say. My hand shakes when I put the tub of hummus in my refrigerator.

We stretch out our muscles in Studio B waiting for Morkie and Pavlovich to begin our first *Swan Lake* rehearsal. It's every dancer's dream. The story—a princess falling under the spell of an evil sorcerer and being transformed into a swan—is one of the most famous. Long before I knew any of the variations that made up the ballet, that story replayed in my dreams.

To be cast as Odette or Odile would mean I'm on track to be a principal and earn those roles. It shocks me, deep down inside, how much I want it. The endless hours of physical therapy, the extra rehearsals in the old basement studio. They've completely blocked it off now and padlocked the Light closet. There are no secret spaces here anymore. But still plenty of secrets.

Madame Dorokhova comes to the front of the room. A hush falls over all of us. She walks back and forth. Her little heeled ballet shoes click ever so lightly. We all look around for Morkie and Pavlovich. The frantic energy stretches between us like a web.

"Most of you know me, I hope," she says. "I am Madame Dorokhova, and I will run your class today."

We all nod and curtsy, and hold our breaths. The shock settles into us.

"*Swan Lake* is the ballet that makes or breaks you. It reveals the stars, casting the rest to shadows. This classical ballet shows the beauty of the Russian technique. It is the best platform for the Vaganova training." She touches a nearby girl's shoulder. "In this ballet, you must be able to be both light and dark, good and evil. That is why only the best get to dance the role of Odette or Odile." She waves to Viktor and he takes a seat. "You all know pieces of these variations, but now I must teach you how to put it all together. We are depending on you to make it beautiful."

No one takes their eyes off her. Her presence reminds us that this is it—every move we make now can affect our chances forever.

"This ballet is beloved. Each of the four acts are anticipated by the audience: from Siegfried's birthday party in Act One to the most famous White Act at the lakeside to Act Three and the party where Odile dances her famous *pas de deux* to the very last second. Your stamina must be perfect. Your feet must last." She circles us. "We will start from the White Act and work our way backward."

Morkie joins her, and I want to breathe a sigh of relief, but instead I hold it in, trying to channel the tension into my movements. "We will start with four swans in the front to work on *la danse des petits cygnes*, dance of the little swans. Most famous." She motions at Viktor. He plays the melody and I can feel my feet move the steps automatically. Four ballerinas, arms interlocked, will glide across the stage in perfect synchronization with sharp and expert timing.

"Let me have little Riho," Morkie says.

Riho leaps up like a tiny firecracker, then makes her way to the front. She's much smaller than all of us and could blend into a pack of *petit rats* with ease. I hear a groan, but don't know where it came from.

"Cassandra," Madame Dorokhova says.

I see Cassie blow the Madame a kiss—a bold move—as she makes her way to stand beside Riho. Her long limbs make Riho look like a tree stump beside her. Both teachers pause before selecting the other two dancers to start off rehearsal with. There are twists in my stomach, like it's a spool of ribbon that's come undone and knotted itself into a mess. I don't want to dance this part. I want to dance the role of Odette or Odile. But to do that,

I need them to see me. I need them to call me forward, want to use my limbs, feet, and arms as demonstration tools. I need them to see that I'm okay now.

"June, come."

Madame Dorokhova looks around the room, trying to decide on her final victim.

June walks to the front with her head down, showing respect, but I can see the tiny smile in the corner of her mouth. Her hair is all spiky. The headband she's wearing pushes it up awkwardly, and it's barely enough to gather into any semblance of a bun. I flush with satisfaction.

"Gigi," Madame Dorokhova says, and my heart monitor buzzes on my wrist because I can't stop its fluttering.

Morkie uses her hands to remind us of the footwork that goes into the dance of the little swans. Tap, tap, tap. Our feet move in a successive shuffle. Point the toe. Bring up the leg. I tune her out after a while. I know this variation. We did it at my old studio for a winter performance when I was eleven.

We crisscross our arms. I hold one of June's hands and one of Cassie's. Viktor starts the famous plinking melody on the piano. Up, down, up, down, up, down. We work together to move across the middle of the floor, all of us gazing toward the window. We stretch our legs out like a fan of swords, all together, then pull them back into a straight-line formation as we head back in the direction we've come from.

Madame Dorokhova and Morkie point to where we should be. June's hand sweats. It's strange to hold it again. Cassie tightens her grip on mine.

"No elephants on the stage," Madame Dorokhova yells. "You are *petit cygnes* not *petit éléphants*."

"Look to the left. To the right. Now forward," Morkie says, demonstrating as we struggle to stay in sync. "Watch the *echappés*. Cleaner."

Madame Dorokhova is right in front of us now. "And a down, up. And a down, up. And a down, up. Faster."

The corrections blend all together and we're a few seconds off from one another. Riho breaks the chain. "We're moving too slow," she complains. I think it's the first time I've heard her speak.

June's eyes are daggers pointed at her.

"It's only the start," Morkie says. "You don't break formation until I tell you." She cups a hand under Riho's very pink face, and I feel like she'll slap her. Instead, Morkie excuses us from the center, ending rehearsal altogether. She seems embarrassed by us. We weren't ready to be seen by Madame Dorokhova. I should be ashamed, but I feel relieved.

Eleanor plops down next to me as she unties her pointe shoes. I feel Cassie's eyes on us. I look up and she lifts her eyebrows in a question. It's time.

"That rehearsal killed me." I pack my shoes away and slip my feet into mukluks. The soft fur helps stop the aches. I try to be nicer to her this time.

"I know." She shoves her shoes into her bag and reaches down to stretch.

"Want to go get a bite? I feel like we should talk."

She looks caught. "I, uh, have an appointment." Her face is

bright pink, and she won't look me in the eye. "But maybe we can hang tomorrow?" Her eyes are desperate and flashing with eagerness.

"Okay, in the morning? We can have a snack, then stretch, and maybe work on these variations?" Cassie overhears me, and smiles.

"Sure."

"Great," I say. "I have just the thing."

15.

June

THE ROOM IS STILL DARK when my alarm blares, and I rush to turn it off before Cassie wakes. I can't take another argument. Not today. But she doesn't stir at all, her light snore echoing in the small space, piles of pink blankets muffling the sound. I tuck my cold feet into slippers, then head into the bathroom to start the shower, turning it all the way up to screaming hot. I need the scalding right now. I need to not feel Morkie's pinch.

I wipe the steam away from the mirror and take a good look at myself completely naked. I touch my too-short hair and force down a swell of emotions. I run my fingers over my collarbone and chest to my ribs. The bones used to stick out more. I used to be able to count them. My hands find their way down my stomach to my hips. I push a finger against my skin and feel the squish around my thighs. I flush red—not from the growing steam and heat in the bathroom, but from the unwanted weight there. I find the spot, the extra flesh, pinching it tight like

Morkie did. I hold that extra inch between my fingers until the skin burns, a cry of pain working its way through me.

I'm not quite as bad as the beginning of the year—some of the definition is back. But there's still that unwanted curve to my hip, and a little extra padding in the chest. It has to go.

The last weigh-in I had was a week ago in Nurse Connie's office, and she sighed as the numbers stopped on 104. "You're on a slippery slope, E-Jun," she'd said, that condescending tone settling into me. "You must get back on track and get your weight up."

I step gingerly onto the silver scale Cassie keeps in the corner of the bathroom, leaning down to reset it into pounds rather than kilos. Everything she owns is British, and she'll definitely know it was me if I don't remember to reset after I step off. The numbers jump, up, down, frantic, then slowly stop—103, 105, 104, 107—before landing at 105.

Morkie's words repeat endlessly in my head: *This will not do. This will not do. This will not do.*

I step off, but the number flashes in my head.

A voice inside asks: *What would be small enough?*

100. 99. 98. 97.

I go back to the mirror, wipe away the new layer of steam, and stare at it. "You can do this!" I need that rush, that powerful feeling of control, like when I'm at the barre telling my muscles how to move and bend. I stand and look at the toilet. I touch my stomach again. I crouch down over the sparkling porcelain bowl, the familiar gargling of the water welcoming me as I lean in close. My breathing goes shallow and heavy all at once, and the familiar lurch moves my whole body.

But nothing comes. I lean in some more, my head hovering over the water below, and wait. Still nothing. Impatient, I stick two fingers in my mouth, and gagging triggers immediate results—even though it's mostly water and bile. The coughing brings tears to my eyes. A pink tinge stares up at me. Worry zips through me for just a second, but I can't stop myself. My fingers have a mind of their own.

I give one more smooth stroke with my finger and the rest erupts, coming fast and furious. I'm empty and full all at once, the relief settling over me, slick and satisfying.

I shower quickly, letting the rush of the water drown out all the thoughts that won't quiet in my head—about my hair and Cassie and college and our upcoming auditions. It washes away all the stress about Morkie's pinch and Riho's perfection and Gigi's butterflies. By the time I'm done, I've let it all go, sliding down the drain with soapy water.

When I step outside the steaming bathroom, Cassie's awake and standing at the door in her pink bathrobe, her face matching it.

"What is it now?"

"You think I don't know?" She's pointing a finger at the door. "I'm not stupid. You spray that hideous air freshener, and oh, Cassie's oblivious. But I can still smell it, June! It's *disgusting*. You're disgusting. And you have a problem."

"I don't know—"

"Oh, you know exactly what I mean. You better figure out how to take care of yourself, or I'll tell them all—Connie, Mr. K."

Would she really rat out another dancer? She wouldn't. But

Cassie's so angry, her usually pale face is turning a livid red, from her roots to her ears, just like Alec's. I know then that she would do it in a second, and be glad to see me go. I wonder if she'd treat me like this—like a gross, foreign thing—if she knew we were cousins. Somehow, I believe she'd react exactly the same. The whole thought of being related to her strikes me as funny, and when I laugh, she's stamping her feet like a petulant poodle, her blond curls frizzing around her face. "What do you think you're laughing at?" She grabs her things. "You think I can use that bathroom now? Between the steam and the smell—"

Part of me wants to just say "you're my cousin" out loud, let the words slide between us, watch how they change the shape of her face.

My ringing phone cuts her off. I don't recognize the number, but I answer it anyway, just to get her to stop talking and leave.

"June?" a voice says. "I need to see you. Now. Can you come over?"

"Who is this?"

The voice laughs. I recognize the sound immediately. Bette.

"Whatever," I tell Cassie, leaving her in her pink bathrobe and slippers and fit of rage. "I've got to go."

Fifteen minutes later, Bette sends a car for me. Because she's *Bette*. The Lincoln Town Car has heated leather seats and bottled water in the back just for me. I don't take taxis in New York, let alone hired luxury cars with suit-wearing drivers who open the door for me.

Manhattan changes as we leave school and go where Bette lives. We pass expensive shops, the Fifth Avenue windows full of well-dressed mannequins and overpriced purses. The car rolls to a stop in front of a white-brick town house. Even the outside looks like Bette.

The driver gets out and opens the door for me with a stupid little smile. I grumble out a thank-you and reach in my pocket for a few dollars to tip him.

"Already included, miss." After he's gone, I kind of wish I was back in the cozy seat of the car and that I took it all the way to Jayhe's house in Queens instead of here. She didn't say what she wanted, and I was too curious to turn down her invitation. Anything was better than staying in that room with Cassie. I open the little wrought-iron gate that leads to Bette's front door, imagining what it must be like to call one of the most expensive blocks in Manhattan home. I ring the bell. The chime is delicate, like a sequence from our performance music.

Of course, she doesn't answer. A maid ushers me down the stairs and into the basement, which is a well-lit, mirrored dance studio, complete with smooth floors and a long barre. *Swan Lake* music tinkles in from various built-in speakers, and Bette's in the center of the floor, practicing *fouettés en tournant*. She's still aiming for the lead despite her exile. Even though she hasn't been at school in almost six months, she's maintained her skill—the turns are sharp and flowing. She's still got it.

"Would you like something to drink?" the maid asks. "Tea, lemonade?" I shake my head, and she disappears. Bette continues to dance, ignoring my presence. She spins and stops, spins and stops, spins and stops, never quite hitting the complete thirty-two, but getting close.

The last time she does it, I clap, more to get her attention than to show my support. But she takes it as a compliment, giving me a deep bow and rising, then running to turn off the music.

"Thanks for coming." The flush that starts in her cheeks and runs down her bare arms makes her look like an undercooked sausage, especially in the leotard and tights. She walks toward me, her toe shoes clomping against the hardwood. She sits on a bench that lines one wall, and gestures for me to do the same. She's breathless. She presses a buzzer on the intercom. Her maid comes running in again, with tea, even though I said no, and Bette waves the tray away. "Justina, I need lemonade," Bette informs her. "The one infused with electrolytes."

The maid just nods and leaves, taking the tray with her.

Bette inspects me, her eyes flitting from my head down to my feet. She reaches for my hair. Immediately, my hands fly to my head—my once-long dark hair is now cropped in a short bob. "Cute?" she offers. It's not a statement, but a question, as if she's not quite sure what to make of it. All I know is, it's too short to pull back into the standard, mandatory ballet bun, and too long to just let it be. It's useless. The RAs still haven't figured out who did it. But I know it was Sei-Jin.

Everyone keeps reminding me that it's just hair, that it will grow back. I know one thing for sure: Mr. K will not let me onstage looking like this. Just thinking about it makes the tears sting my eyes again, and I find myself wondering where the bathroom might be. But I can't do that here.

"It's good to see you," I tell Bette, even though it's really not. "Things aren't the same without you at school." Which is true.

She nods. "I heard about all the changes." She grabs the lemonade off the tray as soon as Justina returns with it. She guzzles half the glass, and the maid refills it immediately from the pitcher. Bette nods to her to fill up the second glass for me, but I shake my head.

She waits for Justina to leave to continue. "I need to clear my name. You do know I didn't do it, right? That I wouldn't do that."

"I know." Bette may be a lot of things, but she's not a killer. "But someone sure wanted to make it look like it was you."

She grins, which I wasn't expecting. "Right, and I know exactly who. That's why I need your help." She stomps across the floor, then she hands me her laptop. She sits down, unlaces her ribbons, and removes her pointe shoes. Her feet are so bright red and bruised, they're distracting me from whatever I'm supposed to be watching on the screen. Despite the horrible shape her feet are in, her toenails are perfectly painted a deep purple. Naturally.

"Click the video."

I watch us pour out of the club that night. I see myself with Jayhe, holding hands, beaming. I watch Gigi, Alec, and Will stumble forward, drunk and laughing, and Bette and Eleanor not far behind them. Then comes Henri, smirking as usual. Just as they take their first steps toward the cobblestones, it cuts off.

"Where's the rest? What happened?"

She takes a deep breath. "I don't know. I'm waiting for the guy who took the video to get back to me. But in the meantime,

I need help from inside the conservatory. Finding a way to get Henri to show that he's guilty." She takes another quick breath, convincing me, convincing herself. "Isn't Cassie your roommate? That's what I've heard."

"Unfortunately. Everything's pink, I have to stay out of her space, but she's always in mine. And she's mean." It feels good to share it. "She's so cold. Like she's the queen and I'm a fly buzzing in her territory. And Henri is always there and they're all over each other. It's gross."

"But sort of perfect."

"How?"

"The video will prove that Henri pushed Gigi, once I get the rest of it. But I need something else, more proof, in case I can't get it. You have twenty-four seven access to Cassie and her stuff. And Henri, by association." She looks down at her foot and retapes a Band-Aid in place.

"He's definitely twisted, but trying to hurt Gigi? I don't know." I tell her how strange they are together, him and Cassie, probably doing disgusting things on my bed just for kicks when I'm out.

"He blackmailed me last year. I'm not proud of the stuff he made me do."

"What?"

"Yeah." She sighs. "That's why I really need to make him pay." She goes over to a file box near the mirror. She returns with a tiny camera, like the kind you'd attach to a computer. "I need you to put this in your room, facing Cassie's side."

I thumb the camera between my fingers. "The thing is,

everyone thinks you did it. I heard you even settled with Gigi's family." What I don't say: *What's in it for me?*

"We did pay her for the bullying stuff. But I didn't hurt her. That's not what it was all about. Listen—"

"If I help you—and I'm not saying I will—then I want something in return. Morkie's been on me, lately. She says my technique is good, but I'm not giving in to the music and the story. You know how to do that."

"Deal." She smiles. "I'll give you the password to the video app, so you can watch it, too." She takes my cell from my bag and asks for the passcode, typing it in. Two minutes later, the app is downloaded.

She's handing my phone back to me when it starts buzzing, a string of notifications. At first I think they must be from Jayhe, but they're pictures some of the girls at school posted to social media—ambulances pulled up in front of the conservatory building. I scroll through, trying to figure out what happened.

There's a post on that new girl Isabela's feed—*"Oh shit! Eleanor's headed to the hospital. Allergic reaction."* A string of comments and sad smiley faces follow. The picture pops up on a dozen more feeds.

Nuts. Allergies. Eleanor. Hospital.

"Oh my god." Bette just keeps repeating those three words.

Bette texts Alec. She's pacing while she waits the few minutes for him to text back. "This can't be happening," she keeps saying. "Eleanor's super careful about her allergy."

The thought sends shivers down my spine. Everyone knows

Eleanor is allergic to nuts—we've known since we were kids. She's never had an incident at school—until now. Which means one thing. The pranks are definitely getting worse. This time, it's definitely not Bette.

When Alec texts that it's Mount Sinai West, Bette's already halfway out the door—throwing a coat and scarf over her leotard. She puts me in a cab, pays for it, and grabs another one, heading straight to the hospital.

16.

Bette

THE HOSPITAL WAITING ROOM IS a nightmare of crying babies, cranky nurses, and teary-eyed adults. Eleanor's mother is at the nurses' counter. Her hair is streaked with gray. I hardly recognize her. The last time I saw her was during our ninth-grade *Nutcracker* performance, when we were in Level 4. All of Eleanor's four siblings were sitting in one long row, and my mother complained that their mom struggled to keep them quiet and contained.

Mrs. Alexander was never one of the mothers who helped Madame Matvienko with the costumes or peered through the glass windows of the studios to watch our classes. With all those kids, she just didn't have the time. I haven't gone up to Mrs. A. and she hasn't seen me yet. Her eyes are too red to see straight. I listen for snatches of conversation when the nurses come over to her. "Eleanor didn't have her EpiPen." "Eleanor is still being stabilized." "Eleanor's reaction was severe."

I fuss with my phone to keep myself distracted. I click open the app that is connected to the video camera feed in Gigi's room. Still nothing.

Someone touches my shoulder. I look up; it's Eleanor's mother. "Bette," she says. "I'm so glad you're here."

She wraps me up in a hug. Her jacket smells like chicken soup and baby lotion, and what I imagine a real mother smells like. Her arms feel strong but soft. She kisses my head several times. She rubs my back, her strokes telling me everything will be all right. I let myself sink into it. Like she knows that these past few months have felt like a series of bad reactions and I need to be stabilized, just like Eleanor. But she needs me to be strong. No tears.

When she pulls away, she can barely hold back her sob. "She knows to check for peanuts. She's known her whole life. I don't know how this could happen."

"Must be an accident, Mrs. Alexander," I say. "Has to be. She's the most responsible person ever."

She squeezes my shoulder and I hold her elbow because she feels light and wobbly, like she might just topple over. "She looked so small in there."

"What happened?"

"Nurse Connie called. Said she'd accidentally eaten hummus with peanuts in it."

Peanuts in hummus? She always buys the exact same fire-roasted peppers kind. There's no way any of those could have nuts in it.

"I'm going to tell them you're her sister, so they'll let you see her. I mean, you pretty much are, anyway. She needs someone here. I have to run to Brooklyn and pick up the twins. There's no one to get them from their dance classes."

She looks at her watch, worried. She's got a ways to go. Eleanor's family lives deep in the heart of Brooklyn, and it's a good hour on the subway. I want to offer to call my mother's car service for her, but I think she might be offended.

"Promise me you'll stay here until she wakes up?" Mrs. Alexander asks.

"Yes, yes," I say. "I have nowhere to be." Which is the most truthful thing I've said in the past few days.

"I'll be back as soon as I get a sitter for the twins." She kisses me again and returns to the nurses' desk. I hear my name and they both glance over at me.

A few minutes later, I settle into the chair next to Eleanor's bed and gaze at her. She looks like one of the round-faced dolls my grandmother used to send me every Christmas. But her porcelain skin is covered with a deep red rash—forehead, nose, and chin. Her lips are cherry red and swollen two sizes larger than normal. Her eyelids are so puffy it looks like she got punched in them.

"Eleanor?" I whisper. "You okay? It's me." I don't know why I expect her to open her eyes, sit up, and tell me what happened. "You're going to be fine."

I babble on for a bit about my lessons with Yuli, about the new coffee shop I found down the street, about how much I miss her and Alec and school. I tell her about the video, how it could be what I need to clear my name.

I take her hand and rub it. "I'm sorry for everything. All those times when I wasn't good to you."

Her chest lifts up and down with her shallow breathing.

"I'll get *Breakfast at Tiffany's* sent over so we can watch it."
I lean over and move her hair around so it looks nicer. "You're
going to get better."

One of the nurses bursts in, shooing me out for a few minutes
while she changes Eleanor's IV bag.

I go back into the waiting room, where a few sad-faced
grown-ups sit, and an old grandma snores in the corner. I take a
seat near the vending machines, and wait until I can go back into
Eleanor's room. I get impatient and return to the nurses' station.
"Can I go back now?"

"There's another guest already in there. I know your mother
said you could stay, but only one visitor in the room at a time."

Another guest? "Okay, but I left my scarf. I'll just grab it."

She waves a hand at me. "Be quick! Better see you back in
this room in less than a minute."

"Okay." I head down the hall to Eleanor's room. I wonder
who is in there. I didn't see anyone come in asking about her. I
look through the slats of the blinds and see someone standing
close to the bed, holding Eleanor's hand, touching her face. It's a
man I recognize immediately by his build, by the close-cropped
hair, by the curve of his back.

Mr. K.

I'm happy that he's checking up on her, and that he cares
enough to make sure she's okay.

But then he leans down, too close, in a way that makes me sick
to my stomach. He kisses her hand, and then, hovering over her, her
forehead, and her lips. My breath catches in my throat. But before I
turn around and walk away, I snap a quick picture with my phone.
I've learned enough to know that no one will believe me otherwise.

17.

Gigi

THE WORDS LEAVING ALEC'S MOUTH don't feel real. They bounce off the glass walls of Studio C and slap me in the face.

"Wait, what?" I push his hands off my body, and untangle from inside his arms, away from the barre he had me up against as we stretched.

"I went to see Bette, and I'm just letting you know about it." He states it like he's just telling me he ate a quesadilla for lunch.

"Why? And when?"

He reaches for me again, but I swat his hands away. "Earlier this month. It wasn't a big deal."

"It's been weeks." I try to keep my voice from going shrill. My stress level is high after what happened with Eleanor. And now this. "When were you planning on telling me?" I search his face for the hidden answers to these questions, buried in the look in his eyes or the way his mouth curves.

"It's not a big deal," he says. "I just went over to check on her. See how she's doing. We spent a lot of time together over the years, and you can't just turn caring about someone off. I'm telling you because I didn't want you to freak out." He erases the distance I put between us and now I have nowhere to go. My back is pressed up against the studio wall, and I feel a bit like we're putting on a show. "I love you, Gigi. That hasn't changed." He grabs for my face and kisses it. His touch is rough and forced.

"Her life sucks right now," he says in defense of his visit.

"I *asked* you if you were still friends. You *lied* to me."

"I didn't *lie*," Alec says, his face angry now. "I just—"

"Did you forget—she tormented me last year? And others? That she's a bad person?" I shove him off. "I can't do this anymore, Alec." The words leave my mouth half-formed and I don't realize their weight and magnitude until they're out, hanging there between us. "I asked you straight-out. You lied. If it wasn't a big deal, you would've told me beforehand, and if not then, right after. You carried this secret around for weeks."

"It's not a secret. I've known Bette for like ten years. And, yes, we dated, but before that, we were just friends. Our families know each other."

"And you don't think I know all that?" My voice rises and I feel my heartbeat start to pick up speed.

Alec's entire face is red now, even his hairline. Anger shows so easily on his pale skin.

"She hurt me, Alec. She shoved me in front of a taxi." It's the first time I've said those words out loud. The first time I've really believed them. I bite back tears. I won't cry. I'm too angry to cry. I push them down.

"Excuse me." One of the Level 6 ballet teachers steps into the studio. "Your noise level is unacceptable." She shakes her head, then presses her finger to her lips. We ignore her.

"I don't believe she did it," he says in a low whisper.

"Really, Alec?" I say. "What more proof do you need? For them to do a documentary on it?"

I leap up, snatch my dance bag, and stomp away from him. A cry claws its way up my throat and I swallow it down three, four, five times. My bottom lip quivers and I bite down so hard I almost break the skin again.

"Gigi, wait!" Alec calls out.

I head for the guest bathroom near the front office. I lock myself in the bathroom and let out a scream.

I clench my hands. Bette's face pops up in my head, and for the first time ever I want to physically hurt someone, to take it all out on her face. Every angry thought, every tear, every upset. After all this time, after everything that Bette put me through, and he's still defending her. Well, he can have her. Maybe they deserve each other. Or maybe I deserve this. Maybe it's karma after what I did to Eleanor. Guilt and anger hit me in waves.

But I thought this was something that might last. Something in the way that we dance together. Something that would bring out the best in both of us. I guess not. I wipe my nose and take deep breaths.

"You're fine," I say out loud. "You will be fine."

I splash my face with water and fan my eyes. No one can

know I've been crying. I pull eyedrops out from my ballet bag, as well as a little makeup. I put myself together again, and reenter the hallway with a smile. It's time for rehearsal. I've got to keep it together.

I am fine.

"Gigi!" Will barrels into the studio. His grin is so wide it looks like it hurts. He waves around one of those celeb magazines he's always reading, and it takes me a minute to realize why he's so excited. "*People.* Page fifty-two! You are *gorgeous*!"

He squishes right up next to me and we pore over a four-page spread, with shots of me dancing with Will, hanging with Cassie, and even in class. Along the side of the third page sits a strip of photo booth pictures of me and Alec. He wouldn't talk to the reporter or be in the shoot, but I handed over these photos to work the "it couple" angle as part of the story. The headline shouts "American Ballet Conservatory's Phoenix Rising!" The Q&A talks about my struggle to recover. I didn't mention Bette's name, but the magazine speculates about her involvement and her dismissal from school. Right there, in black and white, it quotes Mr. K calling me "a real contender for the American Ballet Company apprenticeship."

"It's amazing!" I take a few quick photos of the spread with my phone, and compose a group text to Mama, Aunt Leah, and a few friends. As I hit send, I have the perfect idea. "Will, do me a favor. Get me a hundred copies of this magazine. I'll give you the money. I need to send them to a very special someone." We smile at each other.

In the studio, the Level 8 boys and girls are spread out, waiting for Mr. K and Damien, who enter with Morkie and Pavlovich, the male ballet teacher Doubrava, and others I've never seen before. They take their seats in chairs set up at the front of the studio. Mr. K claps his hands to call us all to attention. We're on our feet and huddle together like his flock.

"An update on Eleanor: she's home and doing better, and will return to school in a week. Tonight, I will meet with each of you individually in my office. Damien will observe the meetings. We will discuss where you're at and chart your progress. The *Swan Lake* audition is two weeks away. You must be ready."

Mr. K takes Sei-Jin first, then Henri. The girl-boy pattern continues while the rest of us wait, and eventually they run out of boys. The teachers watch us, and some dancers are afraid to even talk. They stretch and take deep breaths. These surprise individual meetings have everyone rattled. I hear Alec's voice and I decide to sink into a face-down stretch to tune everything out. I can't rid my thoughts of Eleanor. I think about what Mama would think if she knew what I'd done. I think about whether I should tell Eleanor and apologize.

The secretary returns to the studio door and announces the next dancer. I try not to look at Alec when his name is called. I try to ignore the ache inside of me now that we're not talking, and sort of broken up. I decide to meditate while stretching. My body sinks into the floor and my breathing steadies. The deep pulls in my hamstrings and back relax me. The noises in the room disappear, and all I hear is the steady thrum of my relaxed heart.

Eleanor's name still echoes in the room. It sends a tremor through my body. I close my eyes and try to forget how red her face turned and how she gripped her throat and how her lips ballooned within seconds of dipping veggies into the hummus. I try to forget the sound of her losing air as her throat closed. I try to forget the way she looked at me. Helpless. Afraid.

"She's okay now," I mutter to myself. "She's fine."

Cassie laughs. I catch glimpses of her and think about how I'm going to confront her about the hummus she gave me and the lie she told me about Eleanor's allergy. I don't know what calling her out will feel like or how she'll react. I'm terrified of losing her as a friend.

I shake out my arms and legs, and try to focus on dancing instead.

I will be picked to dance Odette or Odile in Swan Lake.

I will be given a spot in the company at the end of the year.

I feel Cassie's hand on my arm. "Gigi, they've called you like four times."

I sit up too quickly and all the blood rushes to my head. People laugh a little as I scramble toward the door.

"Sorry," I say to the secretary. "I didn't hear you say my name."

I feel terrible that I don't know her name, but she doesn't answer or acknowledge that I've even said anything. She takes long, rushed strides. I keep opening my mouth to ask her a question or two. I can't get any words out and she's not turning her head to give me a reassuring smile or to make sure I'm even there. We're down the hall and through the lobby in what feels like a second, and then down the corridor.

She holds the door open to Mr. K's office.

"Have a seat, Gigi." He doesn't look up from his desk to ensure that it's actually me. Damien sits in a nearby chair, taking notes and reviewing paperwork.

I slide into the chair and sit on my hands so they don't shake. Mr. K turns over several pieces of paper, then finally looks up at me.

"How are you feeling?" His brow furrows and deep wrinkles crease his forehead.

"I'm fine."

"Hmm." He takes the longest pause ever. I swear I can hear the tiny clicks of the clock that sits on his desk.

"Gigi, you aren't dancing like you're fine. I spoke to your physical therapist. She says you've healed nicely, and are getting the strength back in your left hip. But I can tell you aren't confident in your dancing right now."

My head drops down. "I'm working on it every day. I'll be strong again."

"You must fight for it if you want it back. It would be easy to just stay where you are right now—a decent recovery of your technique. But you, unlike many of these other girls, have the one thing ballerinas need to have a career. You have the *danseur russe* flame. It's why I picked you during auditions in San Francisco. I could see you more than the others." His words force tears to drop down my cheeks. I try to wipe them away before he can see them, but I'm too late.

He gets up and puts a hand on my shoulder.

"I'm going to work harder. I promise. I'm going to be that dancer you saw in San Francisco."

"I am confident you will be."

I don't return to Studio C with the others like Mr. K has told me to. I take the elevator to my room instead. A headache punches its way up the back of my neck and settles into my temples. I open my room door and fling my dance bag forward. I don't bother to turn on the lights. My hands find all the origami Alec's ever made for me tacked on my board. With each rip of the paper, my heart thuds with anger and my monitor beeps faster. I curl up on the bed in the dark and wait for the throbbing to slowly drift away like sad, soft music.

18.

June

I'M IN THE CAFÉ, FINISHING up homework and slurping a bowl of broth, when Sei-Jin and her pack of followers walk in. They carefully inspect the various options in the different food stations, all settling on a dinner of grilled steak and veggies, and gather around a table close enough that I can hear their chatter. Much of it is in Korean, so I only catch bits and pieces. But two words I recognize out of Sei-Jin's mouth: Jayhe and love.

Ever so casually, she turns her head my way, catching me in the act of eavesdropping. "Oh, June, she doesn't know yet," she says with that practiced, lip-glossed smile.

I choke after hearing her say my name. "Yes, yes, I applied to three schools already," Sei-Jin tells them. "You know, just in case I don't get a spot here." She stands and walks over, leaning heavily on my table, bringing her face down close to mine. "I think I want to go to school in Providence. It's so lovely. The foliage, the artists." She waits for a reaction.

Stupid. She doesn't know that Jayhe's focusing on NYU, on me. She doesn't know about anything. I gulp down my broth, trying to grin despite the too-hot liquid shooting down my throat. She adds, nearly spitting, "I guess Jayhe and I will just have to enjoy it together."

Trying not to give her the satisfaction, I focus on the little slivers of onion in the yellow liquid, and pick at the small plate of broccoli on my tray. *Eat*, I tell myself. *You have to. Ignore her.*

"Oh, yes, I know. You worry. How will you and Jayhe manage, you here—probably living at home with your mom—and him there, all that distance between you? Especially with me so close by?"

I take a bite of stiff, flavorless steamed broccoli. It scrapes my already raw throat. In that moment, I hate myself for all of it: the undercooked broccoli; the broth; and, worst of all, letting Sei-Jin get to me. "I don't think you have anything that interests him," I tell her, my teeth clenched, my jaw tight. "I mean." I look up, pointed. "Just look at yourself lately. Giving up on being a dancer already?"

She smacks her small fist on the table, but it's laughable, her lack of strength. She barely makes a sound. "Shut up, June." She turns on her heel to walk away, her troops already gathering around. "If anyone should be worrying about their weight, it's you. You think Jayhe will want you? Look at you, with your bowl cut. You look like a little kid."

I stand up, splattering my soup. Her pack gasps and disperses a bit as the rest of the room stops to stare—Sei-Jin doesn't move an inch.

"You did this to me." My hands tug at my hair, and my voice is low, heavy with a threat. "You think you're going to get away with it? You just wait."

"Oh, June." She slams the table again so the hot broth splashes on my arm. "What are you going to do? Shove me down the stairs when no one else is around? You tried that once already, and it didn't work."

I pick up my fork, and I want to stab her with it. A slow smile spreads across Sei-Jin's face, and she knows she's won this round. She sees it in me, this dark side, and she pokes at it on purpose.

"All right, ladies. Cut it out now." The lunch RA finally lumbers over to the table, but the pack scurries before she can quite make it, leaving Sei-Jin and me in our standoff. The woman pries the fork from my hands. "End this now, or I'm going to write you both up. And you don't want that, do you?"

Sei-Jin backs away from the table, but she's still wearing that stubborn, straight-mouthed expression, so I know this isn't over. "You'll see, June. I'll get back at you for all that you've done to me."

As she rushes off, I gather my soup-soaked notebook and head to my room, taking the stairs. When I get to the twelfth floor, I walk right past Cassie and let myself into the bathroom. I run the water in the shower, letting the steam fill the room. I lean over the toilet and stick my fingers in my mouth. This time, it doesn't take more than a second for it all to come up—the broth, the broccoli, the anxiety. All the tension swirls away; and the anger, the hatred I feel for Sei-Jin is just a dull ache now, like

SONA CHARAIPOTRA & DHONIELLE CLAYTON

a muscle stretched a bit too far.

I walk over to Cassie's scale. I reset it to pounds, and step on. The numbers scramble as they always do, and they settle at 102. That's with clothes still on.

A wave of warmth washes over me, relief and something oddly close to joy. It's working—the skipped meals, the extra workouts, the vomiting. It makes me feel invincible.

When I come back out of the bathroom, Cassie's plopped on her bed, her math book set in front of her, her headphones on—they're always on when we're both in the room, so she doesn't have to entertain the idea of talking to me. She looks completely zoned out. She doesn't seem like she's about to go to bed anytime soon.

I click off the overhead lights and climb under my covers, waiting for the impending rage.

Even though her desk lamp provides more than enough light for her to see, she rushes over, and flips them back on.

I get up, walk to the switch, and flip them off again.

She turns them back on.

"Can't you see I'm working?"

"You can work with your desk lamp on. I'm going to sleep."

"Oh, is your eye mask suddenly not enough anymore?"

I stand up, and put my hand on the light switch. She rushes forward and puts her hand on my shoulder. "You could probably boss Gigi around, because she's nice, but I'm not. If you keep messing with me, I'll let Mr. K and Nurse Connie know that you're puking up everything you eat. And every time you use my scale, it records your numbers. You're so obvious."

I remove her hand from my body, as if it's the most disgusting thing that's ever touched me. I walk back to bed, slip the eye mask over my eyes, tune her out, and go to sleep. I know her kind: all words, no action. She doesn't have the guts to tell.

I hope.

The next afternoon, Morkie puts me and Riho side by side again. It's like she gets off on the contrast between us: Riho's small proportions, the flowing grace in all her movements, making me look stiff beside her. I feel like Morkie's setting me up to fail. Mr. K's words from the assessments last week ring in my head: "It's not enough to have perfect technique, June. You have to have passion."

Riho gives me this awkward smile as we both walk to the center. It looks more like a grimace, really, and for a minute I feel sorry for her. "You okay?" she asks in quiet, perfect English. It's the first time she's ever actually spoken to me. I panic about all the things I said about Sei-Jin around her, thinking she couldn't understand. A flush creeps up my chest. "I could ask Morkie to let us go last."

I shake my head, and she smiles again. "I hate going first," she says, making me think about why I automatically slotted her into my nemesis category, why I didn't just let myself warm up to her. She's like me, an outsider—not one of them but not one of the white kids either. There aren't any other Japanese kids this year. She's such a good dancer, she could've commanded her own clique, instead of hanging with Sei-Jin and her pack.

But I know why she does, and I feel a pinch inside, wanting to have my friends back.

I raise my eyebrow at her, signaling I'm ready, not quite willing to commit to a smile. We settle into our spots, waiting for the music.

Morkie shows the class the next part of the Odette variation. Everyone marks it. Except Eleanor, who is still recovering from her terrible allergic reaction. The movements are fast-paced and staccato, all quick, precise feet and big arms. I force myself to relax, not to overthink it. "Ready?" she says to Riho and me.

I bow. The music starts. We spin into the movement, lifting, then turning, lifting, then turning. Morkie hollers out corrections, but she doesn't stop us. We must be decent. I push myself to show her I want to be Odette.

The studio door opens. Morkie waves her hand in the air. We stop. I press my hands on top of my head and will my breathing to slow.

It's Mr. K's assistant. "E-Jun Kim, Mr. K wants you in his office."

Hearing my name makes me jump.

I look from the woman to Morkie and back.

"Go," Morkie says, irritated.

She immediately turns back to Riho. "Excellent. Lots of emotion," I hear her saying as I walk out.

I follow the assistant down the hall and to Mr. K's office, wondering what he could possibly want. My brain is a storm of panic. Maybe they figured out Sei-Jin cut my hair. The RAs said they'd investigate. Though it's been almost a full month since it happened. Or maybe Sei-Jin told them about the butterflies.

When I get to Mr. K's office, he's sitting at his desk, wearing a serious expression.

That's when I see Nurse Connie. She's sitting across from Mr. K, in the seat closest to the wall. My stomach clenches. "Have a seat, E-Jun," she says, patting the chair next to her.

I sit across from Mr. K, who has my file spread in front of him—I can see the numbers on my weight chart, the triple digits as they fall to doubles, getting smaller and smaller.

"When you got back to school this year, E-Jun, I was so pleased by your progress," Nurse Connie says. "You were up to a solid one hundred and eight at the first weigh-in. We thought you were doing so well. Anorexia and bulimia are usually lifetime struggles."

I wince at the words, not willing to accept them. My stomach clenches as I unravel where this is headed. During the past few weigh-ins, Nurse Connie frowned every time I stepped on the scale, the deep line on her forehead getting bigger as the number on the scale got smaller.

I try to tell them I'm fine, but the words don't come out.

"Sadly, E-Jun," she says, "your numbers have been steadily dropping." She looks down at the file, the numbers upside down and all wrong.

Mr. K interrupts then. "We don't tolerate these habits. You've been here long enough to know that. You've seen other girls—stronger dancers—get dismissed from this institution for this behavior." The exasperation is heavy in his voice.

Nurse Connie asks what I've eaten today.

"Chicken soup and salad." It was broth, really, but soup sounds better. Heartier. "And coffee with cream." Cream always sounds so lush.

"And did you purge it?"

I panic. Cassie told them, just like she said she would.

Mr. K's eyes burn into me. The silence stretches around me. My skin warms. I don't know why I do it, but I nod. I tell the truth. I can't bear the weight of their stares or the silence. I don't know how to lie to this man.

"Should she be hospitalized?" Mr. K asks, shaking his head, his tone defeated, as if I'm the latest conservatory catastrophe. An eating scandal is the last thing the school needs right now.

There's a knock on the door, loud and insistent. Nurse Connie opens the door.

"No way. You cannot talk to my daughter like this without me." My mom stands in the doorway. "You were supposed to wait to start this meeting—"

"Ms. Kim, please come in. We really haven't started the entire meeting." He's using that familiar, coddling tone he reserves for parents. I want to interrupt and tell her that he lied.

Mr. K's assistant offers my mother her seat. My mom glares as she takes it. "Now, Ms. Kim, Nurse Connie has been worried about E-Jun's numbers for months. Due to previous incidents, we have no choice but to take immediate action. This type of behavior spreads like a virus."

"I can fix this, Mr. K," I blurt out.

"Lots of dancers have struggles with food." Mr. K sighs, like this conversation is exhausting him. "But to be a ballerina one must be strong. All muscle. And you cannot do that without eating."

"I know." His words settle into me, and shame floods my body.

"I want to talk with June alone," my mom says. "Please

excuse us one moment."

Mr. K nods and says, "We'll step out for a bit."

Nurse Connie follows him out the door.

My mom stands up and looks down, towering over me for once, as I sit slumped in the chair. "I know your fears. I had the same ones." She takes a deep breath. The quaver in her voice makes me look up at her, seeing her clearly for maybe the first time ever. "I know you want this. I know you do." She takes my hand, and hers is cold and frail. "But this will kill you. Make you so sick you won't be able to dance anymore." She's looking at my hand now, and it takes me a minute to see the similarities—how bony and taut it is, so much like her own.

"You trust me?" she asks.

I nod.

Mr. K knocks. My mom reopens his office door. Mr. K and Nurse Connie come barreling back into the room. Mr. K takes his seat, and gets straight back to business. "As you already know, Ms. Kim," he says, addressing my mom and not me, "this has been a difficult year for American Ballet Conservatory and for my Level 8 dancers. June's eating, well, as we all understand it, this has been a problem for quite a while. One that Nurse Connie here has tried repeatedly to address with June."

Nurse Connie nods. "For a while there, I thought we'd truly turned a corner, that June was getting better—that she wanted to get better. But the downward spiral is starting again."

My mom nods, but if she's startled she doesn't let it show. She waits for them to continue.

"We have to make a tough decision here about whether to

dismiss her or not," Mr. K says.

"You will not dismiss her." She hands him an envelope, and in it I see what looks like conservatory letterhead. "Take a look, Mr. K. You'll see, according to the letter from the board, that June will remain at the conservatory through the end of the year, when she graduates. She will audition for Damien Leger, just like the rest of the students, and dance in *Swan Lake* performance." She looks at me, her face still firm. "Make no mistake, her weight is a problem, and she will fix it. But Nurse Connie will not be involved. Per my discussion with the board, June will work with a professional counselor I hired, with a custom menu for her meals with Korean food, not American food. She will meet with her twice a week."

"But—"

She doesn't let him finish. "What you're doing doesn't work. This will."

When he opens his mouth again, my mom adds: "Also, Mr. K, June has invested lot of time and money into this conservatory. It doesn't make sense for her to finish elsewhere, whether she chooses to dance or decides to go to college. You see trustee board approvals, correct?" She doesn't say my father's name, but we all know it's there. "Then we should be all set."

With that, she rises, motioning for me to get up, too. "June, *yobo*, come now. I'm sure you have class."

We walk in silence back to the elevators, and she buttons up her coat, ready to leave. But as she turns away, I grab her arm. "Thank you." I'm trying my best not to cry. I know my dance class will let out any second, and I can't let the others see me like this. "For everything. I'll get better, I promise you that. I'll work with a counselor, I'll do whatever she asks, I'll be strong and sturdy and do you proud."

She nods, silent for a minute. "I want to tell you something, E-Jun." She's standing so close to me, we could embrace. But we don't. "What happened today is not your fault. It's mine. When you were a small girl, you saw a ballerina for the first time, and your face lit up. And—" She chokes a bit on her words, wipes at her face with her gloves. "And I thought, she's like me. A dancer. It made me so, so happy. I admit, it meant you were like him, too. We could prove to *him* that we were good enough—that you were good enough. So I push you. Hard. And realized my mistake too late. You love to dance. You live to dance. But dying to dance? No, E-Jun. This I will not allow." My mom looks square at me. "So prove you can be healthy. I will not support ballet if you're not healthy."

I nod, and for a moment we just stand there, staring at each other. Then she pats my shoulder, and pushes the button for the elevator. When it dings, she watches me as I get into the elevator, pushing the button for the twelfth floor. My eyes stay on her as the doors start to close, and for the first time in months, I feel like I can do this. I stick my hand between the elevator doors just as they're about to lock shut, and they retract.

But when I step back outside, she's already gone.

19.

Bette

DAD SITS AT OUR TABLE for the first time in years. The Christmas tree behind him washes his cream-colored sweater in reds and greens. Even though it's Thanksgiving, the tree has to be up. It's an Abney tradition. Justina brings him a fresh glass of Scotch and pours my mother another glass of wine. I guess they're going toe-to-toe tonight. The stress of having to deal with each other is too much for both of them. The puzzle pieces might be too warped to fit.

"It's nice to have us all here," my mother says, and I can't fight the feeling that I agree with her. I almost reach for her, to pat her hand, but she's still my mother. She's still untouchable and unpredictable. A server appears in the room, and I realize my mother has pulled out all the stops for tonight. My father looks pleased when Adele finally settles in at the table, across from him and next to me. "Auditions soon. How are things going?"

"Fine."

"How are your roommates?"

"Great."

"Are you seeing anyone?"

"No," she says. She's here, she's committed, but if he thinks she'll make things easy on him, well, he's in for it.

The server places butternut squash soup in front of us. I watch my dad eat. He spoons soup into his mouth and holds it there for a few seconds longer than everyone else at the table, as if he's savoring it. I wonder if he likes the Thanksgiving menu my mother settled on. She and Adele fussed over it in the kitchen for days. I wonder if he misses this, misses us.

"How's Howard?" my mother asks about my father's business partner. I wouldn't recognize him if I walked past him on the street.

"Howard is great. Their oldest, Benji, just got engaged. Eugenia is busy helping her future daughter-in-law plan the wedding and driving him crazy. Eugenia asks about the girls, and you, all the time."

"Does she now?" My mother downs the rest of the red wine in her glass. "Well, she stopped calling after you divorced me."

Adele drops her soup spoon. The clatter rings out but isn't loud enough to cover up what my mother has just said.

"That's a most unfortunate thing." Dad paves right over it, like she's just commented that the soup is too cold. "Adele, my secretary called ABC today to purchase a block of tickets for the anniversary performance. Should we invest in one of the sponsor packages as well?"

Adele doesn't look up from her bowl. She shrugs her shoulders. I guess she's done talking for tonight. If you could call what she's managed to say so far actual talking.

"It can't hurt." I try to fill the silence. "Every little bit helps."

"It's nice for us to show our support for Adele, too," he says, totally missing the point.

"Yeah, I mean, that's obvious." Although you could support me, too, I want to add. But I don't. "I've almost figured out who really pushed Gigi and—"

My father slams down his spoon then, and looks at me. He really looks at me, for the first time in months, maybe even years. I think he's going to say "Great" or "You'll be cleared in no time." Instead, he sighs. "Bette," he says, like he's talking about some petulant, six-year-old version of me, "the settlement is done."

I want to pout. Honestly, that's my gut reaction. But I can't. It'll just make him continue to think it's okay to talk to me that way, like I'm not nearly an adult who's been living on her own for almost a decade. We sit in silence as soup bowls are replaced with salads and slices of turkey. No sweet potatoes for me this year, I guess. Then the plates are cleared, and dessert is presented to us.

"So now you're giving me the silent treatment?" My father laughs. It's painful.

"What else should we say?" I scrape the plate, just to piss them all off.

He finishes his drink. "Well, I thought it would be nice for you guys to spend some more time with me, so I arranged a brunch for tomorrow. Your mother"—he looks pointedly in her direction, as if she should confirm—"said that it would be fine, and that both of your schedules are clear. There's this woman I've been seeing, Sara Beth. She's lovely. It's getting serious, so I'd like you girls to meet her."

My mother pushes away from the table, startling everyone.

"I'd rather not—" I start to say, but she interrupts.

"You didn't tell me that." She turns to my father, her voice cold as the November air. "Not happening. Not anytime soon."

"Rebecca, you can't be serious about this."

"Oh, I'm dead serious. You are welcome to take your daughters to brunch. Alone."

"You know I've been seeing Sara Beth—"

"Way more than you see your daughters? Yes, we're all well aware of that fact. Especially given that Bette has been suffering enormously the past few months, and you've barely been around. And frankly"—she waves away the staff—"maybe it's better that way. This whole 'family Thanksgiving' was an error in judgment on my part, girls." Her words feel directed at Adele, who has been silent this whole time. "Robert, I think it's best if you leave."

My dad looks floored, but he doesn't wear humiliation well. "Girls, you know, honestly, that I'm just a phone call away, right?"

Adele chooses that moment to speak. "That's just it, Dad, isn't it? You're just a phone call. That's all."

My father looks devastated as he walks out. So why am I the one who feels like I've been socked in the stomach?

Adele starts on her pie, and aside from the clanging of the

fine china, we eat in silence. All in all, it feels very much like your typical Abney holiday celebration.

The next day, I sit at the desk in my bedroom in front of the lawyers' boxes, poring over files again, when Justina comes in with a large box. The postmark features the conservatory's zip code, and my heart leaps. I tear into the heavy cardboard box. Inside is a stack of *People* magazines, probably about a hundred copies, all identical. I don't get it. There's some random country star on the cover. I flip through the pages, trying to figure it out, and there is Gigi, beaming up at me.

I always wanted to see my name in this magazine. Now, I finally do. But in this heartwarming story about this phoenix's rise from the ashes at the American Ballet Conservatory, Bette Abney has been cast as the villain. Not by Gigi herself. Oh no, she's too "nice" to point a finger like that. The article mentions the settlement, though, implying that it was in the seven figures. Implying my guilt.

I expect tears, rage, fury. But all I can manage is exhaustion. Maybe the battle is really over. Maybe she's really won. I run my fingers over an image of her as the Sugar Plum Fairy, and she really is luminous.

That's when I see the pictures of her and Alec, a cutesy, lovey-dovey photo booth strip running down the side of the third page of the story. They look smitten. Seeing those photos of her cuddling up to Alec, my heart sinks all the way down to my toes, and I realize, maybe for the first time, just how much I really miss him. How much I really miss us. Especially on a thankless day like today. I shiver and pull my wrap sweater tighter around me. I want to curl up in my bed and not wake up until after New Year's.

I know Will sent these to me. Or worse, maybe Gigi. They pulled that trick right out of my playbook.

I open up my phone. I click on the camera app even though I know Gigi went to California and Cassie is probably home with the Lucas clan for the Thanksgiving holiday. The dorm rooms are empty. My father's words echo in my head like they've been said through a megaphone: *The settlement is done.*

I throw my phone across the room. It crashes into a stack of CDs on the shelf, then rings. I've probably messed up my phone, but it still blares out. I scramble for it and answer.

"Hello?"

"Hello?" the voice replies. "Who is this?"

"How'd you get this number?" I ask.

"You left it for me. On YouTube."

I suck in a breath and hold it in my chest. I don't know what to say. Maybe: *Hi, my name is Bette Abney and I think you have footage of the night when a girl was shoved into a car, and it got blamed on me, and I need to see whatever that is.*

"You there?"

"Yeah, yeah, sorry. Here." I put on my mother's most professional tone. "My name is Bette Abney, and I'm a dancer with the American Ballet Conservatory. You might have—"

"You're one of those girls from that night at the club. The accident. Right?"

This guy doesn't mess around. "Yes. I don't know if you've

been following the situation but Gigi—Giselle Stewart—the girl who was hit, she's doing much better. She's one of my friends." I slip in the tiny lie.

"Oh, that's good. She was beautiful—you all were. I was worried about her."

"We're trying to figure out who pushed her. Did you have the rest of the footage?"

"I saw it all go down." There's a gross smirk in his voice.

"So who did you see? Can you clarify for me?" I use words like the lawyers did. I squeeze my phone so tightly I can feel it start to bend under the weight of my grip. All the bits of my life lay shattered, a mess that I'm painstakingly trying to put together, on the top of my desk.

"I have the rest of the footage, but it got flagged on YouTube for being too violent."

"Can I share it with her?" This could be it. This could be exactly what I need to clear my name. I work hard not to sound overeager, not to scare this guy off. "It could be super helpful in resolving this matter."

"Yeah, I don't need it. I'm emailing it to you right now. Same address as the one in the message, right?"

"Yes." I try not to sound breathless and desperate. I flip open my laptop and click on my email. "Thank you. I really appreciate it." I try to stay calm. I wait for him to ask for money or something in return. I don't believe in Good Samaritans.

But a few seconds later, the email pops up from Jeff Waters.

"Enjoy." He hangs up.

I click on the attachment. I watch us stumble out of the club.

My heart thuds as I fast-forward to the place where it cut off online. I hear Gigi's laugh. I see Alec, Will, and Eleanor and me, not far behind them. June holds hands and steals kisses with Jayhe.

The camera wobbles. My cheeks flush and I grind my teeth. The taxi lurches down the street. Gigi flies forward. In the next moment, she's sprawled out in the street, in front of the taxi. It was that fast. I rewind it and try to catch who did it. But I can't quite make it out. I rewind it again. It's still too quick. I open a new tab and search for a slow-motion app. I download it and open the video file through that. Then I watch it all happen again, slowly unfolding on my screen. I see the hands on her back.

I fight the upward pull of a smile across my mouth.

I know exactly who did it. And for once, on this otherwise desperate holiday, I have something to be thankful for.

20.

Gigi

TODAY I GET A LITTLE peek at my future. The one I've been dreaming of since I was just a little girl. The *Swan Lake* auditions are held in the new American Ballet Company building, which is across the plaza from the conservatory. Sunlight washes the marble in rich golden yellows, and for a moment the space looks less intimidating than it is. The place I want to be cast as a lead in *Swan Lake*. The place I want to be called a rising star. The place I want to spend my career.

In my head, my life as a professional ballerina plays over and over. Shows at night. Traveling all over the world with the company. Working my way from the corps to soloist, and then to principal. I haven't made room for any other life. I wouldn't know what to do.

I'm a whole three hours early. I needed to be able to come over here alone, to get away from stretching dancers and girls running around the hall trying to figure the best black leotard for the auditions and all the chatter about Damien Leger and his preferences. Old worries creep back into me, but I don't have Alec to talk to now. We haven't talked since our argument.

The doors slide open to the company lobby. It even smells different in here than in the conservatory. A rush of heat warms me up from the cold December wind outside. Floor-to-ceiling portraits of company stars line the walls. Elevators ping open and shut. Dancers move in and out of them, many wearing company logoed sweats. Glass-walled studios reveal dancers in various stages of movement. There's modern dance in one. Folk dancing in another. Hip hop in a third. When I look up, I can see four more studios full of ballerinas working through classical choreography. Skylights let in so much sun I'm almost blinded.

There's a man sitting at an info desk. "Excuse me, can I help you?" I don't realize he's talking to me until he repeats himself. "Hey you, miss. Can I help you?" He isn't angry, but annoyed.

"I dance at the conservatory. I'm here for the *Swan Lake* audition."

"Do you have your ID?" He's walking back to his desk now, and I guess I'm supposed to follow.

"I don't have it. It's back in my dorm room."

"So how am I supposed to believe you?"

I can't tell if he's joking or not, so I sort of laugh and motion to my clothes. I'm dressed like a ballerina—hair in a bun, mukluks on my feet to keep them comfy, sweats, dance bag, and even a little audition makeup. I take off my winter coat to show him my conservatory hoodie.

"People just show up here, you know? Crazies obsessed with ballet." He starts to trail off on a tangent about the ballet weirdos.

"Gigi?" Someone behind me says my name. I turn around. Bette's face stares back at me. Except it isn't really her, it's her sister, Adele, who's just walked into the building. They look so much alike that my heart accelerates and my monitor buzzes.

"Don't you look lovely today, Adele Abney," the guard says.

"And you're lovelier than ever," she coos back. Even her voice has the same melodic lilt that Bette's does. "Are you giving one of the conservatory's finest a hard time?"

"Little thing doesn't have her ID," he says. "Policy. Can't let her in."

"Well, she'll be coming with me. She's here for the auditions, I'm sure of it. And there will be many more flooding in. They start at six p.m."

Adele leans over his desk and they whisper about something I can't hear. As annoying as he is, I'm actually glad he doesn't recognize me from the articles or the TV segment that ran earlier in the week about the school and the accident.

"Gigi, let me show you where you all will be." Her hand finds my shoulder and she ushers me away from the desk, farther into the lobby of the American Ballet Company. "Don't mind him. He's overzealous and takes his job way too seriously. He's been here a million years." She turns down a hall.

"Oh." That's all I can seem to get out. Walking this close to Bette's sister, Mr. K's favorite dancer, the star of the American Ballet Company, feels weird. She even smells like Bette—a powdery, sweet, and light perfume mixed with the scent of expensive clothes.

"Auditions will be in here." She points into a studio that's being set up with extra barres through the center and chairs along the mirror. "And the dressing room is around the corner for you to change."

"Thanks." I'm not sure how to make any sort of meaningful conversation. This is the woman we all want to be. "Also, I appreciate you helping me out back there with that guy. I just wanted to be here early to get ready."

She strokes my shoulder. "Oh, I get it. And—" she pauses, "I just wanted to apologize for anything my little sister did to make you feel uncomfortable. All this"—she motions around with her hands—"can really get to a person." She waits for me to say something. "I mean, that's not an excuse for whatever she may have done. Just saying."

I nod. Do I say thank you for apologizing for Bette, or tell her I hate her sister? Do I remind her that those little pranks turned into me getting seriously hurt? That Bette shoved me in front of a moving car?

She changes the subject before I can even get anything out. "Our cast lists go up tonight after your audition is done. So we'll be watching you."

"You will?"

"Yeah, don't worry. It won't be a big deal."

Several company members rush down the hall and start talking to Adele. Their eyes flit over me, brightening with recognition—probably from the newspapers rather than any talent I might have—but they say nothing as if I'm not even standing there. They sweep her away.

"See you in there later, Gigi," she calls out.

Just like that she's disappeared. Heading into one of the practice studios, I text Cassie about the run-in and Adele's apology. She texts back a WTF. I send Will a message, asking him to come over here early to warm up, but he doesn't answer. I head to the lockers to change, then find a place to stretch and think about the audition. I plot out in my head exactly how things will go.

Two hours later, all the girls are outside the studio, preparing to be invited in. Cassie sits beside me. We shake out our legs and bounce on our heels and smile at each other. Neither of us says a word. We both have to dance well tonight, and it's getting hard to concentrate as the room fills up with dozens of bodies.

The studio doors open.

"Good luck," she whispers. *"Merde."*

"You, too."

All the Level 8 girls line up, along with a few select lower levels, like Riho and Isabela. We are each given a place at the barre. A few company members stand outside the glass walls. There's waving behind the glass. I squint to see.

It's Mama and Aunt Leah. An embarrassed flush covers me. Mama smiles and blows me a kiss. Despite the hovering, I'm glad she's there. Better than any lucky charm, her presence makes me stand taller, feel stronger, more like my old self.

Damien marches into the studio, then Mr. K right behind him. There are two rows of chairs in the front of the studio, and it feels like the most important audience I've ever danced for.

Damien gives us barre combinations in rapid-fire succession from *pliés* to *tendus* to *ronds de jambe* and turns at the barres. We do twenty minutes of exercises, then he comes around to inspect each one of us on the last combination. "*Tendu* front. *Demi-plié*. Then, *tendu* back. Turn away from the barre, arabesque."

I can feel him getting closer, but I try to focus on pointing my toe and working through the positions fully. I try to center myself in the here and now, knowing every second counts. Damien gazes at me for a moment, but he doesn't say anything. He gives us twelve more barre combinations, and we work until our feet are warmed up and sweat drips down our backs. I try not to watch the company members in the mirror, but their faces are distracting. So I focus on my breathing, listening to the rhythm it makes. I tell my heart to be strong. I remind myself it has to be all effortless turns, soft fingers, and the cleanest positions.

Damien motions to the pianist to stop. "Please remove the barres. Put them in the far corners. Change into pointe shoes."

I quickly change shoes, take a gulp of water, then warm up my feet.

Madame Dorokhova shows us the adagio routine she'd like to see. It's based on one of Odette's *Swan Lake* solos from Act Two. She goes through the complicated series of arm lifts, combinations, glissades, and turns. We mark it twice with the music. Then she splits us into small groups of three. I'm up first, with Eleanor and Cassie and a few others. I don't make eye contact with Eleanor. I haven't been able to apologize to her yet—and maybe after a month, it's too late. Guilt creeps up every time I see her, and I have to work to push it down. June's among girls in the second group, left to wait in their pool of anxiety and panic. I can feel her eyes boring into me, nearly throwing me off-balance.

Focus, I tell myself. *Relax*. I know I've got this. I position myself in front. I close my eyes until the third chord beat and I let myself forget that anyone else is in the room. I sink into the melodies. Madame Dorokhova's adagio is sad and slow and we have to hold poses for long stretches. I explode out of my stance with big leaps and sweeping arms, catching everyone by surprise. I dance long after the adagio has ended and the other girls have stopped. I build on to Madame Dorokhova's beautiful choreography, and the company pianist gives me another full chord to finish.

When I'm done, no one looks particularly pleased. I know I shouldn't have done that, but I smile, curtsy, move out of the center for the next group of dancers. I should go, but I need a minute to just revel in the flush of heat inside me and my labored breaths.

That was just for me, and for Mama.

21.

June

FOCUS. THAT'S WHAT I KEEP telling myself. In thirty more minutes, this will all be over, and my fate will be decided, for better or worse.

"Out of the center," Madame Dorokhova tells Gigi. I wish I could be like Gigi in that moment, just happy to be here, embracing the journey as much as the destination. But it's not about that for me. I need to do well here. It's now or never.

"Next batch," Dorokhova shouts, and I leap forward.

Eight of us shift from the studio's edges into the center. My legs are steady and strong, even as my heart thumps so hard and fast I feel like the whole studio must hear it. I look at the familiar faces all around me, some wrecked with nerves, others calm and determined. I wonder where I fall on the spectrum.

Dorokhova positions all of us, putting Sei-Jin, Riho, Isabela, and me at the very front.

"Ready?" she says.

I take a deep breath and steel myself. Eyes stare in from behind the glass and the ballet masters and mistresses sit right in front of us, taking notes, whispering assessments. The light in here is so bright you would think it was the sun. I arch my back. I flicker my hands out so they look soft and delicate.

The music starts. My heart drums alongside the syncopated beats from the piano.

You deserve this, June, I tell myself. *You've worked hard to be here.*

I step up on pointe and into *glissade* and arabesque and then *piqué* turns. The music builds into a series of crescendos. I turn, lift, and glide; turn, lift, and glide. I hear Bette's voice in my head, reminding me to relax, to smile, to enjoy myself, all while keeping my lines lean and endless, my jumps graceful and controlled. Her advice anchors me. I take a moment to listen to music as we move, letting it envelop me, letting myself forget that Damien, Dorokhova, and the others are here. I imagine myself basking under the bright lights of Lincoln Center, the warmth of the audience's applause as they celebrate my movements, fluid and flawless.

At the same time, I concentrate on lengthening, showing how far I can stretch my legs and arms in these movements. When I was little, I used to wish I'd been made of gum so I could bend myself into impossible shapes. Ballerina shapes.

I buzz with adrenaline. The rush leaves me breathless and flushed, a pretty ballerina pink. I beam outwardly, embracing the final thrums of the music as I spin into the final, impeccable pirouette. As we all curtsy into deep *révérences*, I'm still smiling.

No one claps or comments or even looks up. They're too busy scribbling notes in their files as if we're strangers—as if they hadn't spent the last decade grooming us.

"Company dancers, cast list shortly!" Damien Leger shouts, and we're escorted off center. Just like that, it's all over.

As we exit the room, Sei-Jin and her gaggle embrace one another in a relieved, exhausted group-hug thing. For just one second, I want to join them, wrapping my sweaty, shaky arms around the pack. Instead, I take a seat on the floor near the door, not far from where Adele and the other company members are settling in. Their cast list is about to go up, and my curiosity won't let me leave this space, this moment, its gravity.

I watch the company apprentices gather, their excitement heady and sweet. They're all beautiful, stunning in their easy grace. There's Russian import Katarina Plotkin, with her dark eyes and hair framing snow-white skin, lithe and elegant. She's whispering with all-American Becca Thomas, who looks like she stepped out of *Dance* magazine, all long, lean lines and bright green eyes. Then there's Ting Wu, a Chinese-born Cali girl, an inspiration to Sei-Jin and her crew. And to me, I guess, if I let myself admit it. She gives me hope.

If she can make it to the American Ballet Company stage, maybe I can, too. I imagine Damien looking at these beautiful dancers and picking them apart—putting together the perfect ballerina, piece by piece. He'd pair Ting's strong legs and Katarina's flawless feet, and add Becca's corn silk crown. They all fly now toward a flushed, happy Adele, who throws her head back laughing.

"Odette and Odile, can you believe it?" she says, and the others wrap her into a warm, congratulatory huddle. "It hasn't hit me yet!"

Damien made a great choice in casting her. She's a melding of form and technique, of beauty and charisma. It's a rare thing she has. I see a raw version of it in Bette.

My phone buzzes once, twice, three times, an endless stream of texts from my mom, ranting about the fact that I've missed yesterday's appointment with Taylor, the therapist.

That's three in a row.

You need to get better.

This is costing me money.

Do you want to get better?

Of course I do. But I also want to be here, to do this. Preparing for auditions has taken up all my focus the last few weeks, and rehearsals will take over soon. If I want what Adele has, I can't afford to focus on anything else.

22.

Bette

MY FATHER DOESN'T COME INSIDE when he arrives. He stays in his car and has the driver honk. When he called, he wouldn't give me many details. He just said that he'd talked to Damien, and that I should be ready for an audition. I was too busy shrieking with glee to catch much of the rest of it.

Audition. That word pulses through me like my own heartbeat. My hair is pulled back tight into a proper bun, and I have on a brand-new leotard. I always buy new ones at the start of every school year and I was cocky enough to think that I would be back for the first day of school, so I bought a bunch of new ones. I chose a long-sleeved one that dips low in the back. I can feel the cold pushing in through my down coat as I walk out to the car.

"What's happening?" I slide into the back of his car.

As the driver pulls into Central Park, headed for the West Side of Manhattan, my father's staring out the window like a tourist.

"Dad?"

"You haven't called me that in so long." He laughs.

I lightly hit his shoulder and start to laugh, too, even though I'm mostly a bunch of nerves and questions and worries. It feels good to be with him like this after the disaster that was Thanksgiving.

"It's over. You're clear," he says, and he's grinning, even though I can tell he's trying not to.

"You went to the school?"

"I went with the lawyer, and showed him the video you sent to your mom and me. He called that stuffy Russian man at the conservatory, and he came to my office. Then I got it done."

"Got it done?"

"Done." The car pulls up to the light across from the school campus. "Suspension is gone. Your record is cleared. And your audition is for a role in the anniversary ballet. *Swan Lake*?"

"Just like that?"

"Yes."

The driver pulls up to one of the entrances to the plaza. Seeing the building now with this new information and all dressed up, a flicker of excitement rushes through me. Getting back here always felt like some far-off *thing*. I could see it in the distance like a blinking light, always there and always just a little bit out of reach.

The driver opens my door.

"I'll be waiting here when you're done. Have a conference call to take—" The phone interrupts. "There's my call."

"Dad." I want to hug him, but I feel awkward. The distance

between us might be too far to cross, even after this. "Thank you." I slide out of the car. He smiles at me, and I realize that his mouth curves up just like Adele's does when she smiles. I think about asking him how much it cost or what promises he made or if the video actually took it all away. Instead, I hustle across the Rose Abney Plaza and into the company building before the whole moment disappears.

The man at the front desk looks at me and smiles. "You must be Adele's little sister 'cause you look like she spit you out."

"Yes. I'm here to see Mr. Leger."

"They told me to send you upstairs to Studio Four. Take the elevators to the fifth floor, then turn right once you're off it." I let him tell me all these details, even though my sister is the new face of ABC, and I know this building backward and forward.

It's eerily quiet upstairs. The company members are long gone for the day, and most of the studios are dark and empty, only reflecting bits of light from the street across the barres. But the very last one at the end of the hall is bright, glowing, almost like it's on fire. I inch closer, moving more slowly than I've ever walked. For once I'm scared, and it vibrates through my whole body. I take a pill out from my necklace, and swallow it down without a sip of water, wishing I could feel that hum of focus immediately. I close my eyes and ask it to help me get through this, help me to get all the things I've worked for, help me remind them (and myself) that this is where I'm supposed to be.

Inside the studio are Damien and Yelena Dorokhova, another company director. I stand in the doorway, unsure of what to do with myself. Should I announce that I'm here? Should I stand here and wait for them to invite me in?

I'm Bette Abney and I belong here.

I smooth the edges of my hair and walk in.

Damien turns around. "Well, aren't you a little Adele?"

"I'm Bette." I want to add that I'm strong, not delicate like my sister.

He shakes my hand, and I curtsy. "I'm pleased to meet you. Your sister said wonderful things about you and your technique. And she did say you were different from her."

The way he says the word *different* makes me wonder exactly what Adele said, and if it was positive. She never tells me what she thinks of my dancing.

"We are different."

"Well, then, I'm looking forward to seeing that."

They give me fifteen minutes to warm up, even though I really need at least an hour, but I don't dare complain.

"Start at the barre, please." Damien takes a seat at the front of the studio. Madame Dorokhova shows me combinations, working through the positions, and then signals a pianist to play. She doesn't let me mark it, but now the sharp focus of my pills rushes through me and I don't miss a word from her mouth. I do every motion perfectly—elongating my neck, softening my hands, fully pointing my toes, extending through each position. Morkie's instructions are on repeat in my head—her familiar bark echoing like she's standing right there in the corner of the studio. Extension, grace, clean footwork, beauty, precision.

After they're pleased with my barre work, I move to the center. She gives me classical combinations from Odette's first act solo. I remember seeing Adele cast as a little swan when Mr. K did the ballet with the Level 8 girls during her ninth-grade year. She was pulled from Level 5 ballet to rehearse. She showed me her variations in our basement ballet studio whenever she came home for the weekend. She reminded me that the trick is in the contrast—the light, airy goodness of the white swan, versus the dark seduction of the black. If you can't pull them both off, you're not cut out for this at all.

Swan Lake is the most beautiful ballet there is, and my time with Adele in our studio together, working on these very steps, is one of the reasons I wanted to be a ballerina.

I lengthen my line so that I have the perfect reflection of a ballerina in the mirror, and when I turn I make sure to point my foot as far as it can go before getting a cramp or triggering a muscle spasm. I dance as if someone is pulling me up toward the sky. I smile with each *piqué*, pirouette, and arabesque.

Damien claps when Madame Dorokhova is done with me. My cheeks are pink and I'm that good kind of exhausted, the kind that makes you sleep better at night.

"You have your sister's feet, but a sharper edge." He circles me like a vulture, hungry, pleased. "It's an interesting combination. I can definitely cast you. And I don't know what you did in past years, or even what your role in the conservatory scandal with the other dancer was, but leave it behind. Start over."

"Yes," I barely get out. And just like that, I'm back.

23.

Gigi

A WEEK AFTER THE *Swan Lake* auditions, we're in the lobby after ballet class, waiting for the revelation of the cast list. Parents shuffle in through the doors. A heavy snow starts to fall outside the windows. The wind slams up against the panes. It feels like last year. Except this time I revel in the whispers. My name is whispered alongside *Odette* and *Odile*. It gets louder and louder, like the crescendo in a wave or orchestra music. It's all I can hear as the teachers start to file in. It's all I can think about. How different it will be. How rare it is—nearly impossible—for dancers of color to earn the lead in the "white" ballets dependent on the ballet *blanc*. How I'll be the first one at the conservatory if I'm picked.

I look for Will and spot him near the front desk. His back is to the crowd, and even from here I can tell he's tense. I wave my hand in the air, hoping he'll turn around and come to where I'm standing. I've carved out a little spot with my dance bag plopped on the floor.

Alec is to my far right. I can hear him talking to the boys, saying, "May the best Siegfried win." Each word seems to hit me, makes me miss him, the warmth and safety of his arms wrapped around me, having someone to share this moment with.

Eleanor is the only one of us sitting on the floor. She's stretching with her eyes closed and her lips mumbling. June is somewhere behind me, but I don't want to turn and look. All I think about when I see her are my butterflies and cutting her hair. A knot twists in my stomach just thinking about it. I remind myself that she deserved it. I remind myself that her hair is already growing back, so it's fine.

Cassie comes up. "You ready?"

"Yes."

"This is it." It's weird talking to Cassie about everything. In the few months she's been here, she's really been a friend to me. But in this moment, as much as we'd like not to think about it, we're competitors. Still, I tell myself, it's good to know that there's someone in this cutthroat world that I can just relax with, trust a little. I still haven't worked up the courage to bring up what she had me do to Eleanor with the hummus. I'd rather not lose her.

The next fifteen minutes drag out for what feels like hours. I keep waiting for Will to turn around and find his way over to me. I look for him again.

"Alec craving?" Cassie winks.

"What's up with Will?" someone says.

We both look at the same time. He's still at the front desk, shoulders slumped forward, but now he's sobbing into his hands.

I spot Mr. K. No one else seems to notice him over there talking to Will. We've all been too wrapped up in waiting for the bulletin board to fill with the cast list and making predictions about who will dance what role.

"He deserves whatever it is." Cassie's words startle me.

"What?"

"I never told you, but he dropped me on purpose because of Bette." She's so cold, I can almost feel it coming off her.

"That can't be true," I say.

"Oh, yes it is." Cassie's eyes narrow. "He and Bette used to be best friends. If she wasn't with Alec, she was with him." She crosses her arms over her chest. "You don't know Will or Bette like I do. She has a way about her."

I think of Eleanor. Bette has a power over people. Still, I have to think the best of Will. "I'll be back, okay?"

"Yeah," she mutters.

I weave through the crowd of bodies toward Will. Mr. K and a few guards surround him, blocking everyone else out. I flush with worry. Is he getting in trouble for the pranks I pulled? I try to get a closer look. The lobby is so thick with people.

A hand lands on my shoulder. It's Alec.

"Hey." His fingers graze my skin, sending a tingle through me.

"Hey." We stand there for a long moment, just looking at each other. He shifts back and forth. I try to say something, but it all gets jammed up in my head. Part of me wants to slip past him, to see what's going on with Will. And the other part wants Alec's hands wrapped around my waist, my head on his shoulder, as the cast list is revealed. I want to erase our old fight. I want things to go back to the way they were. It's easier to be mad at him when I can't smell him, when he's not looking at me, when his hands aren't raising goose bumps on my skin. It's easier to erase him and distract myself with ballet.

"Good luck tonight." He touches my cheek.

"You, too. I know you'll be Siegfried."

"And you'll be Odette."

"I hope."

"Oh, I know you will."

A rush of cold air comes in from the front doors. I crane my neck to look around Alec. I spot Will being led toward the exit.

I race forward, almost there. "Will!"

Will stops and looks at me for a second, his face shocked, red and apologetic. He steps in my direction. I feel Alec right behind me. All eyes are on us now.

"You have to leave the premises." The guard pushes Will outside. Alec and I look at each other, confused.

"What's happening?"

"I don't know." Alec's eyes look heavy.

Clapping starts. Mr. K and Damien Leger walk to the front of the crowd laughing, like this isn't the most important day of our lives.

The crowd parts for them as they make their way through. Our other teachers, Morkie, Pavlovich, and Doubrava, come out of the offices to the right in perfect synchronization, like it's all been choreographed. Madame Dorokhova comes through the conservatory doors next. Behind her is Adele Abney, the company's new Odette. My heart leaps a little and my monitor buzzes. She does a little half wave at me and hovers near the back of the crowd. *Why is she here?*

I head back to my spot. Alec follows. Henri stands with his arms around Cassie, his mouth in her hair. I try to focus on the teachers' whispering and the piece of paper in the hands of Mr. K's secretary.

"Good evening, everyone," Damien says.

Sweat beads on my forehead, like it does when I'm warming up, even though I'm standing still. A strange flush of heat flashes through me as he speaks.

"Good evening, my butterflies," Mr. K says. "Tonight is a very important one for the conservatory. Choosing the student cast for *Swan Lake* was one of our hardest decisions yet. I know you're all dying to see the final list. But first, I must welcome back one of our very own." He extends a hand out. The main office door opens.

Bette steps forward and turns to face everyone. In that moment, I feel like I might die all over again.

24.

June

"AS YOU ALL KNOW, THE accident last year has been the subject of investigation for many months," Mr. K says, waving his hands around dramatically. "But Bette Abney has proven beyond a doubt that she was not at fault. We welcome her back with open arms." He claps, and the room joins in, but the applause is slow and light.

Everyone is still stunned. They've clumped up into little groups of shock and support, but I find myself standing alone and aside, friendless again.

Gigi is shaken, her mouth paused in a small pale-pink O. Her eyes are wet, though tears have yet to spill, and her hand grips Cassie's arm. She looks broken, devastated. Alec, too, seems tense, his shoulders stiff. He keeps a safe distance from both Gigi and Bette, clearly caught off guard, as if he didn't know about this surprise return. And Eleanor, well, she's deathly pale, panicked, like she's about to make a run for it. But why? Are she and Bette still not talking?

I knew when Bette found that video that it would only be a matter of time before she returned. A few days ago, when we rehearsed at her place, she told me about her audition with Damien. It must have gone well for them to bring her back so quickly.

An odd satisfaction settles into my stomach. Now we can get back to normal, sort of. And for once, I have an ally. Who would have ever thought it would be Bette?

Bette does a little curtsy. She looks around the room, enjoying her moment, basking in it like a small, feminine version of Mr. K. "I'm excited to be back where I belong."

We all wait for her to say more, but she just steps aside, letting Mr. K continue his speech. "Thank you so much for returning to the fold here, Bette. We're so glad to have you back."

The whispers start then, like a strong undercurrent, threatening to pull the whole night under. I hear the words *Will* and *crying* and *gone* spreading throughout the room. Could it really have been Will? But he and Gigi were friends, so close. It must be a lie.

Mr. K turns his focus to the bulletin board, and that gets everyone's attention. "Now, the moment you've all been waiting for." He flourishes his hands this way and that, like a confused magician. "I present to you the *Swan Lake* cast list."

His assistant nods and walks over to the bulletin board, where she pins it up with a red thumbtack.

Dancers rush past me, bumping me left and right. A small crowd forms around the bulletin board instantly, but I can't bring myself to move. My legs feel like lead, heavy and useless.

Bette appears by my side. Excitement radiates from her skin. "You ready?" Her teeth gleam as she grins, blinding like an unforgiving sun. "This is it!"

That's what I'm afraid of. My future is whatever's on that paper tonight. I'd almost rather not know. I catch Gigi's eye as Bette leads me away, and the look of devastation, of betrayal on her face when she sees us together sends my heart plummeting to the bottom of me, making my feet feel even heavier and more unyielding.

"C'mon." Bette pulls me along. It's only a few feet, but it feels like miles, like slow motion, as I listen to others call out and cheer, to Alec whooping it up in the background while Henri rubs Cassie's back, comforting her.

Sei-Jin and Riho are whispering to each other when I get to the front. I hear them mention the Little Swans. "That's amazing!" Sei-Jin's telling Riho. "To get that when you're just a Level Six? You're on your way!" I can't help but wonder who else will round out the quartet. It's not a true solo, but given the footwork, the coordination, the synchronization, it's a challenging variation. It means Mr. K sees something good in Riho. They jump up and down with glee, and I figure Sei-Jin's happy with being a Little Swan, since this performance marks the end of the road for her.

Sei-Jin smirks at me as Bette and I push our way through, and she doesn't back away. She wants to see my reaction to the list. She wants to watch my future unfold, good or bad.

The single page pinned to the wall is already crumpling with the dashed hopes and dreams of many, and the beaming cheers of so very few. Bette's head blocks it for the first few seconds, and I can't see anything but her golden halo. When she turns around, her cheeks are flushed and she's shouting. "I'm Odile! I'm the Black Swan. Can you believe it?"

Yes, I can believe it. It's the perfect part for her, capturing that dark, sharp edge that separates her from Adele, as much as they may look alike. She'll bring something to Odile that no other dancer here could—it'll be a career-defining turn. If she's Odile, that means Mr. K's cast Gigi as Odette. It will be a study in contrast, no doubt bringing him glee. But if the role was traditionally cast—with one dancer as Odette/Odile—who would've been chosen?

I finally work my way up to the front. I'm listed alongside Eleanor, Sei-Jin, and Riho as one of the Little Swans. I'm also cast as the Baroness, another semisolo turn that requires some skill.

"That's not bad at all." Bette's looking at the list again, finally realizing that this moment isn't just about her. She nods at me with some appreciation. "I mean, it's not Odette or Odile, but you'll do well in those roles. You'll show them you can shine."

But even as she says it, the truth echoes in my head, my future laid bare in black and white. I'm not in the top three here. I'm barely in the top eight. Most of the other girls who're cast as swans or lower will be smart about things and consider college, or set up auditions at other companies—Boston, San Francisco, LA—which will start right after the holidays.

Maybe I should, too.

Maybe this dream is over.

SWAN LAKE CAST LIST

Odette: Gigi Stewart

Odette Understudy: Eleanor Alexander

Odile: Bette Abney

Odile Understudy: Riho Nakamura & Cassandra Lucas

Queen (Princess Regent): Cassandra Lucas

Prince Siegfried: Alec Lucas

Wolfgang (Siegfried's Tutor): Eddie Rothstein

Von Rothbard: Henri Dubois

The Baroness: E-Jun Kim

Prince's Friends: Rebecca McAllister, Isabela Pereira-Carvalho

Benno: James Zhabin

The Cygnets: Eleanor Alexander, Sei-Jin Kwon, Riho Nakamura, E-Jun Kim

Two Swans: Ming-Lee Chang & Cassandra Lucas

Spanish Dancers: Svetlana Novikova-Chastain & Jin Park; Riley Washington & Ahmad Lawrence

Neapolitan Dancers: James Zhabin & Emily Stein

Hungarian Dancers: Christopher Griffin & Eleanor Alexander

Mazurka: Riho Nakamura & Zachary Lim; Fredo Martinez & Hye-Ji Yi; Sara Rosen & Thomas Cauman

Swan Corps: Level 6 & 7 Dancers

ACT II

Spring Season

25.

Gigi

AT LUNCH THE NEXT DAY, all anyone in the café can talk about is Bette.

"I can't believe she's back."

"She looks really good. Different, sort of."

"How did she get a role without being here at school?"

"Do you think she's still evil?"

"She might not have pushed Gigi, but she's not innocent."

Through every spoonful of soup I eat and in between every bite Cassie takes of her salad is her name. It gets louder and louder, like the rumble of the subway under your feet. It's all I can hear. Then there's an awestruck, curious silence as she walks right into the room with Alec and goes straight for the fruit bar.

Cassie pets my arm like it's the back of a cat. I try to focus on my carrot soup and the slice of toast on my plate. Bette's eyes flutter over me as she passes. She and Alec sit at an adjacent table.

She smiles and laughs, acting as if it isn't a completely huge deal that she's back.

"You okay?" Cassie says.

"Would you be?"

"No, and I'm not. I hate her just as much as you do."

The *petit rats* whisper and smile in her direction. Some even venture over to say hello and welcome her.

"We should leave." I start to pack my things.

"No, I refuse to do anything differently now that she's here. You should do the same. She'll get what she deserves." Cassie says the word *she* loudly, and Bette looks in our direction for the shortest second. Her eyes seem even brighter, even bluer, like she hasn't missed one hour of sleep since she's been gone.

I snap the plastic spoon in my hand. Orange flecks shoot all over my tray and the table.

"Chill out. You can't let her see that she's getting to you. She gets off on it." Cassie wipes up my mess.

Two of the new girls sit at her table—Isabela and Madison—and they fawn over her like she's a superstar. Maybe she is.

Alec looks up, and our eyes lock. I wish flames could flash in my pupils to let him know just how upset I am.

"Cassie, I don't know how you stay calm." Anger bubbles up in me. I remind myself that it's not good for me, that it could affect my heart.

"You have to know what you want." She sips her tea, unfazed.

What do I want? This was supposed to be my moment—I'm playing the lead in *Swan Lake* at the American Ballet Conservatory. Which means I have a chance at an apprenticeship. I should be reveling in this. Instead, all I can focus on is *her*.

"I want her gone."

"She will be. Trust me, Gigi. Her being back is the best thing. Because she'll do it to herself." Cassie winks like she's the villain in some movie. "Have you talked to Will?"

The sound of his name sends a shiver through me. Bette spread the rumor that Will pushed me. She said it's the reason she's back and the suspension was revoked. I think about him crying and being dragged out of the building. I can't forget the look on his face. He won't respond to my calls and texts.

"No." I flick the broken spoon around in my soup.

"I bet you it's true. He'll say she talked him into it. But that boy has a mind of his own."

How can someone be talked into shoving another person in front of a car? My phone beeps. A text from Mama, who's still crashing at Aunt Leah's: *I'm downstairs. Mr. K's office. Now.*

"My mom's here." I swallow the last few spoonfuls of my carrot soup. I look over at Bette again. She waves at me.

I leap up. My chair bangs into the table with a loud thud. People stop eating and stare. I feel Alec's eyes on me, too. I slam the chair into the table and storm toward the café exit. I hear Cassie call out from behind. I take the elevator down to the first floor and march myself right to Mr. K's office.

Mama leans forward in her chair and wags her finger in Mr. K's face. Her necklace slaps against a picture frame on his desk. His eyes bulge a little, and I hope he doesn't think she's as completely crazy as she looks. I stare into my phone, texting Will a question mark over and over again. I've sent him an average of three per day, but no answer.

"How dare you not have the common courtesy to inform me before announcing that girl's return. Gigi called me in tears. This is simply unacceptable."

"Mrs. Stewart, I tried calling you several times. But I couldn't reach you or your husband. This is not something you leave on an answering machine. And I wanted to tell Gigi, but there just wasn't any time to set up a meeting. It all happened too quickly and—"

"And nothing, Mr. K. You didn't try hard enough." Her tone gets louder and louder. "I want to meet with her. I won't be comfortable until we do." Mama finally sits back in the chair with a thud. I try to touch her arm and get her to stop, but she brushes away from me. When her mind is set, it's an arrow, never veering off its path.

"I don't think anything that we do will make you feel comfortable." He sighs and crosses his hands over his chest.

"Is my daughter's safety not important? And you split the role between the two of them, so they have to spend all this time together. Perfect for the girl to harass my child." She rises from her seat again. Her anger stirs into mine. My heart races. My monitor buzzes.

"The role was always going to be split. It's a student ballet. We must give all our students an opportunity to be showcased. The Level 8 year is about exposure, especially for the company directors to see their talents. And since the roles are divided, they'll hardly be rehearsing together at all."

"These two have history. Couldn't another girl have split the role with Giselle?"

"Mrs. Stewart, I assure you, this will be fine. We make our casting decisions based on the dancers' skill and what they bring to the roles. Giselle is the perfect Odette. Ethereal, light. Bette is her opposite. We took the opportunity to cast this ballet as it should be danced."

"I want a meeting with Rebecca Abney. This is all ridiculous." Mama slaps her hand on his desk.

"I can call her and see if she'd be willing to meet. That's all I can promise."

"I'll be staying at my sister's in Brooklyn as long as Gigi needs me. So I can be here anytime."

When Mr. K doesn't respond quite fast enough, Mama motions her hand forward at the phone on his desk. He sighs, picks it up, and dials Mrs. Abney's number from memory. In that moment, I know just how important Bette is.

I sink back in the chair. I plug my ears, pull my legs up into the chair, cross them underneath me, and try to get comfortable. I'm in my leotard and tights for afternoon ballet. I imagine the four of us in that little room—Mama and me and Bette and Mrs. Abney—and the shouting match it would trigger. The mean words and dark intentions and secrets spilled. I have my own secrets now. I have to protect myself.

"I don't want to meet with her." I stand up.

Mr. K hangs up the phone. Mama grabs at my arms, trying to get me to sit back down.

"I just want to know how she got to come back, after, after . . . all she did." I fight back a storm of angry tears welling just under the surface.

Mr. K leaves his desk and walks over. He takes my hand in his.

"This world of ours, ballet, is so—what's the word?—complicated." He rubs his chin, and the sound the bristles of his beard make against his hand distracts me. "Bette Abney did not push you. That's what her suspension was for. A violent act. She already paid for the other things she did to you, the suffering she caused. Handsomely, as I understand it." He lifts my chin up and wipes away one tear that's managed to escape. "So chin up, *moya korichnevaya*. You are strong. It will all be okay."

"I've got to get ready for class," I say. Mama kisses me, and I slip out of the room. I head for Studio A to drop my bag off and find a place to stretch. The studio's empty aside from one girl, facedown in a stretch. She looks up. It's Bette.

We stare at each other. I let my gaze burn into hers. I don't move until Morkie and the other dancers drift in. I want her to know I will always be watching now.

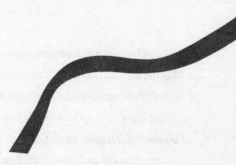

26.

Bette

I CAN'T WAIT TO SEE Eleanor's face. I moved in earlier this week, but she's been too busy, apparently, to welcome me back. I can't wait to plop down with her on the sofa, pop in *Breakfast at Tiffany's*, and fall asleep under the same fuzzy blanket. I can't wait to hear the soft, consistent up, up, down rhythm of her snores, so familiar to me they're like a lullaby. I feel like I'm finally home.

When I open the door, the room is dark, quiet. Empty. She's not there. It's 11:30 now, way past curfew, way past lights-out. I flip on the lamp. I walk around "our" room, trying to get comfortable.

This year, Eleanor's definitely claimed her space, draping the little sofa with a teal throw and pillows, scattering piles of dog-eared dance mags on the floor near her bed. There's an open, half-eaten tub of hummus—that she definitely shouldn't be eating, not after the peanut incident—sitting on top of the minifridge. In my absence, Eleanor's inner slob has come out. I thumb through her dance notebooks, with the Odette and Odile movements marked out lovingly, as I wait for her to come home.

Settling in on the couch, I shove Eleanor's tattered copy of *Wuthering Heights* to the floor. There's no space for me here. Maybe that means there's no space left for me in her life either.

Thirty minutes pass. Then an hour. I've had enough of the waiting. I stand up and gather the book and the magazines. I stack them neatly on her desk, mopping up crumbs with my disinfectant. I empty two of the dresser drawers—still annoyed that she thought she could just have the whole thing, that she didn't realize this room was also being saved for me and put her bras and underwear in a laundry basket on her bed. Underneath them, though, are a few lacy ones that definitely look like they've come from a lingerie catalogue, that are meant to be seen. A panic hits me.

I remember that night at the hospital, the kiss I wasn't supposed to see. I scroll through the pictures on my phone to the ones from that day. I zoom in on Mr. K kissing a sleeping Eleanor. I click off my screen, shuddering. I have to talk to Eleanor. I practice the words in my head, how I'll ask her.

I grab my toiletry kit and robe and head into the bathroom. I need to wash the weight of today off. When I come back out, an Eleanor-shaped lump is in the bed across from mine, the covers pulled from head to toe, her deep snore cutting through the quiet.

"Eleanor?"

I'm answered by a whistling snore.

"El?"

I push down the lump in my throat. I climb into my bed, and let that familiar rhythm soothe me to sleep.

Gigi's all over me before class. We're at the barre and she keeps turning her head to look at me, as if every moment is surreal. I guess it is, because no one thought I'd be back, especially not her. Even after I told everyone the truth and Will had to leave, it's like they're still waiting for that to somehow be untrue.

I hold my gaze straight ahead, which only makes her crane her neck more, like if she gets her face right in front of mine I'll give her whatever it is that she wants. Morkie's calling out orders, so I'm in military mode. If necessary I'll salute her. I'll do anything to get my old life back.

"Is it weird to be back?" some new girl behind me whispers while Morkie grabs June's arm and pulls it practically out of its socket to get it into position.

"No." I say it under my breath. She should know better than to have a conversation in the middle of class. We turn to face the other side of the studio. With June's arm in place, Morkie goes back to yelling out positions, and I watch myself in the mirror on the opposite wall as I move through each order. I've missed the way we look all in a line, reflected in the mirror. It's almost meditative, getting lost in the swish of toes brushing the floor, the bending and straightening of knees in perfect time, the triangle of space between all our thighs making a distinct pattern in the mirror.

Mostly, I like the way my own body fits into the perfect

synchronization in the mirror. When I am truly focused on the precision of the movements, I can forget which legs belong to me, which feet are mine, and the fact that I almost lost all this.

I'm just about in that state when Eleanor's feet get out of time with the music and with Morkie's staccato demands. Her feet flex when they are supposed to point, the left foot drags on the floor instead of the right.

I let out an aggravated huff of breath, but it's too late to get back in the zone. I'm a beat behind. I trip over my own feet just in time for Morkie to catch me. I don't just slip up; I catch my left foot on my right ankle and my knees bend and I have to fight a full-on drop to the floor.

"*Bette!*" Morkie says. Then she's right up in my face, her nose almost touching mine. Her breath smells like coffee and cough drops, but I stop my nose from wrinkling.

"Sorry." I try to just enter the movement, the pattern, without another word. Morkie stands directly in front of me, though, so I can't see myself or anyone else in the mirror, and my heart thumps with awareness at her singular focus on me. "You are making a mess. Too much time out of my classroom."

I can't get my breathing under control and my limbs don't seem to be listening to Morkie at all. I should've taken a pill before ballet class. I can't trust my brain or my body anymore.

"Sit this one out." Morkie has a curl of disgust in her voice.

I slip out of line and don't argue. But I do let my gaze land hard on Eleanor. She bites her bottom lip and her eyes go wide. She won't look back at me though.

Morkie turns her attention to Gigi's feet, not touching them,

SONA CHARAIPOTRA & DHONIELLE CLAYTON

but rather conducting them, the way one would an orchestra. Her fingers dance in the air, and Gigi's flawless feet align themselves in response. Morkie grins, like she herself is making Gigi's delicate movements happen.

I look away. Gigi doesn't exist to me. That's what the lawyers said. You don't even look at her. She is a ghost.

The piano music stops when Morkie stops calling out orders, and we exhale as a group, except I am on the sidelines and everyone else is at the barre, working their legs through slow movements and experiencing the momentary euphoria of having driven through hell. Morkie releases them to stretch.

"Bette, you come," she yells, which means I'm going to have to work on technique with her whispering in my ear and the other girls watching as they cool down.

I nod and approach the barre. It is my best friend and my nemesis. We spar and we make up.

"Toes!"

I rise up, gripping the barre with the hope that today it will be a lifeboat. I tell my mind to stay quiet so that I can hear Morkie and respond with my body without a hitch. Eleanor wisely stays out of my sight line, and June is in her corner, lifting her leg to the ceiling as usual. But Gigi is right in front of me. Her legs are spread and she keeps inching them farther and farther apart until they are practically a straight line that her long, lovely torso grows from.

I fight looking at her, but my gaze drifts to the dark ringlet of hair that's escaped from her bun and the beautiful way her neck meets her collarbone. I can see Alec's fingers on the symmetrical bones, his palm fitting perfectly around the curve of her shoulder. I feel like I'm back in that same place I was last year. What is it about this girl?

"You want to be a ballerina again?" Morkie breaks into my thoughts and grabs my thigh with both hands. "You want to dance, again, yes?" She isn't as gentle as Yuli as she forces a turnout, making the bones and muscles spread more than is physically possible. Her fingers are tight on my flesh, and I'm aware of the imperfections I've developed the last few months: the slight shift in ratio from muscle to fat, the extra few fractions of an inch that the costume mistress will measure in our upcoming fitting, the laziness of my hips not wanting to turn all the way out, the half-second lag in my feet. An almost invisible change, but not to someone like Morkie who has been poking and prodding every inch of my body since I was six. "This is not the way a dancer moves," Morkie says at last.

My muscles scream with pain. Her hands move to my hips, forcing them open. Then she puts a palm to my shoulder blades, pressing until they touch behind my back. "You work harder." Everyone can hear her. Their faces all light up, dozens of pairs of eyes twinkling at my humiliation.

"Yes, madame."

I do not blush. I do not tremble.

"One more time." The edge in her voice is cutting, but there's kindness in her eyes. Or if not kindness, then certainly generosity. She wants me to do well.

She claps her hands, the music starts, she calls out what she wants my body to do, and I do it. I watch my body in the mirror like it's someone else's, and for a full three minutes, I am a prima ballerina again. I am long limbs and a blond halo and alabaster skin. I am a series of perfect shapes, slipping into each other: a curve to an arrow-straight line to a wide V shape to an impossible slope in my back. Morkie claps again when she has seen enough of this series.

"There she is." A smirk plays at her lips, and her eyes betray what her touch will not. I know I'm back. And that at least one person is happy about that fact.

It's way past midnight and Eleanor still hasn't come to the room. She's avoiding me again. She's been mostly missing every night this week since I got back, doing her homework in the hall lounge, dancing late into the night, crawling into bed hours after I'm asleep. She's pulling the same thing tonight, creeping in now, quietly pulling on her pajamas, not even brushing her teeth for fear of waking me. For fear of having to even speak to me. For fear of confrontation.

But I'm not sleeping. Tonight, she's going to have to talk.

"What the hell, Eleanor?" I sit up in bed. She startles, stumbling as she gets the nightshirt over her head. "You've been avoiding me for days."

I'm halfway across the room when she rushes to the bathroom, locking herself inside. I just don't understand it. I didn't push Gigi, and even Gigi knows that; most of the other girls have been cordial, if not friendly. But here's my best friend since we were six, avoiding me like I'm the most disgusting person on earth.

I bang on the bathroom door. "Open up. We have to talk."

"Why wouldn't I avoid you, Bette?" Her snappy voice is one I've never heard before. It radiates through the door. "You come back here—with your big surprise—and think everything's going to be the same again."

"Why can't it be?"

She comes slamming through the door, and I can see she's shaking. But I'm right in her path, and I'm not letting her walk away. Not this time.

"I'm not your friend anymore. I'm not that person you can boss around again."

"I tried to fix it all. I tried to tell you what was happening. You wouldn't answer my calls." I'm balling my fists. "Even the lawyers—"

"I don't want to hear about you and your innocence and your lawyers. You knew you'd be fine. You're Bette. You're always fine. Before you're even back, you land Odile. I've worked for years and do everything I can, you don't even know—"

"I know." I let the words stand and take on a life of their own.

"You don't know. You don't know anything—"

"No, listen, I'm telling you. I know." She's staring at me hard, desperate, trying to erase what I've just said, its implications. "I know everything."

I hold her gaze. "I know about Mr. K."

A thousand emotions wash over her face: anger, sadness, confusion, disbelief. And finally embarrassment. "You can't. How could you? Did you—"

"I saw you with him. On Halloween. And then again at the hospital."

"Did he see you?"

"No, he didn't. I didn't let him. Eleanor, you've got to—"

"It's nothing. It was just . . . You don't know anything. He's like a father to me, he worries, ever since—it's nothing at all." She turns her back to me, her shoulders shaking with sobs.

"I don't believe you, Eleanor." I'm just inches away from her, and I want to hug her, but I can sense that it would be the wrong thing to do right now.

I step closer to her. My hand touches her shoulder. Her panic rises again. She's shoving me away, then lunging at me. She's full of rage, her nails clawing the flesh of my wrists, digging deep enough to draw blood. I back up all the way near our beds, until there's no place left to go.

"Listen to me." I grab her hands, her shoulders, making her stop, trying to get her to focus. She shoves me all the way to our room door. My head bangs against it. The pain shoots through me. "I know. It's okay. I told you, I'm not going to tell anyone. I'm not going to say anything." She's crumbling to the floor, so I go down with her. "It's okay, Eleanor," I whisper into her hair. "It's over, right? It's done with? So no one has to know."

As much as it might thrill me to finally get back at Mr. K for all the years of torture he's put me through—and everything he still has planned for me—this time, I mean it. I'll keep Eleanor's secret as if it were my own. I need her to need me. I need her to want to be my friend again. "It's me, Eleanor. It's Bette. You know I wouldn't—"

"Oh, but you would. You will." She's still shaking, snot running down her tear-streaked face. "You don't know what it's like to have to work this hard, to have to give all of yourself over to get just a tiny fraction of what you want. You've never known that, and you never will."

She stands, her fury fueling her as she storms past me, bumping against the chair and the desk as she throws her body toward the bathroom again, slamming the door behind her. I can hear the cries on the other side of the door, the shattering sound of tears no one can stop, and all the power I felt the last few days, weeks, years, drains out of me. All this time, I'm realizing now, I was so focused on me. Even today, even just now, as Eleanor devolved into an ocean right there in front of me. I was worried about what this meant for me: my hold on Mr. K, the safety net of my friendship with her. I wasn't thinking about her at all. I never do. And that, I realize, could just cost me my best friend.

27.

June

ON THURSDAY AFTERNOON, I WRAP myself up in my warmest scarf, hat, and gloves, and take the 1 train downtown, switching to the N at Times Square. Even now, I'm startled by the grime and the crowds. I haven't ridden the subway in forever, even though we're in the heart of Manhattan. My life is set in a four-block radius around campus.

Not today though. I've asked Jayhe to meet me in the East Village—he thinks we're going to this Szechuan place called Xi'an that he's talking about nonstop. He's been craving their cumin lamb noodles for months now. But I have something else planned.

My stomach grumbles, swishy and empty, as the train lurches forward. It feels completely foreign to be riding in this overheated metal box with a million strangers. I feel eyes on me, and most of them probably think I'm a high school kid or maybe a tourist from Korea. The train screeches to a stop, and I'm pushed out the door along with a throng of people.

I look down at my phone, checking the time and location. Then I walk east until I hit Second Avenue. The vibe down here is hipper, old but new, and there are a gazillion kids—most just a bit older than me—hanging out, eating, playing basketball on the court across the street even though it's freezing. When I finally get to the address I gave Jayhe, he's not there yet. Late, as usual.

I can't believe I'm here. It feels surreal, like walking into some kind of vision of the future. But college could be my reality in a few short months. Jayhe's already applied, early decision. He asked me months ago to think about it, but for the longest time, even looking at the website made me feel like a failure—a has-been, a would be, a never could.

Still, after seeing the cast list, I know I have to keep my options open. The dance program at NYU is very respected, but it's not where real ballerinas land. So I'm auditioning elsewhere, too. But maybe those companies are still long shots. Maybe this is my only option. If it is, I have to make it work for me, for us.

A tall, muscular guy in tight black jeans and a slim peacoat is standing in front of the building, texting on his phone. A sprinkle of freckles splatters across his nose. He's got on red warm-up booties, and a beret sits perched on his otherwise bald head. The effect screams dancer.

"You here for the tour?" he says with a broad smile, square white teeth gleaming. "You're my one thirty, right?"

I nod my head and look at my watch. Jayhe's still not here yet. Should I go without him? But that would ruin my surprise.

And really, defeat the whole purpose of today—showing him that we're in this together.

"I'm June. I think we're waiting for one more."

I'm trying to figure out what to say, what to do, when Jayhe runs up, backpack slumped on his shoulder, out of breath. His cheeks are flushed from the effort, and he grabs my hand. "Here. Sorry I'm late." He leans in and gives me a big, sloppy kiss, not noticing we have company. "What are we— Oh, hey."

"I'm Fred. Dance major. A junior at Tisch and your tour guide. Welcome to NYU." Fred looks from me to Jayhe, noticing his hand on my arm. "You guys both dancers?"

Jayhe shakes his head. "I draw. I already applied, early admission, and I got in. But June's deciding whether to apply." He smiles at me, and then at Fred, and then at me again. "And I guess the fact we're here—"

"I thought we could check it out." My cheeks are blazing. "Just to see."

This isn't how I planned this at all. But Jayhe's grinning and holding my hand, and the hope in his eyes tells me that maybe, just maybe, I've made the right decision.

Fred starts walking, and we follow him. "Well, you're both gonna love it here. NYU is known for being a renowned center for the arts. We live and breathe it here. And our alumni are everywhere."

He opens the door and we walk into the building, riding the elevator up. "We've got classrooms and practice rooms and rehearsal studios on this floor," he says, pointing things out as we pass.

It's all modern, bright, state-of-the-art. There's a student lounge, an orchestra room, and an alumni meeting room. He shows me the dance department offices. They all look lovely, sprawling and endless. He walks us back to Broadway, where the main school of the arts offices are, showing us big auditoriums and a café and finally the admissions office. But I can't bring myself to pick up an application. I grip Jayhe's hand the whole time, letting him lead as we follow Fred, trying to picture myself in these halls, in this life. I want to love it here, to be excited and enthusiastic and ready to embrace it all. But I can't. Not quite.

"How many hours a day do you dance?" I ask Fred.

"It's different for everyone—some are in the studio for like four hours a day. Others, it might just be an hour or two. We start broad and then specialize. Plus, you round out your schedule with academics and electives."

I try to stop the frown from taking over my face. I don't want to take random electives, like Shakespeare or pottery. I want to focus, to dance, to be the best ballerina I can be. Maybe this isn't the place for me.

"That sounds great, doesn't it, June?" Jayhe says. "Maybe we can take a class or two together."

His voice gets me out of my head. He's right. That's why I'm here in the first place, right? This is the only place where maybe I can have both—Jayhe and dance. I have to keep reminding myself that.

When we get onto the elevator again, Jayhe pushes the button for a different floor. "I'm going to go check out the drawing studio and art offices for a second."

Before I can stop him, he steps off the elevator and disappears. Fred waits for me to say something. But I just stand there silently, trying to look bright and interested and happy.

As we get off the elevator, he grins. "You're a ballerina, right?" His question is on the edge of a chuckle. Like he'd be laughing at me, if he could get away with it.

"How do you know?" I ask.

"So composed, so serious. So above it all. You're all like that," he says. "And you walk turned out."

I look down and laugh at my feet. Permanent V.

Just outside the building, Fred sits, patting the spot next to him. I take a seat, looking down at my feet again, covered in cozy boots. Do they look out of place here? Do I?

"I do some jazz, some modern, I've even taken some Odissi, which is like an old-school Indian regional thing."

"What about ballet?"

"Yeah, that, too. But it's a bit too stiff for me." He looks at me again, sizing me up, and I grin. "You dance uptown, right?"

"American Ballet Conservatory," I tell him.

"Tough spot. We get a couple every year, and it's like they're resigning themselves. But let me tell you something: if you land here, that's definitely not the silver medal. That's you going places."

I try to believe his words, trust his judgment, but I know that in the ballet world, there are only a few places that count. College dance is just not one of them. "I don't know if I'm cut out for college," I say. "I don't know if I can give up ballet."

"Well, that's why you're here, right? At NYU, you won't have to."

"But it's not the same."

"I'm just saying it's not a bad problem to have, NYU." He rises. "Come on, I have one last thing to show you."

We walk west a few blocks until we end up on Sixth Avenue. We're standing in the heart of the city. A big, majestic castle-like building towers on one side of the street, a more mundane cityscape sits on the other. He points up to an endless wall of windows on the top right corner of the street, so I look, shading my eyes from the glare of the sun. "The Joffrey. Right here downtown. For when you really miss it."

I grin at him. He may not be a ballet dancer, but it seems like Fred might really get it. "So should we go get an application?"

I nod. Ten minutes later, I'm standing in front of the admissions office with paperwork in my hands.

"I hope you give it a thought, June," Fred says.

He hands me a Post-it. "Call me if you need help," he says, then walks away. *Maybe NYU could be a place for me*, I find myself thinking. *Maybe it could be just what I need.*

I sit on the bench, waiting for what seems like eternity. Broadway bustles around me, students, tourists, and cabs with horns blaring. Artsy types, all tattoos and pink hair, come out of the building, nodding in my direction like maybe I'm that girl from their art appreciation class, that small glimmer of recognition that doesn't really exist at all. There are endless waves of people coming in and out of those doors, just in the span of a few minutes. The ballet world is so small, so intimate. Just this one building here is teeming with dancers.

When Jayhe finally shows up, he's grinning from ear to ear. "I met one of my professors and showed him the drawings I did—the ones of you that I put up on my website. He said they were an excellent start, that they should definitely become part of my freshman portfolio. Isn't that great?" He beams, then remembers to ask. "What did you think of the dance school? It looks pretty badass, right?"

"It was awesome." Then I blurt out what's been stressing me. "But maybe it's too much—I mean, there are so many people. How would I fit in?" More important, how would I stand out?

"June, don't you know by now?" He's leaning down, looking at my face in that way that sends my heart spiraling with joy every time. "You're not meant to fit in. You're one of a kind."

He bends lower to kiss me, taking my face in his hands, letting his fingers run through my hair. He leans back a bit, looking at me again. "And this was an amazing surprise."

"Don't get too excited. I'm still thinking about things. I'm looking at my options." I can't make any promises. "I do know one thing, though."

He raises an eyebrow.

"It's lunchtime."

He smiles, and we head east. But even as we walk away, hand in hand, one thought repeats in my head: all we really have is now.

That night, I spend hours poring over the NYU catalog online. I've filled out the application already, but I still can't decide if I want to hit the official submit button. They've got all different styles of dance—ballet, tap, jazz, modern, and different regional stuff like Fred said. They've got acting and musical theater and music. They've even got dance studies, where you can spend endless days analyzing the way other people move. It seems so broad, so overwhelming, like I'd never figure out how to make a decision about anything there. Like by the time I figured things out, I'd be too old to really do any of them well.

I have to dance. I need to dance. If it can't be at ABC, it has to be somewhere else that takes ballet seriously. I open up the websites for other major ballet companies. I look up Miami, San Francisco, Los Angeles, Salt Lake City. Some have auditions right here in New York, but others are only in the company's city, which means I've got to get moving if I want to audition. I spend the rest of the night filling out applications. I even book a ticket to San Francisco using the emergency credit card my mother gave me.

See, I tell myself. *That casting wasn't the end of the world.*

In fact, it might be just the beginning.

"Sorry, there was traffic," Jayhe says as I climb into his van. We're heading to his little cousin's first birthday at the main restaurant in Queens, and I know he's nervous. Or maybe I'm nervous. I buckle my seat belt, settling in, so his lips land on my cheek. "Gimme a kiss."

"Drive," I say.

"Kiss!"

As he pulls to a stop at the next red, I lean over and give him a small peck, a teaser. I pull away as his hands reach for me. "The light," I say, as horns blare behind us. I lift up the little red-wrapped box that sits in my lap. "I got her earrings. Are her ears pierced?"

He shrugs and leans heavily on the gas. We're late, and the van smells like the pork and chive dumplings he probably had to deliver to the new restaurant branch in Brooklyn, which means we will, too. "So you applied?"

"Filled it out yesterday," I say.

"You excited?"

I nod. I don't tell him that I think it might be a mistake, that maybe it won't work out after all.

"Oh, c'mon, June, you're going to love it there. We're gonna love it."

"I hope so."

"I know so." Pausing at the next light, he takes my chin in his hand. "All right, say it. *Boe heh joo seh yoh.*"

"I don't love you today." My voice is playful, my mouth a pout. "Because you're late."

"Yes, you do. So say it."

"Will that get you to just drive?"

He grins. I say the Korean phrase. It actually sounds the way it's supposed to. I'm grinning as he kisses me, and he takes my hand, his other resting on the steering wheel.

"That's better." He starts to drive.

"I'm excited to see everyone. It's been so long," I say.

"Are you nervous? Don't worry. You've met most of my family already."

"I was little."

"You're still little."

The restaurant is the first two floors of a three-story red brick building in Elmhurst—the oldest branch, the one his grandma still runs. The moment I step in, the nerves disappear. Even though I've only been here once or twice before, this feels like the place I belong, as if I'm just heading home. The celebration room is decked out in a deep burgundy and gold, sparkling streamers cascading from wall to wall, balloons floating up toward the high ceilings.

Baby Mi-Hee sits in a swing that's been decorated like a throne, gurgling and giggling in a maroon *hanbok* dress. I remember seeing pictures of a tiny version of myself dressed up like that, in a little blue and gold *hanbok*.

Jayhe hands me a plate of dumplings as the ceremony starts, watching to make sure I'm eating. Has he talked to my mom?

Jayhe's uncle makes a few announcements in rapid-fire Korean, then picks the baby up, holding her forward for all to see. I recognize the words: *congratulations*, *family*, *fortune*, and *blessed*.

"Introducing Mi-Hee." The room erupts in cheers. "Time for her to pick her fortune." It's an old tradition, letting the baby choose her own fate. A bunch of objects—a pen, gold coins, a sewing kit, a thermometer—sit on the table, each predicting a different future for the lucky one. Everyone leans in to watch. Whispers and laughs burst through the room.

Jayhe's uncle lets the baby hover over the table, her chubby hands landing on this object and that, until she reaches down and finally picks up the coins. "A banker, a banker," the cheers go up.

I watch the baby playing with her goodies, trying to eat the coins, and I wonder what I picked. I smile at the thought that maybe, just maybe, my mother would have put a ballet slipper out for me to choose.

"Hey!" Jayhe pops up behind me. He pulls me close to him, whispering close to my ear. "What're you grinning about?" He spins me around to face him.

"Do you know what you picked at your fortune ceremony?" I ask. Light glitters in his dark eyes, washing out any reflection of me.

He frowns. "Ma always says it was the coins, but I think it was probably a pencil."

I take his rough hands in mine, and I feel like a child, they're so big and calloused. "I wonder what I picked," I say. A dark thought settles over me. I wonder if my mother had a fortune ceremony for me at all. My mom was a single mother, and her family was all in Korea.

"What's the matter?" He squeezes my hand tighter. "You used to be one of the happiest people I knew. And now, it just seems that place makes you sad."

"I am happy," I say, shrugging. Why is he bringing this up now?

"You don't seem like it." He tries to pull me closer, but I can feel eyes on us again.

"Stop."

He realizes people are watching, and lets me go. "Why are you being like this?"

I bite my lip, thinking about what he's said. I'm trying to

figure out what to say when he speaks again.

"Okay, then. Maybe this will make you happy. I talked to my dad, and between the scholarship and what he would have paid for Queens, I can make NYU work. Probably." He waits for me to say something. "So it can all work out."

"Congratulations."

He seems angry. "That's it, that's all you have to say? Not 'we're on our way'? Not 'I can't wait till we're together'? None of that?"

I nod my head, but I can't force the words.

"Okay, then, I guess that's that. I guess asking you to have Valentine's dinner is useless, too. You have to rehearse. I know."

Actually, that's the weekend I have to fly to California to audition for the San Francisco Ballet. "I'll be out of town. Auditions." I ease the words out slowly, waiting for him to erupt. "We could do the weekend after? Or before. Or maybe you can come with me?" I let myself imagine that for a minute—the two of us on the trolleys and in Chinatown. But I can't quite picture it because I know that's impossible. He's got school, he's got art class, he's got endless hours at the restaurants.

"Auditions?" He takes a deep breath. "For what? I thought you said you were applying to NYU. I thought you said—"

His grandmother ambles over, and Jayhe goes silent. When we were little, I spent hours with her and Jayhe at their house down the street, playing, watching Korean dramas, and eating mandu. Her whole face lifts when she smiles at me. "*Yeppeo gangaji,*" she says, touching my cheek. Pretty little thing.

I wrap my arms around her and kiss her soft, wrinkly cheek.

The skin is papery, like it will tear if I push too hard. She feels and smells like home to me. She puts a warm palm to my face. She says a bunch of stuff in Korean, but the only thing I understand is the word *eat*. Then, she tries in English. "Eat more. Too small."

"Yes, yes." I kiss her again. She takes a dumpling from her plate and pushes it toward my mouth. I take a bite and then a second. When it's gone, she starts on another, but I excuse myself. "*Hwajangshil.*" Bathroom. I hope she understands.

Am I really that bad? I wonder as I look at myself in the mirror. There are hollows under my eyes, and my arms are string beans. The dress makes a line straight down, no curves anymore. In real clothes, ones you wear outside ballet, I look sick, underfed, not like a normal girl. In leotards and tights, with my hair slicked back and my face powdered, I look like what I am: a ballerina.

I can feel the dumplings and other junk floating in my stomach, the thick, salty soy sauce coating my insides. I can't even walk into the bathroom anymore without wanting to purge. My body does it on command, the smell of the disinfectant and the coolness of the tiles an instant trigger.

I run into the stall and let it all out. The dumplings, the drama, the tension that's been weighing me down for days. But the guilt doesn't leave me like it usually does. It sits heavy and solid in the pit of my stomach, a reminder that, despite this one little bit of control I may have, everything's far from okay. Maybe it'll never be okay. I can't just sit here on the cold hard floor, so I paste on a smile, ready to head back into the party. When I open the bathroom door, Jayhe's standing there. His face is stone, his lips pressed together tight, unyielding. His eyes are confused, crinkling with pain or revulsion.

The party still spins around us, but it feels like we're in a bubble. "What?" is the only thing I can get out. But I know that's not nearly enough.

"How—were you—" He swallows the rest of his thought. "We don't talk about this stuff, so—"

"And we aren't going to talk about it right now either," I snap.

"I just thought you were working on it. That you were doing better."

"Are you kidding me? Do you know how much pressure I'm under? You don't get it, do you? This is it. These next few months are all I really have to make something of myself. I'll do whatever it takes—give up whatever I have to—to make it happen. Even if I have to do this."

He pulls me in close, a hug I can't escape, and I'm clawing at him, at everything, trying to get out. I can't. I can just hear his heart pounding against my ear, the thud, thud, thud of it fast and exhausting and soothing all at once, making me realize something for the first time. "I know you want this, June, but this isn't worth the struggle," he whispers into my too-short hair. "This isn't worth it. June, you don't have to—"

I shove him away. "No! You have to understand. I can't eat dumplings and noodles and pizza and hang out and watch movies and hook up. If you want that girl, go back to Sei-Jin. She's who you wanted in the first place."

His face is bright red now, and everyone in the room has

paused. "June, keep your voice down." His hands are on my shoulders. He's looking me straight in the eyes, trying to calm me down, saying soothing, hushed things in both Korean and English.

"I can't—I can't do this anymore, Jayhe. I'll do whatever it takes to dance. And you'll never understand. I'm not giving this up. Not even for you."

I storm out of the restaurant, racing down the block. My heart is pounding as I run, the winter air whipping my hair back against my face, the chill seeping into my skin.

An hour later, I'm standing in front of my mother's apartment building. I can barely remember how I got here, and I'm hoping this is all a nightmare, a mistake. But I know somewhere deep inside that it's over with Jayhe.

I stand there for a moment that feels like hours, finding it hard to believe what I've done. I walk toward the building and let myself in. I climb slowly up the three flights of stairs, carrying the weight of a broken heart with me.

It's only nine p.m., but it feels like the dead of night. It's cold in the apartment, the single-paned windows letting every draft in. I put on a sweater and socks. I crank up the thermostat. I even turn on the oven. But that's not enough, and I bat away the thought that being cold is a symptom of low body weight. I go into my mom's room, where she's snoring slightly, that same familiar rhythm she's always had, and crawl in right next to her, cuddling close. Like I used to when I was little.

28.

Gigi

"TAKE A LOOK AT THIS patheticness." Cassie passes me her phone. She's sprawled out on the extra bed in my room after curfew. I'm on a mat on the floor, doing my physical therapy exercises. I zoom in on the picture. It's June bent over their toilet, vomiting. Her face is twisted into the ugliest expression. Liquid spews from her mouth.

"Gross. How'd you get this?" I give her the phone back. I remember catching her throwing up last year. The embarrassment, the shame of it all, floods back to me.

"I set up a camera right above the toilet bowl. If she half paid attention, she would've seen it." She clicks through a few others, flashing them at me. "She stinks up the bathroom, too. How did you deal?"

I shrug. Back then I liked June and didn't mind putting up with her quirks and habits, however damaging they might've been. But now, every time I see her, every time I hear her name, every time I think of her, I see my butterflies pinned to the wall. The gleaming needles pierced straight through the space right under their heads and their eyes, where a human heart would be if it were that small and fragile. The wings pushed forward and brushed up against the walls. I feel my cheeks flush and the pressure build up.

"I need to ask you something." I dredge up courage.

"Yeah, what's up?" She doesn't look up from her phone.

"Did you know that Eleanor would end up in the hospital?"

She looks up. Her eyebrow lifts. "No."

She stares at me so hard, I can't ask another question. My stomach knots. The question has been burning inside me since the incident.

"You think I wanted to send her to hospital?"

"I'm not saying that. Just wanted to know if—"

"I thought she'd just look funny, okay?"

"Okay. Forget I asked." I jump up, take her phone, and try to change the weird mood in the room. "I have something fun we can do."

"Oooh, what?" She nibbles her bottom lip.

"Let's remind the girls not to throw up what they eat. Make sure they know how ugly it makes you look." The mean words pour out of my mouth and erase a little of the anger inside me. I can't stop. The cruelness fills me up.

She breaks out in a smile, like she's just finished a particularly difficult variation and is basking in the applause. "This will get her to clean up after herself or, better yet, get sent home."

I plug the phone into my computer and select those photos. I print about fifty of them. I hand her a bunch of the papers and clear tape. "We're going to let everyone know her nasty little habit. Ballerinas love their secrets."

We put tape on the photos, ready for posting, then open the door. The hallway is silent. It's just after midnight, and most girls are asleep or on their computers.

"I'll start on the eleventh floor—the Level 7 girls will find this hilarious." She slips down the stairwell.

I start putting the photos up on every door and the wall space in between. I even plaster them over the Level 8 bulletin board, June's ugly, pained face covering up announcements about changes in dorm rules for the new year. I imagine what her face is going to look like in the morning: twisted, weepy, shocked. I imagine how loud the laughs will be. I imagine her racing through the hallway, trying to tear them all down, only to find a dozen more. I imagine how long it will take her to find all of these. I imagine how many tears will stream down her face.

The guilt doesn't bubble up this time. Maybe it's all gone now. Maybe I am completely different now.

I go to the kitchen area and climb on one of the chairs. The streetlamps leave shadowy beams of light across the floor. I open the cabinets and tape them on everyone's cereal boxes and food containers. This feels addictive. A rush goes to my head.

"What are you doing?" The lights startle on. "You know there's a camera in here."

I almost fall out of the chair. The nighttime RA has her hand on her hip. She looks around at all the pictures, then starts tearing them down. My heart monitor buzzes on my wrist. Worry floods into my stomach and I start to shake.

"Get down, right now."

I ease down and put the rest of the pictures on the counter.

"What the heck are you doing?"

"I—I—just—"

"This is bullying and harassment." Her mouth is a hard line. "What's happened to you?"

"I was messed with, Miriam!" I shout. The anger shoots out of my mouth. I want her to feel it. I want everyone to feel it.

She closes the gap between us and puts a hand on my shoulder. Her sleepy eyes brim over with concern.

"June killed my butterflies. Will pushed me in front of a car."

She shakes her head, whispering "I know" a few times, and rubs my shoulder. She puts the rest of the photos in the trash. I can't move. My legs are frozen in place. I can't stop staring at the hall where I've put up all those pictures. I think about Cassie downstairs doing the same. I wonder how much trouble we'll be in.

"Help me take them down."

We remove each photo in silence. No one comes out into the hall. No one discovers the pictures. They end up in a pile in her arms, ready to be deposited into her trash bin. I text Cassie to do the same and warn her about the RA.

She finally says something just as I'm about to go back to my room. "Gigi, I'm disappointed."

I wait for the punishment—a meeting with Mr. K or a suspension or worse, possibly being banned from performing? The weight of it crashes in on me. Sweat drips down my back. My lips start to quiver.

"You've always been better than this."

I bite my bottom lip to keep from crying.

"Don't let the worst thing that ever happened to you define your life. Don't let it eat you up. You're back. You're dancing better than ever. You will be successful here. You don't need to do all"—she waves her hands around—"of that petty little kid stuff. Be better than it. Just dance. Doing all this makes you no better than Bette."

Her words hit me square in the chest. Bette's name slaps me. I think about Eleanor's face after she got sick eating the hummus, June's beautiful hair all over the PT room floor, Sei-Jin's pointe shoes, and mailing all those magazines to Bette. I've wasted so much time trying to show everyone that they shouldn't mess with me instead of pouring that energy into dancing, making sure my body is strong again and my technique is still there. I think about what Mama would say or do or think if she knew what I'd done.

"Fix it, and this will stay between the two of us. You do anything else, I'll make sure you're done at this school. Understand?"

"Yes," I say.

I close my room door and slide down to the floor. I press my knees into my chest. I'm wracked with pain and tears and anger at myself now. I've become Bette. I've become the person I hate. And that's the thing that shifts it all, the thing that snaps it into place.

The next morning I'm sitting in Mr. K's office again. The scent of his tobacco, the buttons in the chair, and the noise of ballet music pushing in through the door mix together and make me sick. Or maybe it's because Will's sitting in the nearby chair. His eyes glare down at his lap. His mother dabs her eyes with a handkerchief. She's got the same pale white skin and bright red hair, and wears almost as much makeup as her son.

Dad and Mama sit to my left. Mama's leg twitches to an angry beat, and it rubs against mine.

I stare at the side of Will's face. I close my eyes and think back to that night. How I laughed coming out of the club. How I felt happier than I ever had in my entire life at that moment. How I thought I'd finally found a place where I belonged, where people loved ballet as much as I do.

I try to remember how the hands on my back felt. I wonder if I should've recognized their size and shape and feel from all the times I'd danced with Will, letting him turn me and lift me and parade me around. All the emotions I'd buried rise to the surface.

How did I not know?

A voice inside says: *You didn't want to know.*

"Please don't press charges. He's sorry. Right, Will?" Mrs. O'Reilly slaps his arm. The sound echoes.

Mama presses back in her chair.

"Say you're sorry." I can see Mrs. O'Reilly's nails digging into Will's pale flesh, leaving red half-moons behind. He doesn't move a muscle. Her southern accent makes the words sound even harsher. "My idiot son's disgraced the family in more ways than one."

"He deserves to be punished by the law." Mama doesn't look

at her. Only straight ahead, like she's spotting for a pirouette. "He almost killed my child."

"And he'll be forever punished by the good Lord himself." Will's mother reaches out to touch my arm. I flinch and pull back.

"I don't know what else there is to discuss, Mr. K." Mama rises from her seat and picks up her bag, ready to go.

Will breaks down in full sobs.

"Now wait." My dad grabs Mama's hand and gets her to sit back down. "We should leave it to Gigi. All this happened to her."

"Gigi doesn't have to do anything she doesn't feel comfortable with," Mama says, but Mrs. O'Reilly interrupts.

"The good Christian thing is forgiveness. Will knows he faces judgment from the above. He doesn't need your—"

I finally look at Will. His skin is the color of his hair. He doesn't look up from his lap. I'm a terrible judge of character. I'm too trusting. I'm too naïve. "Enough," I whisper at first, then yell it over and over again until it's the only word in the room. After last night, I want all this to go away. I want to start the year over. I want all the wounds to close and stop bleeding. I just want to dance and not have to deal with all this. I want to go back to being the old me.

"Why did you do it?" I say, turning in my seat to face Will head-on. My heart knocks against my rib cage, its erratic beats making me light-headed. "Why?"

Will looks up finally. Tears stream down his face, but he's not wearing mascara today. "You have to listen to me. Please. Let me tell you what happened. I was trying to get Bette in trouble. I didn't know you'd actually get hurt. Henri promised me you'd just trip, twist your ankle. Not be able to dance *Giselle*. I didn't see the taxi. He made me believe that he liked me." His words give me goose bumps. The boy he liked and had a strange relationship with was Henri. "I swear I didn't want to hurt you like that." His cries turn to hiccups. "I didn't mean to hurt anyone."

The last phrase reverberates between us.

"I don't care why you did it, but I don't want to talk about this anymore, or even hear about it." I turn to Mama. "I don't want to press charges. I want to move on. I just want to dance." I turn back to Will. The relief on his face is so sudden, so desperate. "And, Will, I don't want to talk to you ever again."

I walk out, leaving Will to his own little version of hell.

29.

Bette

I SKIP BREAKFAST, HEADING STRAIGHT downstairs and out back to meet my dealer to buy more pills. My prescription stash is long gone, and I definitely need a pick-me-up. I've been waiting for him under the dim streetlamp by the Dumpsters for half an hour—and so far no-show. I tuck myself farther in the little alcove behind the back door, stomping my feet a bit to warm myself up. The February air freezes into a poufy cloud as I breathe out.

I check my phone every three seconds. The screen is empty, which has been a trend these days. I smash my furry boot into a mound of snow. Eleanor is still avoiding me, Alec hasn't wanted to do more than grab food in the café, Henri makes my skin crawl when he so much as glances my way, and even June doesn't have any time. Cassie just stares at me.

I shove my phone in my back pocket as Jarred walks up. "Finally!"

He shushes me, but then pulls me into a greasy hug. He's tall and skinny, sickly pale, with a full beard growing in, making him look far older than a junior at Columbia. I've been buying from him since he first moved to New York three years ago, and I know a lot of the company members do, too, because he dated a dancer back in the day. I met him at Adele's apartment.

I scoff. "You got my stuff?"

"Nope." He decides to have a cigarette.

"Need a drink, too?" I cross my arms over my chest. "Stop playing with me."

"Lighten up." He pulls out a couple of tiny paper packets, and it's a rainbow of pills—baby blue, pale yellow, even a pretty lavender.

"What are those?" I pull the purple packet right out of his hands.

"Bonus!" His grin is slimy, hopeful. "These are stronger than the Adderall."

"Just want the regulars." I pull two hundred bucks out of my left boot and hand him the cash. "Thanks. Later." I wave him away, and slip the pills into my pocket.

"That's all I get for coming this early?" He has his arms open like I'm supposed to fold myself inside them.

"I gave you a tip. Now go." I wait until he walks away, then turn back around and freeze. Cassie stands right behind me.

A large grin creeps across her face. "How's Jarred?"

"I don't know who you're talking about." I try to brush past her. She doesn't let me pass.

"Which ones did you buy this month? Are they blue, maybe? Or white?"

"I have no idea what you're talking about."

"Sure, Bette. Two minutes back on campus, and the games have begun again, right? You going to drug Gigi this time? Or maybe you'll try to get me again?"

"I *said* I don't know what you're talking about."

She gets right up in my face now, and I can feel her hot breath—strawberries and cinnamon—hit my cheek.

I back up.

"You don't remember? When you made Will drop me and send me to the hospital and rehabilitation for a year and a half. Or the way you messed with my diet pills. Made me faint in class."

I'm caught off guard, so I back away a bit more, realizing too late that she's trapped me against the Dumpster. My head brushes against the cold metal. I don't know if it's just the lack of light, but there's a gleam in her eye that's making me nervous, something I've never seen before. "Maybe you need to go back to rehab." My fists ball. "Because you're clearly having a break-down."

"I don't know how you did it, Bette. You've got them all wrapped around your finger. But you'll get what you deserve soon. Eleanor's already abandoned you, and Alec will hate you permanently if I have anything to do with it. You just wait."

My heart hiccups in my chest. I can't get it to relax.

She flashes a mean grin again, and then, just like that, she's gone.

People always ask me if I love having a sister. Usually, I do. But on a Sunday morning, as we rehearse Odile's variation together for the eightieth time, I hate her. My mother has decided that I need to rehearse with Adele to make sure I use this second chance to its fullest. Because Adele's heralded as the next great principal of the American Ballet Company, and my mother donates a ton of money, they've reserved a stage at Lincoln Center at six a.m. two weekday mornings and on Sundays, so that we can practice together.

I stamp my pointe shoes in the resin box. It's eerily quiet in here—aside from the stage we're on, the building is draped in darkness. The *Swan Lake* score plays on a loop on Adele's phone. It's the only sound in the huge space, apart from the soft soprano of Adele barking orders.

"Let's go." She waves me forward and clicks the music back to Odile's variation in Act Three. The quick strum of harp strings announces my presence. I parade around in three circles, as if a group of onlookers ring the stage perimeter. I flap my arms, gracious and full, like a dark swan.

"Focus, focus, focus, Bette." She circles around me, watching my every move before I've even started dancing. But I can't focus. Not today. The two blue pills I took with my coffee this morning have my heart racing, my mind frantic. Maybe they don't work anymore.

I lift my arms over my head in big sweeping circles and cross them in front of me. The music starts. I tiptoe forward and swing my leg, then leap into a split jump.

"Bigger legs. Stretch them. Point the toes. You only get one chance to show what your body can do in those jumps."

I want to tell her that I don't have her extension.

"Quick circles and back to center. Leg up."

She claps to push me to jump higher.

"It should be all one motion, flawless, fluid. But I can see every thought about every movement on your face."

I can see every thought on her face: that I'll never quite get this.

I want to show her that I'm not a reflection of her. I don't have the things that make her great. I kind of want to mess it all up, just to show her that I'm not as good as she is.

But I can't.

"Make sure you extend the leg fully in that first turn—that will set the tone for the whole variation." She grabs my leg as it flies up, lifting it further, higher. I can feel the spasms shooting up from my calf to my thigh, making me shiver with pain. "Long, strong arms." She lets go of my leg and lifts my arms next, pulling me this way and that like a marionette. I push her away and then pause, my hands on my knees, to breathe for a second. All my time at home, working with just Yuli, lowered my stamina. I walk to the edge of the stage and pick up a bottle of water.

"What are you doing?"

She pulls it right out of my hands. "You'll lose all the heat, the momentum. We've still got to practice the *fouettés*. That's the most difficult part."

"You don't think I know that?"

"I know that you *know* that. You've seen the ballet a hundred times. But you have to do it." Her eyes burn into mine. "Now, the coda."

We practice the thirty-two *fouettés* for an hour straight. She can get it without stopping, without thinking, every single time. I have to work through it, every single time. "You're thinking too much, Bette." She yells. "Relax into it. Let go. Otherwise you'll lose it, without fail."

She sends me spinning again, and I try to block everything out and focus. But my mind wanders to whether I'm smiling enough and if my hands look soft and if I'm up on my leg. I imagine finishing the final spin and the roar of the applause and how Alec's arms will wrap around my waist, strong and safe, like they used to. At turn number twenty-three, I crash.

"Bette." Adele's voice drills into my head. "If you're going to join me at this level, you have to give it your all. You can't think about other things, no matter what. American Ballet Company will only take two of you, and you've worked so hard for so many years. Don't blow it now."

That stops me in my tracks. Failure is not an option for me. Especially not now that I'm so close.

"I know. I just keep thinking about what you're seeing. My hands, face, you know?"

"Stop thinking. Just do it. Focus on how it feels. You'll know it's right then."

The music is reset and I start again, from the beginning. I let the quickening pace carry me like I'm a dark cloud floating around the room. I'm all impossibly long arms and out-to-forever legs. I'm all the grace of the swan and the frenetic energy of little blue pills and endless cups of strong black coffee. It's like my heart is impatient, leaping, angry, and urgent.

Adele watches, trying to keep the judgment off her face. But there it is, in the narrowing of her eyes and the two little frown lines that have settled in on either side of her mouth. I look at her now and see myself, but with all the softness worked out of me. I feel her exhaustion cover me like a blanket.

"I need some water. Then I'll start over." I head toward the wings, grabbing my bag and a bottle of water. The little old custodian, the one who washes the floor every morning, gives me a wave. I frown in response. He knows we've got the stage till eight. He's not supposed to be up here yet. I plop down on the stage, the opposite of grace, unable to move.

I stretch out my muscles. They still feel buzzy and dead. I can't do it again. "You know what, Adele, I can't dance anymore today. I don't know if I'll ever get it."

"You will." She walks over to me and offers a hand, a consolation. "Let's do it one more time. Then we can call it a day."

I shake my head. "I'm done." I uncap my water bottle and take another big sip, hoping the chill of it will calm me down. But all I can hear is the pounding in my ears. I close my eyes and let the darkness overtake me for a second, dropping my torso between my legs to cool off.

"I'll show you. Sit and watch." She might as well pat me on the head and give me a lollipop.

I start the music for her. She's gone, somewhere far away, inside her head, where it's just her and the sweet melody of the music. She's far beyond my reach, and I feel a pang as I realize that I'll never quite be her equal. I'm barely her shadow. I'll never match the way she extends those legs sky-high, the way her arms arch and flow, with all the grace of a real swan. It's breathtaking.

She starts the thirty-two endless spins that are a signature of this ballet, a challenge for any ballerina. It's almost like it's automatic, the momentum and the velocity of it, like someone's wound up a little knob on her and let her whirl off. Round and round she goes, and I want to look away but I can't. It's exciting and infuriating—to see something that beautiful. And to know you'll never live up to it.

I count the turns in my head. After her twentieth turn, she drops, just disappears out of my sightlines. Half her body has fallen through one of the trapdoors in the stage. Her arms flail overhead, grabbing hold of the edges of the stage, and she's shrieking. I leap up and run toward her.

"Betttttte!"

Her arms and head are the only things above the floor. I try to tug her up, but she yelps in pain, so I let go. I'm trying to pull her forward again, more gently this time, when I hear heavy boots on the hardwood. The janitor appears.

He clomps over. "Wait— Is she hurt? Don't move her. You could make it worse." He's leaning in now, with his flashlight, letting the beam spill on her legs, her torso, her face as she blocks the sharp light. She's whimpering now, her face white with fear and pain.

"Hold on, we're going to get you right out of there." His voice soothing and warm. He pulls up his walkie-talkie and talks fast, requesting help and an ambulance. "They're on the way." He turns to me. "Did you see what happened?"

My voice is shaky when I finally manage to speak. "I—she

was doing the coda, the *fouettés*. But the trapdoor—"

"Wasn't supposed to be open. Nobody's down there this time of morning."

The door was shut tight before. It was just the two of us—Adele and me. No one else.

The EMTs come rushing through, dragging sleet across the stage and leaving wet stains on the hardwood. A tall dark-haired one in a blue uniform carefully lowers himself down into the trapdoor space, as others carry a gurney over, prepping it for Adele. He gingerly lifts her up to the stage, and I see her face explode with pain. That's when the tears come. Hers and mine.

"I was supposed to be dancing," I say aloud.

"What's that?" one of the EMTs responds.

"That was supposed to happen to me."

"You feeling okay?" The EMT reaches for my arm. "You should sit."

I follow her directions. She checks my blood pressure while they strap Adele onto the gurney. Nobody would ever want to hurt Adele.

Me.

Someone would want to hurt me.

Adele cries out.

"Shhhh," the EMT whispers, dabbing her forehead with a cloth.

Another EMT fires some questions our way. "What happened? How did she fall?" Then he asks Adele: "Can you move your foot? Your leg?" She whimpers in response.

"Are you related?" the first EMT asks me. I nod. "How old is she? How old are you? We need to call your parents."

It's all rushing back, the sirens and chaos of that night Gigi nearly died. This feels so familiar. But the real question is: Who did it this time?

30.

June

"E-JUN KIM?" THE LADY BEHIND the registration desk riffles through the stack of papers for a third time. "Are you sure you're slotted for today?"

I nod my head again, and the flush creeps up my neck to my cheeks. There's nothing to be embarrassed about, I remind myself. It's just a clerical mistake. But so far, the whole trip to San Francisco has been one huge mistake.

It's Valentine's Day. I should be at home with Jayhe, celebrating with kisses and even coconut cake. But we haven't talked since that night at his little cousin's birthday party. Now here I am, almost three thousand miles away, and everything's gone wrong. When I got here, the hotel gave me a hard time checking in, since my name wasn't on my mom's credit card and I didn't have a note with her signature. Then I couldn't figure out which trolley to take here this morning, so I took a cab, which cost me fifty bucks. Now they can't find me on the audition roster.

It must be a sign. I can't move to San Francisco. It's the last place I should be. Besides, everything here reminds me of Gigi—I feel like she'll be on the next trolley or in the diner down the street from the hotel or here at the dance company, where she'd fit right in, and I feel so out of place.

"Oh, E-Jun Kim." The woman's dimples swallow her face. "We have you under June. Sorry. I don't know where my head is today. You're in batch B—which goes on in half an hour. I'd warm up now if I were you."

I try not to roll my eyes. Does she think I'm new at this? This is the fifth audition I've done in the last month. But the others—DC, LA, Salt Lake, and Miami—all came to New York for castings. So I just walked to midtown, instead of going cross-country. I don't know if I'm cut out for California, but I'm here, so I'll give it my all. I have to.

She hands me a number—44. The number four is bad luck in Korean culture, at least according to my mother, which means I'm already off to a terrible start. I try not to freak out. "Any chance I can get a different number?" I ask.

"Next," she calls, ignoring me completely.

"It's just a silly superstition," I tell myself as I walk to the ladies' changing room, where I pull on my tights, leotards, and ballet slippers, and put my stuff into a locker. I'll have to deal. I check my phone again, hoping for a call from my mom or, really, a text from Jayhe saying *break a leg*, or *thinking about you*. I miss those. I ponder texting him, just for a second, but part of me knows it's pointless. I don't think he wants to hear from me again.

I look around the studio. It's all glass and metal, not unlike ABC. These companies, they're all the same, but different.

I follow a numbered crowd into a warm-up studio, which is sweltering with the heat of too many bodies. The barre is filled with dancers of every shape and stripe—statuesque blondes that remind me of Bette, willowy Asian girls like me. But as much as I keep thinking I'll see her any second, no one looks like Gigi in this room. She'd stand out, even here.

I plop down on the floor and spread my legs into a V, determined to warm up despite the thick crowd. I lean forward and touch my toes, letting my torso drop between my legs. The stretch shoots down my thighs and into my calves until it reaches my toes. I point and flex, point and flex. Then I lie down like a dead frog, knees apart, flat to the ground, opening up my hips and getting them ready to turn out.

I look for a space at a barre. That's when I see Sei-Jin, in the far corner. She's not facing me, but I recognize the long black hair, pulled taut in a bun, the mole that sits on her neck adjacent to her right ear. I recognize the familiar way her arms move up and over and down, but the fingers curl, never quite extending enough no matter how many times Morkie corrects her. I remember telling her it would hold her back, when we were still friends.

I back away from the barre, hoping to make it out of there without her seeing me. What happened to Princeton and Yale and Brown? I thought she'd given up on ballet. But, I realize with a start, maybe people think the same thing about me.

"Batch B," the lady with a clipboard announces, "you're up."

I rush to follow her out the door, but I can sense Sei-Jin not far behind me. She hasn't noticed me yet, but she will in a minute. The last thing I need here is a scene.

"You five first. Line up," the clipboard lady announces. She points to me and four other girls—including Sei-Jin, today dubbed number thirty-nine. She's magically by my side, her mauve mouth smirking at me, an eyebrow rising when she sees my unlucky number. She does a little wave.

They hand us each a fan, and announce that we'll be doing Kitri's fan variation from *Don Quixote*. We learned this in class back in Level 6. We spent weeks perfecting how to hold a fan while doing simple jumps. "No chicken wing arms," Madame Dolinskaya would holler at us. "Big, bold Spanish arms. Bigger, bigger!" I always had trouble getting into character. But I've been working on that with Bette, so I know I can handle this.

"Wait your turn stage right."

We line up along the edges of the studio. The other three girls in front of me are white, brunettes. They all look alike to me—although they probably look at Sei-Jin and me and think the same. We're mirrors, despite my short bob, now starting to grow in, and her long dark hair, pulled into a proper bun.

A ballet mistress goes over the steps once as a refresher. Then, one at a time, we're called forward to the center.

I mark the movements. I get to review them three times before I go on. Sei-Jin performs right before me, missing a step early on, then staying slightly off the beat for the remainder of the variation. Usually, I'd be filled with glee at this humiliation, but I can see the pain behind her pasted-on smile, and it breaks my heart. I've been there. We all have.

"Number forty-four!" the ballet mistress calls, and I grimace, but manage to pull myself together. I saunter to the center, circling the space. I smile and bow at the line of ballet masters and mistresses sitting in front of the mirror. The music starts, loud and clear. I flash my fan, jump on my toes and prepare. The harp chords deepen. I press my hand against my hip and flutter the fan. The variation begins: arms wide, long steps, leg up. All you hear is the music and the clack of a fan opening. My movements are automatic, step, step, step, extended leg, *plié*. Slide the leg out and up, and turn. I do a quick crisscrossing of the feet and tiny *taqueté* hops with pointed toes.

Remember to smile.

Remember the quick, small fan flutters from the wrist.

Remember a Spanish-style *port de bras*, arms extended over the head.

The joy of the wedding dance lifts up from the center of me, floating like the celebratory bubbles in a glass of champagne. My face is rosy and flirtatious, the smile beckoning. I glide my toes forward, one after another, as I move from the left corner to the center, presenting the fan.

I take a small bow, and exit. One other girl dances after me. We wait for them to let us know who'll go on to the next round. I'm feeling good about my chances, and then the ballet master, a man with a thick Eastern European accent, calls out, "Forty-one, forty-two, forty-three." He pauses. "The rest may go." The rest. Sei-Jin and me.

I don't think I've heard him correctly. "Wait, what?"

Sei-Jin steps forward to leave, and my hand reaches for her arm, holding her back.

"But—" I can't believe the word has escaped my mouth, and she looks as horrified as I feel. It's not proper to acknowledge the rejection, to utter a word of pain or regret. Still, I can't quite believe it. I did well. I know I did.

"Yes, number forty-four?" The man's voice drips with ice and disdain.

"I'm sorry, I just—I thought I performed well." I look at Sei-Jin, and her eyes are dark, desperate, begging me not to drag her into this. But a surge of confidence shoots through me.

There's dead silence in the room. When he speaks again, there's a finality to his voice, which remains neutral, indifferent. "You certainly were spirited, and your technique was strong." His eyes trace all the lines of me, from tip to toe. "Strong pointe, good expression, although a bit too practiced. The passion doesn't scream authentic. But frankly, you're not the right type for San Francisco. The look—too lean." My head drops along with my heart, and he waits for me to lift my eyes, to look at him again before he dismisses me. "Honestly, I think you'll find it difficult to get work without building some strength. It's a risk most companies, financially and otherwise, are not willing to take." He waves his hand, and I feel Mr. K's shadow enveloping me. "Good luck in your search."

I will not cry. I keep telling myself this as I storm out of the room. I feel a hand on my shoulder before I break down. It's so familiar, the touch of those long, lean fingers, the scent of lip gloss. Like a flash of home in this foreign place.

"June." In that moment, I want to forgive everything and let Sei-Jin hug me. "I know this is hard. But I don't think this is about what you think it's about."

"And what's that?" I'm blinking back tears, trying not to give her this moment, the satisfaction. Knowing, then, that we'll never be friends again. Not in the way I've secretly hoped for, all this time.

"I know I did poorly," she says. "I didn't display the fan properly, my leaps weren't great, and my heart wasn't in it. I shouldn't really be here at all, but I couldn't let it go."

I don't know what to say to that—except that she's right, it's all true. So I don't say anything at all.

"You, though." She looks at me so intently, from just inches away, like she did that day when everything ended. "You were probably as good as I've ever seen you. Despite the unlucky number." She swallows and looks down and then looks up again. "But, E-Jun, what he said was true. You're going to have a hard time." She reaches out, touches my chin, and then my collarbone, which is exposed by the scoop neck of my black leotard.

The tears fall, fast and furious and unstoppable. She tries to hug me then—the moment I've been hoping for every second of the past three years. But it's all wrong, and I'm flailing my arms and pushing her away.

She won't let go. I give in this time, and we stand here, heads together. "Come on, E-Jun, let me help you."

Sei-Jin gets our stuff from the locker room and bustles me downstairs. I'm still wearing my pointe shoes when we get into the cab. I can't bear the thought of having to take them off again.

The trip home is a blur. I take a cab from the airport straight to my mom's. She doesn't ask me how it went. We don't talk about it that night or the next morning. But I know she knows. She's been watching me, when I'm not looking, trying to figure out what to say, what to do.

I sit next to her, doing math homework while she knits and watches a Korean drama. When the show is over, she gets up and heads into the apartment's small kitchen. I can hear her chopping vegetables, stir-frying beef. The smell makes me realize that I'm starving—and nauseous. "E-Jun," my mom yells into the living room. "Come set the table."

I rise from the sofa like a zombie. I walk into the kitchen and set out two deep, flat bowls, along with napkins, two pairs of chopsticks and spoons, and two tall glasses filled with water. I see her twirling clear noodles into the stir-fry pan, which still glistens with the grease from the beef. The smell is amazing— salty and garlicky, sweet and sour, like soy and sesame.

Putting everything together, my mother brings the serving bowl to the table. The noodles are glassy and beautiful, surrounded by the bright orange of the carrots, the red of the peppers, and bold green of the spinach and scallions. The scent of the stir-fried beef and shiitakes wafts up. It makes me want to heave, but I sit in front of the bowl and let the steam graze my face, prayerful and soothing. Why can't I just love this like I used to? Why can't I just eat it like a normal person?

I know why she made them. This was my comfort food growing up, when I was all cried out, exhausted and spent. "You have to eat, June," she says finally, sitting at the table across from me. "You have to, *boba*."

I nod again, but don't touch the food.

I imagine myself eating it. I can even see myself chewing and swallowing. I feel the warmth in my stomach. I picture myself asking her for hot sauce.

"I can't." The chopsticks fall from my hands.

My mom picks them up, wipes them off, and digs them into the bowl. She picks up a few noodles and a mushroom. "Open. I will show you how to eat again." With her other hand, she pinches my chin and my lips part. She pushes the noodles into my mouth, like I'm a baby who can't get the food inside. The noodles sit, slimy and salty and gag inducing. My tongue fights them. My mind tells my mouth to spit them out.

"You eat so you can be strong. If you want to dance, you have to be strong." She twirls more noodles onto the chopsticks, lifting them to my mouth. She repeats the word over and over again to the beat of my chews, forcing me to swallow. I want the heat, the strength to sink into my skin and muscles and bones and harden me from the inside out. I want to be strong, like she says. It's just, I don't know how.

31.

Gigi

THE MIDDLE OF FEBRUARY, WHEN Mr. K watches the girls' class, everyone is a mess. He barks at Cassie about looking like a mannequin. And June falls when he makes her do ten pirouettes because she wasn't fully extended. Even little Riho lets her arm slip and her gaze drop and fails to achieve the perfection we all know is expected of us. The left side of me aches, and even though I can see the movements in my head and know where my arm should be, I'm a few seconds behind.

We should be stronger at this point. I should be stronger.

Mr. K doesn't move a muscle, not even in his face. I'm getting better at interpreting his little twitches and squints and almost imperceptible nods. But there's nothing there today. His arms are crossed over his chest. His mouth is a perfect straight line.

I want to make his lips turn up. I want him to see me, the way he used to. His *moya korichnevaya*.

When it's my turn to dance for him again, I try to channel

that old spirit. I make sure my practice tutu is perfectly arranged and there isn't a single hair out of place on my head. My right foot's pointed, torso bending from the hip. I'm ready. I want to do the perfect pirouette, the most delicate arabesque, the most lovely *fouetté*—to make him see me again, to make him tell Damien that I should be one of ABC's apprentices next year.

My music begins. I prepare to step into my first move. The plinks of Viktor's piano keys feel like waves that my hands, arms, legs, and feet wade through. The movements feel good, but there's a pinch in my hip as I turn my left leg, and a new pain in my ankle radiates down through my toes. I push through it and try not to let it show on my face.

"Soft hands," I hear Mr. K say. "Soft neck." His deep voice is a ripple in the waves. Tension seeps into my muscles. I can't stop it. Sweat streams down my back. I clench my teeth.

"Soft mouth. Descend through the toes." He walks in front of me now as his voice rises. "Lighter, lighter! You are a swan, not a cow."

His corrections drum into me, one after the other. The monitor on my wrist buzzes, but I push harder.

"The whole school can hear me, but you can't because you're still doing it wrong!" he shouts. I can't keep tears from pricking my eyes. He makes me dance through the messiness that I am right now.

Finally, he gives up on me, motioning at Viktor to stop. The pianist's fingers crash on the keys. I have shifted my weight too far over, so I trip.

I used to think being a ballerina was special, but in moments like this, it is easy to feel like the least original being on earth. I wipe away the tears, willing them to stop falling.

"Come." He waves me over to the mirror.

I straighten my back and step away a few inches, like that will somehow temper whatever terrifying thing is about to explode from his mouth.

An interruption is never *good*.

The other girls lean in to listen. They know that whatever he is about to say is ten times worse than the corrections he's just hollered at me. He places a hand on my shoulder. I almost collapse under its weight.

"Giselle."

For one glorious moment I lock eyes with his and my adrenaline surges. I try to hold his gaze and not be distracted by the dozens of ballerinas watching our conversation play out in the mirror, trying to read his lips and watch my face.

"Yes?" I settle my body into a comfortable and respectful third position.

"My darling, my butterfly. You've been through so much. But I will not pity you or give you special treatment. I will treat you like everyone else. Can you do this?" His accent is thick and his manner of speaking cryptic.

The four-letter word *this* thuds into my chest. It sweeps together all the recovery progress I've made and how hard I've been working and all the years of my ballet training, like it's so tiny and insignificant that it could fit into such a small word. I want to tell him that my mind and heart know each step, each movement, but my muscles are still remembering. I see myself in the mirror. I'm a mop. I'm that sweaty and sad looking. I catch some of the girls inching forward a little, and Eleanor has her eyes fixed on Mr. K. Her doe-eyed gaze doesn't waver. All the girls hate and worship Mr. K, but Eleanor's current fixation seems to go beyond that. It's like she doesn't see anything—anyone—else in the room at all.

I'm so busy watching her watching him that Mr. K has to repeat his question.

"Yes," I squeak out. I hate myself for the mousiness of the word and the way it gets caught in my throat. "I can. I promise you, I can."

This all feels like some sort of punishment for messing with other dancers instead of channeling that rage into stretching and working in the studios. For thinking about revenge all the time instead of the footwork in *Swan Lake*. For letting this place change me, turn me into one of them.

"I will fix it," I say.

"Good. Show me you're still my little butterfly." He leans down closer to my ear. He touches my cheek. "Let me see that spark again." He turns back to everyone and walks forward. "Gigi, out of the center, and Eleanor in."

After rehearsals, Sei-Jin lets me come into her room without a second thought. I've decided to apologize to her for soaking her shoes in vinegar, so that I can start over and really just focus on ballet and the Odette role. Posters of Korean pop stars swallow the walls, grinning boys peering out from behind all the hanging tutus. A shoe rack sits at the door where I slipped out of my mukluks. The glowing white bulbs of a vanity table cast a glow on her TV.

"I can't believe we've never hung out." She's sewing ribbons on her pointe shoes and icing her ankles. "But I'm glad you asked."

I try to get comfortable in her vanity chair. I don't want to see myself in the mirror when I tell her what I did, when I try to make amends. She's the first on the list. She asks me about California, tells me she auditioned for the San Francisco Ballet, and about her plans to go to college. I ask her about possibly dancing in Seoul or Europe, and tell her not to give up on dancing in a company. There are pauses and lulls in our conversation that I don't know how to fill.

I wind myself up to tell the truth. Get these things off my chest so I can start over, go back to the old me. The one who would never hurt another dancer. "Sei-Jin . . ."

"Yeah?" She pauses her stitching and looks up.

"I'm the one who messed up your pointe shoes."

"Wait, what?" She puts down her half-sewn shoe and slides to the edge of her bed.

"I did it."

"But . . . it was June." Her mouth closes with a pinch.

"No, it was me. I thought . . . or I was sort of told that you were the one who put glass in my shoe last year."

"I would never do that." Sei-Jin leaps up.

My heart thuds and sweat races down my back. I feel like I'm in front of Morkie. Sei-Jin's brown eyes flash with anger and she clenches her teeth.

"After what happened with W-Will"—I can barely say his

name—"I wanted to come clean. Start over. And fix all the stuff I've done this year. I became someone else." I go to the dance bag I left near the door. I take out a brand-new pair of shoes that I ordered from the ABC shoe room. They're identical to the ones I ruined, custom for her feet. "I'm sorry."

She shoves them away. "You should leave."

I say sorry again. I imagined that she'd accept my apology and the shoes. I thought she'd understand. Instead, she holds the door open. "Get out!"

"Sei-Jin, I am so—" The door closes in my face.

I stand there for a minute, at a loss, then gather my guilt and walk away.

The next morning academic classes are canceled for costume fittings. One at a time we file into Madame Matvienko's room. She circles me as she examines how the Odette costume fits. The white tutu blooms around my waist in layers of stiff tulle. The bodice drips with encrusted jewels. The feathery headpiece sweeps over my ears and has a glittering diamond that rests right on my forehead. In the mirror, I feel like I'm wearing such an important costume. One that defines what most people think of when they think of ballet.

She hums and frowns and snaps the measuring tape in her hands. "You and Eleanor cannot wear same costume. Will have to take in too much. Ruin the original."

How am I supposed to respond to the fact that she's saying Eleanor is so much tinier than me? I cross my hands over my stomach and feel much more exposed in front of her than I do anyone else.

She yanks them apart. "Stand still. You American girls fidget so much. Always moving, moving, moving."

"Sorry." She's never nice to me and I don't know if it's because of who she is—a person who doesn't smile much or seem to like many of us—or if she doesn't like me in particular. She goes to her worktable and returns with another pair of white tights. She lays them against my arm, then compares them to the ones I'm wearing.

"Very hard, you know"—she pulls at the fabric—"to match you girls' legs. Color is too dark for the white. You can see through it. It's no good."

I gulp. I wonder if the way she uses the word *girls* refers to black girls and not all girls in general.

"White swans have white legs. Then it would be easy." She turns back to her table, comes back with another pair. "I have had to spend lot of time dyeing these tights. To make them even whiter. And no matter what, legs still too brown and you can see them right through it."

"I'm sorry," I say, and instantly hate myself for it.

She frowns. "It's a big problem, you know. Messes up the whole costume, the whole look, the pictures. I have to special order."

I gaze at my legs in the mirror. Through the thin nylon, I can see the brown color of my legs a little bit.

I want to say that it makes me feel uncomfortable that she'd even say something like that, that she's rude and a little racist for even saying these things. Would she say the same to Bette or Eleanor? No, because their legs are white and blend easily with the tights.

"What do you want me to do about it?" I ask her with caution. She's very powerful here. "I can't change who I am."

I want to add that I wouldn't, even if I could. But I don't say that. Cassie told me stories about girls Madame didn't like who performed in costumes that were just a smidge too tight or tutus with pins left in them, pricking them at every turn. I remember June telling me about a girl who Madame Matvienko thought was a little too plump for the Arabian Coffee costume. The girl snatched it out of Madame's hands and said she'd fix it herself. Three days later, she was dismissed from the conservatory.

Matvienko laughs. "Well, you can't change the color of your legs, and that would be best." She unhooks the bodice and starts pulling it off me. The fabric scratches my skin. "But I will just have to place special order for you."

She snatches the tutu off and leaves me there half-clothed, her eyes fluttering over me and my too-brown legs. I quickly get dressed. Every part of me feels prickly and hot. All the things I'd like to call her bubble up, but I can't get them out.

"You're dismissed," she says. She goes to the back, where her office is, and shuts the door.

32.

Bette

I LIE ON MY SISTER'S bed with my nose in her peach-scented hair. I braid and unbraid it because she says it helps her relax. It's one of the few things my mother actually did for us growing up, and something she was good at. When I was little and refused to cut my hair so I could be like Rapunzel, she could give me any kind of braid I wanted: fishtail, French, crowns. I'd fall asleep, even first thing in the morning before school, head bobbing back into her lap as her fingers worked their way through my hair.

It's Saturday evening, and Adele's leg is propped up on a set of pillows with her foot swaddled in a cast. Two broken toes, a hairline fracture in her ankle, and three stitches to the knee will keep her off her feet for at least eight weeks, right through the spring gala performance. So I'm doing what I can to help her keep her mind off things—bringing her DVDs and food, reading aloud from *Little Women*, her favorite. We'll sit for hours, sharing the latest gossip from school and the company, like who'll fill her role, now that she won't be able to dance it. We're waiting for chicken salads from our favorite local bistro, so when the doorbell buzzes, I jump up.

But when I open the door, Eleanor stands there. She looks exhausted but upbeat—and surprised to see me.

"Hey. I thought—I came to visit Adele." She's got a bouquet of white roses in her hands. Adele's favorite. "I thought she might want some company."

"She has plenty of company." I don't mean for it to sound so bitter, but it's been two months since I got back to school, and we've barely spoken two words to each other since that night I told her I knew about what was happening between her and Mr. K. This should be the happiest time in my life. But it's not. Maybe I can't blame her. But I do.

"Bette? Is that the food? I'm starving!" Adele shouts.

"No," I say back. "You have a visitor." Eleanor follows me back into the tiny living room.

"Oh, hey," Adele says, nearly jumping up before she remembers she can't. Eleanor hands her the roses. "Thank you so much. How are you?"

"I should be asking you the same thing." Eleanor's eyes are on my sister's cast, and they're full of worry. "What, uh, happened exactly?"

"They say it was a switch malfunction—that the trapdoor opened when it shouldn't have. And I fell right in!" Adele laughs, but I can tell that Eleanor is thinking the same thing I am: that this was no accident.

"Can I sign your cast?" Eleanor asks then, and Adele beams at her.

She's scribbling on Adele's leg when the doorbell buzzes again. This time it is the delivery guy.

"Please share," Adele says as I pull out the chicken salads and put them on the coffee table. We all pick at them for a few minutes, and I find myself repeatedly stopping myself from spilling Eleanor's secret. Because if there's anyone who'd know what to do about it, it's Adele. After all, she lived it. Sort of.

The whole meal is awkward and slow and lull filled, like we're strangers instead of girls who have known one another our whole lives. Too much has happened, and too much is being left unsaid. At nine p.m., Eleanor looks at her phone, which has been buzzing for a while, even though she's tried to ignore it. "It's getting late," she says, standing. "I should get back to the dorm."

"Oh, Bette, why don't you go with her?" Adele says.

I start gathering up the leftovers, putting them all into one container. "I was planning to crash," I say, but Adele's shaking her head.

"No, Bette, go. It's Saturday night. You shouldn't be stuck here with me. And, really, I'm about to take a few painkillers and go to sleep."

I open my mouth again, but the look in Adele's eye tells me she's not about to listen. I do as she says, getting her the medicine and helping her into her room. Once she's tucked in, I turn off the lights. Then I hear her say, in the darkness, "You should talk to Eleanor. I think she needs you."

I nod to myself in the dark.

Eleanor and I walk the four blocks back to the dorm in silence. When we get there, I expect her to walk in with me, that maybe we really will pop some popcorn and watch a movie. But she's looking at her phone again. Which means she's still communicating with him.

"Eleanor, don't." I put my hand on her arm, but she's set to walk away. "This—it—it just isn't right."

"You're hardly one to judge." She tosses away my concern like garbage in a nearby street bin. "Look, I know things haven't been easy for either of us. And I know this thing with Adele, it's eating you up. But it's not your fault, okay?"

That's the thing, though. It is. "It was meant for me. I know it."

"No," Eleanor's saying again, and now she's got her arm around me, the weight of it familiar and comforting, like a heavy winter blanket. "You've got to let it go. Focus on ballet. You've got a second chance. You know how rare that is?"

"That's just it." I don't know if it's the cold bite of the wind that's stinging my eyes or tears, but either way, I let them fall. I just want to be in this moment, to maybe fix all the things I broke. "I'm finally getting exactly what I wanted. What I've always dreamed of. But none of it feels like I imagined it would. Adele. You. I'm like little hurricane Bette, taking out everyone in my path."

"You haven't ruined me, Bette." She sighs. "I'm right here. And Adele will be fine."

"But you and me . . . we're a mess."

"I know," Eleanor whispers. She looks down at her phone again. I start to walk toward the building, heading inside and out of the cold.

"Wait, Bette." She slips the phone into her pocket. "I'm so tired. Popcorn? Movie?"

I smile at her. "Only if it's *Breakfast at Tiffany's*."

Damien will be watching our ballet class today. With Adele out and cast lists shifting, he'll probably hire early, like he did last year. Aiko Yosidha left the conservatory last November to join ABC's corps de ballet and start her professional career before graduating. The same thing happened with Adele. But they were both clear standouts, proving themselves over and over.

That's what I need to show: that level of technique, that level of commitment. I have to be perfect. I have to be like my sister. I slip into a new leotard and tights and give myself a flawless bun. I open the jewelry box where I keep my locket hidden away. I open its usual drawer to find empty red velveteen. My heart thuds against my rib cage. Sweat beads my brow.

I comb through the other compartments, then go to my dance bag. I tear through it, throwing everything out onto the floor. The locket is tangled with pointe shoe ribbons. The clasp is open and the pills have scattered throughout the bag. My heartbeat drums through me, making my fingers all wobbly and anxious. I dump everything out of the bag and fish the pills from the mess, one by one, returning them to their safe space inside my locket. The familiar little halo makes everything slow down.

I swallow one pill, then decide to take one more. I need to

be extrafocused during rehearsal. I race downstairs to warm up early.

Damien watches as we do the movements, Morkie barking at this girl or the other. "Extend. Higher. Soft arms. Long, lean lines."

I can feel the sweat seeping through my leotard and dripping down my face. I try to tune Morkie out, focusing instead on my toes, which burn so badly I think they've burst. I let the pain wash over me, pushing me harder. But then all I can hear is the pounding of my heart in my ears, like the bass in a club. I try to slow my breathing, to relax.

Everything is making me anxious: my own reflection, the sound of the variation music, the lower-level dancers drifting past the window, Damien's pen scribbling across a page, the weird smile Cassie keeps flashing my way.

The room swirls around me. Reflections twist and warp in the mirror.

Calm down, Bette. Relax.

I put my hand on the mirror to keep from falling. My head feels like it's floating away, and my chest tightens. I know it's nothing but panic. It has to be that.

"A tarantella, Viktor," I hear Morkie saying. He plays a few chords on the piano, and she stops him to give directions. The noises all blend together into one droning glob of sound. My legs feel like they're going to give out from under me.

Cassie rushes forward. She puts a hand on my shoulder. I can't move away from her. It's like we've plunged under water. Each movement is slow and watery. "Are you okay, Bette?"

I try to answer her. I try to jerk away from her. I try to tell her to get away from me.

Cassie leans in and whispers in my ear: "How does it feel to lose control? To not know what the things you put in your body might do to you?" She smiles and pats my arm, but I don't hear what she says next, because black dots stamp out my vision and the studio goes dark.

When I wake up, an EMT hovers over me, a stethoscope cold against my chest. I'm wearing an oxygen mask.

I try to tell them I'm fine. The words get caught in the plastic. Nurse Connie pets my arm. "Stay still. Rest," she says. "Your mom is on the way."

My mother? That's the last thing I need.

One of the EMTs riffles through my bags—and he comes across my locket. "Pills." He flashes the contents at Connie and Mr. K. The other Russian teachers try to clear out the room, but I can still see faces behind the glass walls, staring in at me.

"What are these, Bette? Diet pills? Help us out." Nurse Connie's looking at them now, frowning. Mr. K is pacing. I can hardly keep my eyes open. They droop and flutter.

I pull off the mask. "They're my prescription. It's in my chart. Nothing I haven't been taking forever."

"Okay," the EMT says. "Ideally, we should take her in. It's protocol. But there's a note in this chart documenting all her meds."

Another one checks my pulse and flashes a light in my eyes. I can barely stay awake. I feel pulled under again. I just want to curl up right here and sleep.

"Her pupils are dilated, and she's barely awake."

They collect all the pills from my bag. I try to watch everything, but I dip in and out of the room. The lights, the voices, the sounds go on and off.

"Bette." Nurse Connie shakes my shoulder. "Are you sure these were just Adderall?"

My mouth goes dry and my brain tries to put this all together. I look up and see Cassie standing directly in front of the glass studio wall. She blows me a kiss and smiles. I try to stand. My legs are too weak to hold my weight. I want to confront her in front of everyone. I want her to get caught for this. I want it all to be over. We're even now.

"She should go to the hospital," one of the EMTs says, holding an ice pack to my forehead. "She needs blood work."

"Her mom is on the way, and doesn't want her moved until she arrives," Nurse Connie says. "She's got a knot on her head that will need examining. Also, we should give her a CAT scan."

"Cassie did . . ." I slur out.

Nurse Connie frowns. "Did what?"

The words sound ridiculous out loud. I look back up. Cassie's not there anymore. The crowd thins out. No one cares about what's happened to me. Ballet class has resumed in a different studio.

"Cassie helped me is what I meant."

"Morkie said she caught you before you hit your head even harder," Nurse Connie says. "What a nice girl,"

I clench my teeth.

The EMTs hover, the gurney ready to go, still insistent on taking me to the hospital. When my mother arrives, raging, they start packing things up, and taking out refusal-of-medical-treatment paperwork.

She storms up to Mr. K. "Just what has happened here?"

Mr. K looks stricken. He can't afford to mess with my mother. Not now.

"Don't you worry, Mrs. Abney," he says, resting a hand on her arm. "We'll have this all taken care of in just minutes."

She touches my cheek, and her eyes get a little watery. A tiny swell blooms inside me and I try to keep from crying. I don't remember the last time she's looked at me like this.

"I think I took the wrong prescription. One of my sleep aids," I say. "It was an accident."

"Still, you need to go to the emergency room, just to be sure."

"I will take her," my mother says.

"I will go with you. I want to ask the doctor about clearing her to dance," Nurse Connie says.

"Oh, you've done enough," my mother says, helping me to my feet. "And not to worry, she will be fine to dance."

"But—"

"She's an Abney, she'll always be fine."

In that moment, I actually love the woman.

33.

June

"I THOUGHT YOUR MOM WOULD have told you." It's after lunch, and I'm dressed in my black, long-sleeved Tuesday leotard with pink tights, ready for class. But Nurse Connie's waiting for me in the hall, her face grim, with a medical pass for Morkie—one I didn't know I needed—excusing me from afternoon ballet. For a minute, I'm scared that someone told them about all my missed appointments with my therapist, Taylor, and the fact that I'm still hovering around 102 pounds. "Did you eat?"

I kind of want to say yes. I wonder if that would get me out of whatever this is. But I shake my head. "What's this for?" I peer at the paper, but it doesn't reveal much.

"You have a doctor's appointment. A bone scan."

A bone scan? I don't know quite what that means, but I know it's scary. I snatch the pass from Nurse Connie's hands, and head down to the front office.

My mom is seated on the leather bench in the administration office. I'm about to ask her if I can go change when she stands. "Good, you are on time. I don't want to be late." She pauses, awkward. "It takes weeks to get these appointments. I had to call in a favor."

I know what she's not saying. My father's the one who called in a favor. So he knows about all of it—the auditions, the eating, the not eating. The bile rises in my throat, knowing that he's in on something so close, so personal, when he hardly knows me at all.

I go change, and we're in a cab headed east five minutes later. The driver goes through the park, which is a major mistake, because traffic is at a standstill. I turn to face my mother, tapping away on her phone. Usually, I would be, too. But the idea of this is freaking me out too much to focus on anything else.

"Why didn't you tell me?" My voice seems to startle her, like she forgot I was sitting next to her.

"It was last-minute." She looks up and around, frown lines forming fast and furious as she realizes we're blocked in. "You should have gone down to Central Park South," she tells the cab-driver, as if it will do any good now. "We're already behind."

"I know you think I need this stuff." I catch her off guard again, the way she looks at me, surprised. "But I'm almost eighteen. I'd like to be in on the decision-making."

"When you show me you are well enough to handle yourself, we can talk about that," she says, touching my leg. "For now, though, you will do as I say."

She taps away on her phone again for the next twenty minutes.

We're half an hour late. The doctor's office feels cold and metallic, with the AC going, even though it's barely March.

"Just another minute," the tall, scrub-suited woman at the front desk says before she turns back to the computer. She's brown, with dark hair and dark eyes. "We're short staffed, and you were supposed to go in fifteen minutes ago. I need to get another nurse."

My mom nods, and I focus on the small flat screen in front of me that's tuned into the cooking channel. It's a chubby, redheaded chick who talks about life on the ranch and cooking for cowboys. She's making fried chicken, potato salad with globs of mayo, and cupcakes for dessert. "Things that will stick to your ribs," she hollers through the screen.

Do real people eat this stuff?

"Can I go to the bathroom?" I ask no one in particular, and when my mom nods, still on her phone, I take off. I walk through a long corridor, with patient rooms off either side. The bathroom is to the right. I head straight for it.

The tall, scrub-suited lady spies me just as I reach the door. "Oh, did they call you already, E-Jun?" She extends both the *e* and the *uhn*, so my name sounds stretchy and loose.

I'm so panicked, I want to cry. I want to curl up on the floor and go to sleep.

"Bathroom." I point.

"Oh, then take this." She hands me a cup. "We need a sample before we start."

When I get into the bathroom, I pee first, filling the cup

halfway, the acrid scent of urine overwhelming the small room. I flush, and carefully wipe down both the bowl and the floor. Getting down on my knees, I listen to the swirl of the water, and seconds later, the bile comes up naturally, friendly and familiar. There's not much to it—mostly water, since I've yet to eat today.

But just the act is comforting. I heave again, trying to be as quiet as I can, but someone's knocking, then pounding. My vision is teary, so I flush and stand, washing my hands as fast as I can. My throat still throbs. I have to swallow and breathe to press down the rest of the liquid in my stomach. "Just a second."

I splash my face and look away from the toilet. I nearly knock over the pee cup as I pull open the door.

It's the scrub-suited lady. Dr. Neha Arora, her name tag reads. All this time, I assumed she was a nurse.

"E-Jun." She pronounces my name more normally this time. My mom walks into the corridor, too. She's wringing her hands, which means they're onto me, although no one's saying anything yet. "The nurse is ready for you now."

The nurse stands behind her. She's a youngish black lady, also in scrubs, with hot-pink spiky hair. "I'm Ericka. I'll be administering the radiotracer for the bone scan." She doesn't look like she's graduated college yet, let alone whatever else she needs to legally pierce my arm. She settles me into a lumbering metal chair, my feet flat on the floor for now, checking my heartbeat and temperature. My mom stands around, observing. I wish she would leave—that is, until the nurse brings in a few tubes and a long, skinny needle.

"It'll only pinch for a second," the nurse says, and I grimace.

"Want me to hold your hand?" my mom asks, then takes it without waiting for an answer.

The nurse ties what looks like a supersize, superflimsy rubber band around my bicep. I try not to watch what she's doing— tempted to close my eyes like I used to when I was a kid—but I can't take my eyes off her.

"Try to relax." She taps my arm, looking for a vein. When she finds one, she sticks the needle in. It burns and pinches, like the time I got bitten by red ants at the beach in Coney Island. Ericka hums to herself as she attaches a tube to it. She draws a small vial of blood—dark and thick—and then attaches another needle hooked to a metal tube. As soon as she's done, I feel something cool and creepy climbing through my veins—like someone is freezing me, part by part. I want to pass out then so I don't have to be in the room anymore. The nurse must sense it, because she tapes the tube in place, then pushes a button and the back of the chair slides down, so it's almost like a bed. "Just breathe and relax. You can close your eyes if you'd like."

I do for a few minutes. I can hear the nurse coming in and out of the room, and sense my mom still sitting in the other chair. I bet she's on her phone, which annoys me to no end, so I lift up my head to look. But she's just sitting there, staring at me. She immediately comes over, puts her hand on my forehead. "You okay, *boba*?"

I nod but don't speak. She hovers. She wants to say something, I can feel it, but it's all bottled up, like a shaken can of soda, ready to burst.

"What?" I finally say.

"I had a bone scan. Back when I danced." It's the first time she's ever brought up her dancing history herself, so my ears perk up. I've tried to ask her about it a dozen times, but she usually won't talk about it. "Back then, it was so different. That massive machine felt like death, like a coffin."

That's what I have to look forward to? I must seem stressed out, because she rubs my face, her fingers gliding over my eyebrows as she smiles. "You'll be okay. They have open-air machines now, like a tanning bed." Not that either of us have ever been in a tanning bed. The thought of my mom lying in one, in her skirted one-piece and compression socks, makes me giggle.

She smiles, then frowns. "I had shin fractures—tiny little ones that would've gotten worse. Then I got pregnant, and had you." She smiles, a bit happy, a bit sad. "I knew by then dance was not happening anymore."

The defeat in her voice makes me want to cry. For the two of us, our tiny little fractured family. But she's rubbing my cheeks again, and though her eyes are wet, she's still smiling. "I'm not disappointed, E-Jun. I never had the same love for dance. For me, ballet was an escape—from Korea. And, back then, I was so, so happy, so in love. With a baby, I thought it meant—"

She goes silent there, but I know what she's thinking.

"I know you struggle, that this is hard. But, believe me, having you, I was happy." Her papery fingers are on my arm now, not far from where the needle has pierced me, where the coldness begins. "But you like this—here, the needles, so skinny, I can't take it. It's killing you, this dream. And it's killing me."

She's holding my hands so tightly, I know what she says is

true. If I don't fix this now, I could lose everything. Dancing, I realize, slowly but surely, is not worth giving up my life for. I nod, and I hope she can see the clarity in my eyes, the determination. I may never be cured, like Nurse Connie said, but I can take control. I can stay the path, and do what I need to do—for myself, for my mother, and for the others who choose to love me.

Two hours later, the bone scan begins. They lay me down on a flat bed, one that I know will go into the huge machine that's been whirring and spitting in this room for the past half hour, as they prepped me. With its screens and the tunnel-like cavity, it looks like a face with a large gaping mouth, one ready to swallow me whole. Dr. Neha is by my side now, and Ericka is on the other side.

"Shhhh," Dr. Neha says again. "Relax."

I am relaxed, because they've clearly slipped me some kind of sedative. Everything feels so slow, so soft, the sharpness gone from it all. As the flat bed moves forward, I know I should be panicking. But I just feel tired. I close my eyes and let the machine do its thing, knowing what it will reveal—the things that the physical therapists have been warning me about for months. The miniscule stress fractures in my shins and feet, the ones that cause me those tiny agonies on a weekly basis. The ones that have been getting progressively worse since freshman year. The ones that might eventually end my dancing career. The lack of strength in my bones from poor nutrition.

I know from all the pamphlets Taylor gave me at our first meeting that my eating problems are to blame—the throwing up, the lack of bone-building nutrients, the fact that my period came

SONA CHARAIPOTRA & DHONIELLE CLAYTON

and went and never came back. I picture the box full of dead toe shoes I've compiled over my time at the conservatory, each pair taking its toll. The thought of them makes me shiver, like the butterflies that stared out at me that night, cold, menacing.

When it's finally over, Dr. Neha talks briefly to my mother in her office, as I sit quietly and wait for her to tell us what she knows. What I already know.

"It's bad," she says, and my mom flinches. "But it could be worse. We won't have the full analysis for a few weeks, but I think we know what we're looking at here. That gives us someplace to start."

My mom breathes then finally, and I watch her hands tremble as she places them on Dr. Neha's desk. "So what's next?"

"Well"—Dr. Neha turns to look at me sternly—"the eating issues are the biggest culprit here—and I know you're working on that, but that is the key. We need to get you healthy, June. You're seventeen, in the prime of your life, and you're falling apart. There's no reason for that—even if you continue to dance. I've worked with dozens of dancers, and strong bones and musculature are so, so critical. You're doing yourself a disservice here—as a dancer and a human."

I nod.

But she's not satisfied. "No, speak. I want to hear you say it."

So for the first time, I say it.

"I'll do what I have to do," I say. "I'll stop." I don't say throwing up, but I know they know what I mean. This time, I know it's true. "I want to dance," I tell them—and myself. "I want to be healthy."

289

The next week, things shift, slowly at first, but then all at once. I visited my therapist, Taylor, for the first few days, but my mom decided instead of me going to her—and possibly skipping appointments—that as of today, Taylor would come to me.

When I get to the café, she's already there at the entrance, waiting with her ever-present clipboard and that menacing red pen, already making notes of my crimes to report back to my mother.

"Right on time." She smiles and gives me a quick once-over, looking for signs that I'm up to no good, I guess. She heads toward an empty table, and we sit. "Tell me what you had today."

"I managed to down a full bowl of congee at breakfast," I say. I can still feel the rice porridge sitting heavy in my stomach, leaving no room for everything she'll make me eat now.

"Junebug, that's a strong start." I cringe as she scribbles some more notes. Junebug? Gross. No one's ever called me that. "I think lunchtime should be protein focused, since you'll be dancing again in the afternoon. And maybe some carbs."

Her voice rings out even over the din of the café, which means everyone can hear her. It's so loud, so obvious, I wonder if I should start planning meals for odd hours, so no one else is here. I don't want them to see how strict Taylor is with me, how she monitors everything I put on my tray, every bite I put in my mouth. I feel like a petulant four-year-old who doesn't want to eat her peas.

"Did you have your snacks today, Junebug?" Ugh, there it goes again. It kind of makes me want to vomit. Which isn't good if that's what she's supposed to be trying to help me not do. "Do you need more?"

I shake my head. She's taken to portioning out little baggies of nuts or trail mix—I'm supposed to eat two packets a day. Taylor says it's perfect postclass food: full of vitamins, minerals, and the good kind of fat, the kind your brain and your muscles need after a harsh workout. I want to get better, I do. But it's just too much for me. So I've been eating one bag, and leaving the other in the rec room, where I've seen the boys downing it during movie night. But that's not what I tell Taylor. "Yes, one bag of trail mix after academic classes," I say, pulling out an empty packet from my backpack. "Saving the other one for afternoon ballet class. I'm always starving then," I lie.

"Excellent," she says. "Let's go check out your options." She stands, heading toward the lunch line. I get up and follow. She carefully observes the day's offerings, as if there will be something new and delightful to eat. "So what will you have for lunch today?" It seems like an innocent enough question, but it's a test. I'm supposed to be learning the art of composing healthy, carefully balanced meals—lean protein, lots of veggies, some carbs, and limited fats, of course.

I know she wants me to pick the fish—all protein and good fats. But it's salmon, the worst kind. It's pale pink and gooey looking in the center, but crispy at the edges. My stomach lurches at the sight of it. I shake my head, maybe a little too violently. "I'll stick to the chicken." I pile my plate high with greens, then toss a few pieces of grilled meat on top, hoping that will satisfy her. I add peppers—pretty much zero calories—and tomatoes and cucumbers.

She's frowning. "Maybe a little hard-boiled egg, too?" she suggests, putting two whole chopped eggs onto my salad and ruining it. "And you can have some balsamic, if you'd like."

I opt for a sprinkle of dressing instead—no oil—and she frowns some more. She adds a roll, butter, and a carton of milk to my tray. I don't protest, although I want to scream. She's going too fast, I'm going too slow. I guess we just have to meet somewhere in the middle. *Recovery is a long process,* I hear her say in my head. *One day at a time.*

Tray loaded, we head back to the table. She says a little prayer over her own tray—which is laden down with the salmon, a few roasted baby potatoes, and some greens. She opens my milk carton, butters my bread, all without asking. I should be used to it by now, but it still burns me up every time.

"So, Junebug," she says, and I seethe. "Tell me about morning classes. You had a history paper due, right?" She's chatting away, as if this is perfectly normal, as if she's not secretly counting the number of bites I take.

I force food down. I've discovered that twelve is the magic number. If I can take twelve solid bites, she's happy. She'll sigh that little sigh and make her notes. Then she'll nod, satisfied, as if she's full, as if she's eaten them herself. It's enough to make me want to sob.

But I get it. I know why my mom is doing this, why I'm committed to following through. My body already feels stronger, more in control, more confident. It's as if the food has made me fuller in every respect, and it actually helps. Every time I've wanted to throw up, I write it down instead—all the thoughts, the anxieties. That curbs the desire. But I'm just waiting for it all to fall apart again. This is harder than ballet.

I'm thinking about that when Bette appears in the café. I duck behind a notebook as she passes, but she sees me.

"Hey," she says, walking over to the table. She's got two sandwiches tucked in their little plastic boxes, along with chips and salsa.

"This is Taylor"—I gesture over to her—"my therapist."

Bette smiles. "Nice to meet you. June says great things."

Taylor smiles, too, and I wonder if she thinks that's not true.

"Just getting lunch for me and Adele." Bette looks at Taylor. "My sister, she had an accident, so she's not very mobile." Her expression is pained, and I know what she's thinking: that it's her fault. It is, in a way, because surely that trap was meant for her.

Bette's eyebrows are perched high, and I know she's wondering if I've overheard Cassie and Henri talking in my bedroom, if I know anything that might help her figure out who hurt Adele.

"You find out anything new?" I ask before she can.

Bette shakes her head. "I was hoping you might have—"

"Nothing," I say, and Taylor looks confused, so she focuses on her salmon. But I know Bette gets what I mean. "Let it go."

"I can't. They—it's personal now. I have to—"

"Focus on what you can control. Isn't that what you told me once? Isn't that what Adele would want?"

Bette nods, still looking defeated. She steals a carrot stick from my plate and charges out of the café, full speed ahead.

"It's good advice," Taylor says after a minute of silence. "You have to take it, too. Focus. Focus on getting healthy. The rest will follow." I nod. When I take another bite, she beams.

"I'm trying."

"That's really what it's all about, June. You'll never be cured, and there will always be triggers." She waves her arms around, excited. "Especially in this world. But you're working hard, you're figuring it out, and look at you. You're already so much stronger."

It's only been a few days, but I can already see a real difference in my dancing. I've been working with Bette on one of the *Swan Lake* variations from Act Three, the ballroom scene, and it's quick and loud, just like she is, with fast footwork and lots of in-character acting. With Bette's—and Taylor's—help, I think I might really have a chance at dancing professionally, stress fractures and all.

34.

Gigi

"HOW'S ALEC?" AUNT LEAH ASKS. She's got a smirk on her face, that *I-know-what-you've-been-up-to* look.

"I don't want to talk about it." It's been weeks since I've talked to her or Mama, and they're severely out-of-date on my life these days, which I guess is my own fault. But I can't tell them about Alec. Not yet. I think back to our fight, to all the origami cranes and hearts and the terrarium he's given me. I can't bring myself to take them down.

It's our first family dinner out in months. I shouldn't be in such a bad mood. "I did do well on that history paper though," I say.

Mama nods, pleased, and Aunt Leah babbles a bit about her new museum job.

"Oh, Dad's got the summer off," Mama says, grinning from ear to ear. She takes another bite of halibut and sprinkles some pepper on her salad. "I thought we could all go on a big trip, rent that old house in Maui for a couple of months. I could paint, you could swim, maybe Leah could come, too."

Aunt Leah nods, her smile matching Mama's. "Maybe not the whole summer, but a few weeks for sure," she says. "I was thinking Gigi and I could learn to scuba dive—I've heard the water can be very healing."

I focus on my plate, taking a small bite, pushing food around like I have been for the past twenty minutes. I let them chatter about this possible, hypothetical trip, even though, if all goes as planned, I won't have time for anything this summer. I'll have intensives, and then my apprenticeship will start.

"Your steak not good?" Of course Mama notices my lack of appetite. These days, she notices everything when she's around. Like she's watching every breath I take or move I make. Like she's treating me as if I'm sick again. She reaches over and pokes at the meat. "It is a little red."

She's motioning toward the waiter when I shake my head. "It's fine, Mama. I'm just not that hungry."

"Let the girl be," Aunt Leah interjects. "She'll eat if she wants to eat."

Mama puts her arm down and focuses on her own plate for a minute. "Maybe Ella could come down, too," Mama says. "She's headed to UCLA—did you know that, Gigi? Microbiology, just like she wanted. I bet she'd love Hawaii. Does she have plans?"

It's a simple question, one I'd easily have known the answer to a year ago. But my old best friend, Ella, and I haven't talked in months, and I feel like I can't definitively say anything about her anymore. The whole idea of California feels foreign and fuzzy, like some vague dreamscape, long forgotten. New York is where I want to be. Ballet is my everything. I need to earn this apprenticeship because I've put all my eggs in one basket. I need to focus on the role of Odette and impressing Damien.

"I don't think I'll make it." It slips out like a butterfly from a cage, quick and unstoppable, filling up the little Italian café with its sudden enormity.

"What do you mean?" Mama's dropped her fork now, her face fierce, concerned. She's not oblivious to my ambitions, but for months she's been in denial about how close I am to making them real. She never asks me about ballet anymore, just calls Mr. K every other week to rant and complain.

"You know what I mean." I don't mean for it to come off as rude, but the bite is there. "I'll probably be needed here. I'll probably be dancing."

Aunt Leah looks worried now. I know she's been calling Mama every week, reporting in on how I'm doing, trying to convince her that I'm fine, that she can stay put in California. Mama's got a mind of her own, and there's no changing it. But maybe I take after her after all. "Gigi, I—"

Mama shushes her with a wave of her hand.

I expect Mama to yell, to fight, but instead her face softens. "Gigi, baby, I know you want this. And I know how hard you've been working. But I think it's time we let it go." It feels like a slap, unexpected and mean. "It's time to come home to California, to regroup and figure out next steps. Work for a little while, maybe. Dad could use a summer intern. Or you can take some summer classes and figure out what you want to do for the fall." Satisfied, she takes another bite, as if the discussion is over, finished.

"I can't let it go, Mama." My voice is shaky, heavy with the weight of tears. "I won't."

Mama sighs, putting her fork down again. "Gigi, I understand your ambitions. I mean, I get it. I'm an artist, too. But this dream, it's become a nightmare. You've barely made it out alive this year, you're clearly depressed, and Dr. Khanna says your heart is holding steady at best. I can't support you anymore if you choose to keep chasing this."

As if on cue, my monitor goes off, betraying my heart. I look down at my plate. My steak sits, cold and congealed, a pool of bloodied grease collecting below it.

"Yeah, bug," Aunt Leah adds. "Maybe it's time for a break."

"There's no such thing as a break in ballet. Drop it. I'm staying here."

I race back to the dorms after dinner with Mama and Aunt Leah. I get to the twelfth floor and run past my room, heading straight to Cassie's. I need to talk to someone who'll understand. When I push the door open, Cassie's not there, but the room is lit and the shower's running.

"Hey," I hear as I'm about to pull the door shut. It's Henri, tucked under the covers on Cassie's bed, his hair sleep rumpled, his eyes heavy. I instantly think of Will and his accusation about Henri making him push me. But one look gives me away. "Gigi. You okay?"

I shake my head, and crumple into a mess on June's perfectly made bed, not caring if she flips about her mussed sheets. "My mom—I can't—she wants—" I'm crying so hard now, I'm hic-cupping through, making no sense whatsoever. I don't know if it's sadness or fear or rage. He rises from the bed and crosses the room, pulling on a T-shirt as he makes his way. I can't help but notice how different his body is from Alec's—fuller, more mus-cular, with small patches of dark hair scattered across his chest. I look away, frantic, trying to figure out how to escape.

He sits next to me on the bed, putting a heavy arm around my shoulders. "Shhh, breathe, Gigi, breathe."

I swallow tears and try to slow myself down—my heart, my mind, my breathing. His arm has dropped, and he's rubbing my back in long, low strokes. My first instinct is to panic, to pull away. I keep thinking back to Will's words. "Henri made me . . ." But he moves his hands as soon as he sees the expression on my face, and I realize too late that there was nothing really sexual about it. "Sorry," he says with a sheepish grin. "I just— What happened?"

"My family wants me to give up dance and move back home to California." A tearful tremor shoots through me, and Henri pats my arm, brotherly. "I can't. I've worked so hard, so long—"

"So you don't have to," he says. I can't even get the *but* out before he continues. "You Americans are so funny. Gigi, you're almost eighteen, a grown-up. And you've been on your own for almost two years now. You've gone through hell. You're one of the strongest girls—one of the strongest people—I know. Do what you want. You don't need anyone's permission."

I'm dumbstruck. As much as the magazines have gushed and called me a rising phoenix and this and that, no one's ever pointed out my own power to me before. Not when it counts. Not when they really believe it. But Henri, I can tell he does.

I think about asking him about Will, but Cassie steps out of the bathroom, wearing pajamas, her cheeks rosy from the heat. "Hey!" She looks at me and is instantly worried. "You okay?"

I nod, realizing how much better I feel. All because of Henri. "Yes, I am. Or I will be."

I think back to last year, those moments when I thought he was too intense, too invasive. I think about how easily I misinterpreted all that concern as something more—and how Will might have done just that, too. How Will might have gotten it all wrong. Just like me.

Looking at Henri now, as he leaps up to give Cassie a kiss, quietly filling her in on my drama, I realize that maybe he was just trying to look out for me. That maybe he was right to.

I open the door, ready to step out of the room. "I've got to go, though, so we'll talk later, okay?" I tell Cassie. She looks from me to Henri and back, but I can't stay and explain.

Right now, I have to go dance. I have to remind myself of why this is so important.

35

Bette

MORKIE HAS ME IN STUDIO B to watch Gigi and Alec's *pas* rehearsal before I have to go work with Cassie. Alec and I warm up at the barre, even though I'm only supposed to be here to watch. I'm supposed to observe what type of white swan Gigi will turn into so I can be the opposite—dark, sinister, dynamic. That's what Morkie said. Eleanor sits quietly on the left side of the studio.

"We will begin from the love duet in Act Three," Morkie says. Gigi still hasn't come to the front. I look at Alec, ready to purse my lips and roll my eyes to communicate how utterly irritated I am with her. But he looks away. For the first time since returning, I realize that we haven't fallen back into our old relationship. I guess it will never be quite the same again.

"Gigi," Morkie calls out.

She tiptoes to the front. She won't even look at me, no matter how hard I stare. In the mirror, we're a mismatched trio. Alec stands in the middle, with Gigi and me at his sides. We're cast as opposites. I look like the classical version of the White Swan, and she should be the black one.

She's sullen, quiet, probably dying to ask Morkie why I'm here. I bet it bothers her. It would bother me.

"Last time, remember, I told you that there wasn't enough of the story in your dancing," Morkie says. "Tell me what the scene is."

Alec doesn't wait for either Gigi or me to answer. "It's the ballroom scene with the princesses, the one where Siegfried comes in, along with Rothbart in disguise with his daughter, Odile, Odette's evil double."

"Yes, Alec. Very nice," Morkie says. "What else?"

Gigi chimes in. "Siegfried welcomes the disguised Odile to the ball and they dance. He chooses her as his bride and swears the oath."

"Gigi, where are you during this scene?" Morkie asks.

"She's off to the side watching from a window," I interject. "She's a mess and shattered."

Gigi rolls her eyes while I speak, so I continue without being asked. "The masked Rothbart reveals his true identity—and Odile's—and they disappear. Siegfried rushes off to search for the real Odette. It's about love and deception and perception."

Morkie nods in approval with my addition. "Great—there is so much feeling, so much emotion. I must see all of that in your movements. Tell this tragedy."

Alec and Gigi take their positions.

"Let us try." Morkie moves to the front to take a seat. "Bette, watch how light and graceful she is. Because you must do opposite for your *pas* with Alec." She waves me out of the center and I stand back.

Gigi flits over to the far corner, awaiting her entrance. The music starts. Alec trots through the studio as if he's searching for Odette. The chords speed up and Gigi enters. Her arms flap and pulsate in beautiful waves like they are wings.

"Beautiful arms," Morkie shouts. "Articulate the feet, Gigi. Alec, strengthen your lines."

Gigi takes tiny steps in his direction, then folds herself down onto the floor. He lingers over her and takes her by the arms, lifting her like she's nothing more than a feather. He turns her as she stretches her arms and legs out in arabesque. A little voice inside me whispers: *She's gotten better.*

"Gigi, descend through the toes," Morkie commands. "Yes, perfect, perfect. Show me you love her, Alec. Gigi, you, too. I need to feel the love."

Morkie stands and motions with her arms, demonstrating what she expects from Alec. A knot coils in my throat as he slides his hands along Gigi's arms and turns her around like a beloved object. It's the way he used to touch me, to look at me. I want to step between them, dousing the fire before it flares again. Instead, I'm frozen, transfixed, unable to move or breathe.

I'm not the only one. Morkie stops shouting corrections and we all just watch them float and glide and fall into the most well-known classical variation from the most beautiful ballet in the world. Level 6 and 7 dancers crowd outside the glass walls like moths to light, everyone drawn to their movements and the flame between them.

They anticipate each other's movements, just like he used to know mine. She trusts him. There's no clenching of her stomach when he lifts her or tightened mouth when he holds her waist. In that moment, I feel like I've lost. Like there's something real and maybe lasting between them.

An hour later, we've shifted studios. I'm with Morkie, Cassie, and Riho in Studio E to work on the thirty-two *fouettés* in the coda.

"Did you hear the news?" Cassie leans over me while I tie on new pointe shoes. Riho is facedown in a deep stretch and meditation. She doesn't even look up.

I ignore Cassie. I pretend that she's some version of an imaginary friend that will just disappear if I think about something else. Morkie lingers up front, talking to Viktor, so I have at least ten more minutes to get my muscles warm and my feet ready to do what she needs them to.

"I would think you'd want to hear it from me." Her grin is so wide I can feel it.

"All I want to hear is the date you plan to jump off a bridge. Or that you're going to leave me alone. I didn't tell. Your little pill stunt could've injured me, seriously."

Her smile doesn't disappear. "You might not have gotten hurt this time, but there's always another opportunity."

"Get over it." I shoot up and bounce on my toes to make sure these shoes feel good. I go to the barre and sink into a stretch. She follows; she's desperate for me to look at her.

"I'll never 'get over it,' as you say. I lost a year of my life. My hip still isn't the same. I'll never forget that, and I'll never let you forget it either." She's not smiling anymore. I'm pinned close to the barre. The wood digs into my back.

"Move," I say.

"No." She steps closer. My back curves over the barre. The pain of it shoots through me. I push her. She doesn't budge.

"Oh, my Cassandra." Morkie turns around, and claps her hands together. "Congratulations. You will be beautiful. This is your start."

Cassie makes a kissy noise at me, then pivots around, and rushes over. Morkie rubs Cassie's cheek, then pats her back like there's a bruise there. "The company corps will be stronger with you in it."

It takes a minute for it to sink in. But then it hits me all at once.

She got the apprenticeship. She's in the company.

There's only one spot left.

I hold the barre so tight my knuckles go white, then my fingers turn red.

Cassie squeals with delight and thanks Morkie over and over again for all her help.

Riho finally looks up from her phone. "What's going on?"

Cassie doesn't answer her. Morkie wraps Cassie up in another hug. "I'm so thrilled," Cassie's babbling as Morkie embraces her. "I'm glad Damien's letting me do both performances, though. I'm proud to be able to finish off my final year with you and all my friends here at the conservatory." Her eyes flash with victory, her mouth a smug smile.

Riho turns to me. "Cassie got into the company," I say as if I'm reporting that she's suffering from a case of hemorrhoids. Her face twitches with anxiety.

As Morkie walks off to consult with Viktor about today's rehearsal, Cassie turns to grin at me again, expectant.

"No one cares, Cassie," I say. Even though I care. A lot.

"Oh, but of course you do," she says.

"Center, girls." Morkie waves us forward. "Odile's *fouettés* are what people who love *Swan Lake* wait for."

Viktor plays the music, and she has us listen to it three times. Rehearsing on my own and with Adele, I've managed twenty-five or maybe even thirty, but I've never gotten the full thirty-two *fouettés*—and that's a feat expected of any future principal dancer, especially at ABC.

"Cassie, I know you have company corps rehearsal after this, so you give a try first. I think Bette and Riho will need more time." She flutters her arms out left and right like she's shooing me to the sidelines.

I step back and turn away, so I don't have to watch Cassie. I see Damien standing in the studio doorway, observing. He winks at me, then joins Morkie at the front.

The piano chords grow louder. Cassie moves her shoulders and arms back and forth like the perfect imitation of a stretching swan. Then she steps into her *fouettés*. One after another she hits them, perfect lines and perfect turns and perfect pointed feet. You would never know she had a fracture in her hip, that she's been through rehab. She makes the turns look effortless.

Damien starts to clap before she's even finished. She beams and spins a few more times. I lose count after she hits number thirty-two.

A few minutes later it's my turn. This is what I've always dreamed of. This is what every ballerina dreams to dance. But today it feels like a nightmare, with all those eyes on me, and Cassie smug with her flawless turns and company news.

I think of Adele, of all the time she spent with me and what happened to her, because of me. I have to make her proud. I have to be a true reflection of her, of the Abney name.

I spin and stretch and curve, taking my body to lengths it's never been before. I prepare to do the *fouettés*, all thirty-two of them.

I step into the first one, up on my standing leg, strong through the hip. I'm spinning and spinning and spinning, almost perfect, counting them out in my head—twenty-nine and thirty and thirty-one. And then, just as I nearly have it, my leg drops and I miss the last one.

Everything comes to a screeching halt as Damien calls out, "Stop! The understudy gets it, but the Odile does not." He's not glaring at me, but I can tell he wants to. He motions at Morkie, as if it's somehow her fault that I missed one. "Bette, you must get the *fouettés*. It's part and parcel of this performance. You have to let the foot go completely flat in order to maintain your strength." His hands land on my calf, adjusting my turnout.

I can practically feel Cassie smirking from the sidelines. I want to turn to her and scream, ask her if she's happy now that she's better than me. Now that she's won.

Damien leaves us with Morkie. We practice the thirty-two *fouettés* for two hours straight—Cassie can get it without stopping, without thinking. But I have to work through it. Riho struggles, too, but lands more of them than me. "You're thinking too much, Bette," Morkie says for the hundredth time. "Relax into it. Let go. Or you'll lose it."

She sends me spinning again, but all I can think about is beating Cassie. About all the things I did to her. Maybe this is some kind of cosmic punishment for being a bitch. Again, at maybe number twenty-three, I crash.

"Bette," I hear Adele's voice drilling into my head, *"if you're going to join me at this level, you have to give it your all."* So I try again without Morkie saying a word.

I only get twenty-six this time.

Frustrated, Morkie ends rehearsal early. Riho rushes out. It's just Cassie and me left in the studio gathering our things.

"So you're not even going to congratulate me?" Cassie's already out of her toe shoes, her bag on her shoulder. "Still sour?" She laughs like she's just said the funniest thing in the world. But my face is stony. "Oh, Bette. Don't worry about the *fouettés*. You'll get them eventually. I mean, you nearly got them that day, when you were working at Lincoln Center with Adele."

I freeze. My hands stop untying my pointe shoe ribbons. "What did you say?"

"You heard me."

"No one else was there that day."

"When are you going to learn, Bette? I've made sure to know exactly what you're doing. Always." She applies lip gloss. "You terrorized me, so it's your turn."

308

"Adele could've died."

"Oh, don't be so dramatic, Bette." She makes popping sounds with her mouth as she rubs in the lip gloss. "She'll be fine, eventually. She's such a wonderful dancer. Or she was."

"Don't ever talk about my sister."

"I'll do whatever I want." She picks up her dance bag. "Tell her I hope she gets better soon. *Swan Lake* won't be the same without her."

My heart beats itself all the way up my throat. "Did you hurt my sister on purpose?"

"Now, why would I ever do that?" She blinks her eyes at me like a doll. A creepy, evil doll. "I just wanted to hurt you. And I will." With that, she walks away, and I'm left there, stricken, unraveling every detail but unable to do a thing.

I reach into my dance bag, planning to text Eleanor, but my phone is gone. Maybe I left it in my room or the other studio? I start combing through my bag, looking around where we were sitting. Nothing.

I look back up. Cassie presses her lips to the glass and leaves the imprint of a kiss behind.

I go down to the student lounge. Henri's right where I thought he'd be—playing pool with a few of the Level 7 guys. I lean into one of the new kids, Lucio. He's Brazilian, with golden skin that sets off deeply brown eyes. I pout at him. "Mind if I borrow your stick?" He blushes, handing it over immediately.

Henri raises an eyebrow, annoyed. "We're in the middle of a game."

My voice is ice when I say it. "So are we. And you know

what, Henri? I'm winning."

That gets his attention. He misses his shot, sending the cue ball right into the corner pocket. The other guys laugh, but Henri's eyes don't even have a sliver of a smile, not even that signature smirk. He comes around the table, grabs my arm, and says, "Come with me."

He pretty much drags me into the ice and vending room, playing right into my hands. What I want to say to him doesn't require an audience. Not yet, anyway.

Once we're in there, he pushes me up against the wall, blocking me in, making it so I can't move. I shiver when his hands land on my waist, cringing at his rough, familiar touch. "What the hell do you want, Bette?"

"I want you to tell your girlfriend to back the hell off. Or I'll give her something real to worry about." I touch his neck. He jerks back a little.

He's glaring down at me now, his breath hitting my forehead, and I resist the urge to squirm, to show fear. I have to make him think I'm not scared, that I'll actually go through with it and tell Cassie everything—the kisses, the touches, the manipulations. Because I will. But that sick glimmer is creeping back into his eyes, and I know how much he enjoys a good power trip. "She won't believe a word you have to say."

"Oh yeah." I let a smirk play on my lips. "Well, I'll just have to reveal some of the things we shared last year. You know, Henri. Those sweet, stolen moments? Or were they all a part of her master plan? Especially when you got into the ice bath with me."

He looks caught, the glimmer gone, anger taking over fast

and furious. "You better keep your mouth shut, Bette, or I'll—"

"Or you'll what? Tell her you just did what you had to do? Or what you wanted to do? What did you tell poor Will, anyway? What did you do to that boy to get him to do exactly what you wanted, even if it meant nearly killing a girl?" His hands are traveling now, vindictive, a graze here, a pinch there. "Was it that old friends-with-benefits line? Because he sure believed it. Enough to let go of a ten-year crush on Alec, even. Enough to risk going to jail."

I lean in close so he can smell the shampoo in my hair and the lotion on my skin. "Did you kiss him? Did you let him touch you? What will Cassie think about that? Are you into girls or boys? Maybe both?"

"Shut up, shut up, shut up!" One arm grabs mine, holding it against my back, and for a moment I'm truly scared. He could do anything right now. Maybe this wasn't the smartest idea.

But I steel myself. I lean in and rise up on my toes, planting a kiss near his neck, right near the fuzzy collar of the cream-colored shawl sweater he's been wearing all winter. Cashmere, I know. My lips leave a hot-pink Chanel signature, one I know he'll have a hard time explaining away.

He lets go abruptly.

Even though I think he gets it, I say it, just to be sure. "Get that girl to back off. Or suffer the consequences."

As I push past him and pull the heavy metal door open, making my escape, I can't help but smile.

36.

June

THE CAFÉ BUZZES WITH CHATTER and laughter. It's pouring outside, and they've set up a hot cocoa station today, complete with marshmallows and chocolate shavings. No one's had any though.

My mouth is dry, my palms sweating. I'm here alone for breakfast, right at eight a.m., after weeks of late lunches or early dinners, trying to avoid the others while Taylor supervised my meals. And I was right to do so. Gigi and Cassie sit near the windows, their plates piled high with fruit salad and boiled eggs. They're leaning in close, whispering to each other, and I know Gigi's seen me. Eleanor sits at a table by herself at the other end of the room, her headphones on, her nose in her history book, oblivious to the noise around her. She's nibbling on dry toast, and there's an apple waiting on her tray.

I scope out the rest of the room, feeling out of place. It's been more than a month since I started working with Taylor, and this week, finally, she's letting me try meals solo again. "I trust you," she said at our meeting yesterday, poring over my food journals. She was pleased that my weight was up to 106. She was positively gleeful that I hadn't thrown up in nearly two weeks, despite all the stressors of the spring gala. "Just keep track, like you always do. Make smart choices."

I grab a tray and lay my tablet right on it as I pick out a balanced meal from the buffet. I examine the food, trying not to count the calories in my head. As Nurse Connie repeatedly reminds me, the café staff has been "made aware of the situation," and will continue to "suggest" healthy options.

I skip the whole wheat waffles, the congee, even the fruit salad, which I know is doused in a honey-based dressing. Instead, I pick two eggs, scrambled with low-fat margarine and chives; a whole wheat English muffin; and plain, reduced-fat yogurt with strawberries. In the food diary on my tablet, I record everything set on my plate, along with how much of it I've eaten and my thoughts—before, during, and after. Tonight, I'll email the daily record to Taylor.

I sit away from everyone, in the other corner that faces the glass wall. April rain streaks down the glass, and I watch all different kinds of umbrellas bob along the street. I try to eat at least some of everything. It's excruciating, the roughness of the bread, the way the margarine coats my throat, the goopy syrupiness of the yogurt.

I'm so focused on my food and thoughts that I don't even realize the shadow over my tray is a human one. I look up to see Sei-Jin.

"Hey." The word is garbled up with the bread in my mouth. We haven't really spoken since San Francisco, and I've been completely happy with that situation. But now she's standing next to my table, her mouth neither a smile nor a frown. I wait for the taunts, the comments about being like the white girls, avoiding the Korean rice porridge the chef set out.

Instead she sits down. "Glad you're—"

"Yeah." I cut off the word *eating*.

"You look better." It isn't mean or bitter or vicious, like it usually is. It sounds sincere. Like someone who actually cares. She smiles. "I mean, you look stronger. Like you're doing well."

I sigh. "I'm feeling better." I look down at my plate, at all the food still on it. "It's not fixed. But—"

She nods, and I think she's going to get up and walk away, but then she stays. I must look startled, because she grins. "I—I wanted to say I'm sorry. I mean, I know I started it. But—"

She leaves it dangling, like a loose ribbon on a slipper, and I wonder what she might have said then—that she was too scared? That she thought I'd give her secrets away? That she couldn't trust me, or anyone? That it was better to protect herself, even if it meant giving me up, hurting me?

"I get it," I say. Not that it's okay or that I forgive her. I do understand, in a way. We all do what we have to in order to get by here. Even if we have to hurt others in the process.

"Gigi told me you didn't ruin my shoes. She did it."

"She did?" I can't quite believe it. I look across the room to where she was sitting, but she's gone now. It adds up, the way she'd been hanging with Henri and Cassie. I can see it.

"Yeah, I didn't think she had it in her. But I guess she was getting back at me for the glass in her slipper."

I nearly choke on my yogurt. "You did that?" I thought that was Bette for sure.

"Yeah, that was me." She's looking down at her fingernails, the same familiar mauve as her lipstick.

"Why?" I ask. I can see her messing with me, but not Gigi.

"She just came in and took everything, all at once. When the rest of us were here all this time, working so hard, trying to—I don't know. It just made me so mad. Like, how is that fair?"

"I was mad, too." We all were. "And we all did things we aren't proud of." I think about the butterflies, and my hands fly to my hair with a will of their own.

"I didn't cut your hair." Even as she says it, Sei-Jin looks worried, apologetic. "I wouldn't do that. Not to you."

I'm surprised, but I try not to look it. When did I start expecting the worst in her, in myself, in everybody?

"But I am sorry about Jayhe." She picks at her nails, a nervous habit I remember all too well. "I didn't mean for anything to happen. I was lonely. I was scared." She swallows hard. "You know him, so funny, so sweet. He was just there for me when I was having a hard time. He brought me little presents, and we'd go off in the van."

I wonder how many times they made out in his van, the way he and I used to. The jealousy stabs me hard. And it's like she can tell, because she looks me straight in the eyes for a moment, completely serious.

"I know it was different for you guys. More real. You should call him. I know he misses you."

She's really going at her cuticles now, and they're frayed around the edges. I want to ask her how she knows. But I know I can't.

When she looks up again, she's wearing a bright smile. "I'm going to college in New Jersey. I decided last week. They offered some scholarship money, and it's near my sister Ji-yoon. She's pregnant." She's beaming now. "So I'll have a little niece or nephew."

I smile back. I make one last note in my food diary, pick up my tray. "I have to go," I say, but take her hand before I do. "Thank you, though."

My heart pounds when I finally make it out of the café. I feel like a heavy, lumbering weight has been lifted off my shoulders—one that I've been carrying now for nearly three years. Maybe Sei-Jin and I won't be friends again. But at least we don't have to be enemies anymore.

I walk down the hall to the mail room, finding myself hopeful for a second. Maybe, if Sei-Jin's managed to figure things out, I can, too. I've been waiting for notices from the dance companies I auditioned for—the New York auditions for Salt Lake, Miami, DC, and the Los Angeles Ballet. Inside my mailbox are a couple of envelopes, all skinny.

I tear them open, one by one. DC says my dancing is promising, but there's lots of competition, so please try again next year. Miami tells me I'm not quite ready yet, but I'm welcome to pay them five thousand dollars for their intensives with their artistic director, Rafaelo Diego. No thanks.

The defeat washes over me like waves crashing, and suddenly I feel like I'm drowning. I've worked so hard now for nearly a decade. It makes me want to cry. Or worse, go and throw up all the yogurt and eggs and anxiety.

I find myself staring in the direction of the first-floor bathroom. I can see the shiny plaque on its door, swinging open and shut with moms waiting for their *petit rats* in morning ballet class.

I take a deep breath and pull out my tablet, recording my thoughts. I'm locking the mailbox, balancing my tablet, when I drop the letters. But before I can pick them up, another hand is reaching for them. It's Riho's.

"Hi." Her voice is low, muted, like it hurts her to say hello.

I take the mail from her hands, say "thanks," and start to walk away. I don't want to be near her. Not when I'm facing rejection and she's probably never been rejected a day in her life. But as I shove the envelopes of doom into my bag, I realize that Riho is still standing there.

"What?" The anger drips from the word like acid. She comes in here, steals roles, then stands around to gloat about it? I want to smack her for a second.

"I just—I wanted to say thank you. You know, for being so kind to me here in my first weeks." I try to hide my surprise as her face lights up with a smile. I instantly regret all the rude things I said to her under my breath, thinking she was just one of Sei-Jin's minions. "I know that you're graduating soon, and I know we haven't talked much, but I thought I'd make you something to show my appreciation." She pulls a small box from her bag.

I open the box. Inside, there's a pair of pale lavender leg warmers, with sequins sewn on by hand. I've seen Riho in a similar pair in pink, and wondered where she might have gotten them—even mentioned them to my mom, who said she'd look into it.

"I made them. My grandmother taught me how to knit." She smiles again, and it's sweet, the kind of little lift that makes you want to protect someone. "I thought you had an eye on mine. So maybe you'd like a pair?"

"Thank you." I'm surprised at how quiet, how grateful my voice is. Ever since Gigi and the butterflies, I've felt even more alone here than ever. It never occurred to me that others might be having the same experience. In that moment, I'm glad—for Mr. K and his stupid mentor program, for Riho and her gift, for Sei-Jin taking the first step toward repairing what we had, even if it won't ever be the same.

The tears come. But for the first time in a long time, they're happy ones, not sad.

Riho hands me a tissue, and I snivel into it, thanking her again and telling her I'll see her later. She nods and smiles. She turns, rushing off to academic classes.

That feeling that had come over me just a few minutes ago—the anxiety, the stress, the sadness—has lifted. I don't even want to throw up anymore.

37.

Gigi

STUDIO B IS SET UP today with backdrops and lights for the official *Swan Lake* costume shoot. The pictures we take today will be used for press materials, programs, and the gala brochures, so we have to look perfect. Ballet moms run around helping Madame Matvienko check costumes and headpieces and help us do our makeup. Mr. K inspects each one of us before we head over to be photographed.

I stand in front of him. He circles me, fluffing my tutu and adjusting my headpiece just slightly. "You look luminous."

The word sweeps me back to last year, when everything was new and untainted and magical.

I join the group waiting to be photographed. I gaze at all of us in the mirrors. This is what I love about ballet—the twirl of the tulle; the long, lean lines of the fitted white bodice; the mirror effect we create when we're all standing together, tutus and jewels and headpieces catching the light.

The photographer shoots me after June and the quartet of the little swans. They look beautiful standing all in a row, arms interlocked. It's lovely, the corseted top giving way to a waterfall of white tulle that flies when they move in sync.

"You look beautiful, Gigi," one of the *petit rats* says in passing. I smile and wave at her.

I feel classic: the white tutu and bodice, shimmering with silver, and a stone-encrusted tiara and plumage on the headpiece. All of it is a stark contrast to Bette's Odile. She waits to the left, enveloped in a black, feathery costume that connotes darkness and despair. It's striking.

I step in front of the camera.

"Relax." The photographer takes his camera away from his eye. "Good. Show me the first movement they asked for."

I lift up in arabesque for the first picture. The flicker of the camera shutter echoes. Morkie gives corrections from the side for the second pose. I lift my leg higher, make my turns a little slower, and push my legs to their maximum. I try to keep my feet from spasming and a smile on my face. I do a few pirouettes, spinning like a top.

"Too much, too much," he says. "It's a still camera. I need you to be deliberate in your posing."

I stop and pause, lifting and swishing the skirt.

"Hold still." He looks down at his screen. "Elongate that leg!"

The comment stiffens me up further. He takes a couple more shots. I decide to ignore that he's there and leap into a split jump, pretending it's just me onstage.

"Great! Beautiful!"

I do another, just to hear those words. I think about my head shot in the program. I think about future articles in *Dance* or *Ballet* magazines, this time talking about how well I danced the role of Odette, the accident a distant memory.

He points to Bette. "Now, the white swan and the black swan together."

Morkie pushes Bette forward. My stomach twists. When Bette's in front of the camera, she's twirling and posing and looking every bit a principal ABC dancer. She's a little echo of Adele, and clearly the camera—and the photographer—loves it. "Heads up." You can practically see the drool sliding down his chin. "Can you do another pirouette? And hold it, one second. Beautiful. Gorgeous. Stunning darkness."

He places us side by side. We don't speak to each other. I hear her deep, heavy breaths. She smells like lipstick and that perfume she always wears. I suck it up and smile, because this is my moment. I'm not going to let her ruin it. I'm not going to let my anger with her affect what I'm doing.

The photographer sets up to shoot Bette solo. I start to walk away.

"Hey." She plants herself in my path. "Can you wait a second?"

I don't want to, but the look on her face is deliberate, determined. "I just—" She's at a loss for a second, but then she finds herself. "I wanted to apologize. For the mirror and the photos. I didn't realize until it happened to me—I mean, well, not really to me, but to the people I loved—just what it feels like to be on the other side of all this. It's terrible. Devastating, really. I'm sorry, really sorry, that I put you through all that."

The old Gigi would accept her apology, try to make amends, let her *fix* things. Just how I did at the end of last year, right before the accident. I'll never get back that innocent Gigi. I take three deep breaths. I can hear my mama's voice drumming in my chest. "Bitterness feeds on the host." I need to let some of this go, the stress that's been sitting on my shoulders all this time.

"Bygones," I say with a shrug. "Moving on." It's not forgiveness, not exactly. But it's all I have to give right now.

Alec brings popcorn into the basement rec room, where I'm working on a history paper. I'm typing up my bibliography and trying to figure out why anyone would want to spend their life or careers writing papers about the past. Some students watch TV in the far corner and others play pool. The attached computer lab overflows with bodies.

He plops down in the next beanbag and starts eating the popcorn and talking to me about the basketball game on TV. I shush him like Morkie would if he was making noise outside the studio. It's enough to get him to come over and stand behind my beanbag chair.

I pretend he's not there. Two white fingers appear in front of my face, then a muscular arm. In the middle of those fingers is an origami rose. A smile overtakes my face and whole body, like it's stretched all the way down to my toes.

He tries to squeeze himself onto my beanbag. "Is there still room for me?"

"No." I can't hide my smile. Since our breakup, we've danced together for weeks without exchanging words. It's been excruciating, feeling him against me but not being able to laugh or kiss or relax.

"Miss me?" He tries not to grin, holding his mouth shut.

"I miss nights when we didn't have so much homework." I'm sick of comparing the governments of England and France, and can't possibly understand why Mr. Martinez would want to read all these papers on the same exact topic.

"Well, I've missed you," he says.

I let him squeeze in next to me. I inhale his familiar woodsy scent, so clean and boyish. The warmth of his skin pushes through my ballet sweater. I reach for the origami rose, but he pulls it back toward his chest and grins. I try again, and he teases me with it, lifting it over his head. I lean forward to sniff the rose, even though it just smells like a mix of paper and his skin, and I let his finger graze my bottom lip.

I move closer to his side and secretly find his hand. I trace my fingers inside his palm and sway a little, leaning closer to him so I can smell him. It sends a warm zip down my spine. I've missed our conversations and texts and him in my room and our stretching together.

"You still mad at me?" he asks.

"Maybe."

"Well, I'm sorry."

"Me, too."

He nuzzles my neck, and tells me again that he's missed me. I fall into a little daze. Henri comes up to us and tells us to check social media. I'm having trouble focusing on the words coming out of Henri's mouth: *photos, ballerina, kissing*. Alec's kisses and touches make me lose focus on the people in this room and what I should be doing. My heart monitor buzzes, and even though it's supposed to be silent and discreet as the package claims, everyone seems to hear it.

Henri flashes his phone at us. There are three zoomed-in photos of a figure—clearly Mr. K—bent over someone in a hospital bed.

I put a little space between Alec and me. "What is that?"

"Everyone's sharing it. Caption says it's a Level 8 ABC student and one of the teachers."

I look at my own phone. All the feeds fill up with the same pictures.

Eleanor and Mr. K.

It has to be. The dancer is in a hospital bed. And after spending two years in a classroom with Mr. K, I'd recognize him anywhere.

Statuses speculate. People are tagged. I scan through the pictures and read some of the comments. They say that Mr. K has gone too far. That he's done this before. That this is the end of the American Ballet Conservatory.

"You can't even tell who it is." Alec zooms in. "Could be a fake."

"Hey, guys!" the RA calls out into the room. "Need you all to come upstairs."

"We still have three hours until curfew," someone complains.

"Mandatory meeting in Studio D," she says. "Let's go. Now."

Alec and I exchange glances, knowing that this is about those photos, wondering what they're going to do now. Others whisper about it as we all pile into the elevator to go up to the main floor. Half the school is moving toward Studio D in slippered feet and with bleary eyes, many in pajamas. Others are yanked right out of extra rehearsals in the studio. I see Cassie in the crowd of people, and walk over to her.

"What's going on? They knocked on everybody's door in the dorms. I was in the shower." Her wet curls smell like mint conditioner. She's been spending most of her time lately with the company dancers, but staying in the dorms. I hardly ever see her anymore.

"It's always bad news." I bite my bottom lip. "Always."

We crowd into Studio D. Alec, Henri, Cassie, and I find a spot to sit. Whispers crash into one another. Some of the students wonder aloud about the photos.

"Of course it's her."

"And Mr. K?"

"Wouldn't be the first time."

I think back to last year, the night my butterflies were killed, and how Mr. Lucas asked if I'd done anything *inappropriate* with Mr. K. The thought makes me shiver. I don't want my name in whatever this mess is.

My legs are jittery and tired from the complicated footwork in *Swan Lake*. I didn't stretch properly after rehearsal because I wanted to get that paper done. Alec's fingers stroke the small of my back. The rhythm calms me. I think maybe we're stepping in a direction back to where we used to be. June sighs a few paces away from us. We haven't spoken, even though I need to apologize to her, and sometimes I feel her staring, hoping for just a flicker of something back. I just can't bring myself to forgive her yet.

I try to curb my impulse to look around for Bette. But I

can't. With all this nervous talking, I don't know what to do with myself. I take attendance and the only dancers missing are Eleanor and Bette.

"Have you seen Eleanor?" I nudge Alec.

"No, but she's probably in here."

"I don't see her."

"You two are getting closer."

"Yeah, I guess."

"Didn't you all stay after rehearsal for extra time?"

"No, not today. But, yes, we've been hanging out a little."

We didn't agree to practice Odette together, exactly, but somehow we started watching each other try out different solos, and have entered into a kind of a rhythm over the past few months, giving pointers, helping each other stretch, running through the most difficult sections together. Which some people would think is weird for the lead and her understudy. But it works for us. And I still feel like I'm making up with her after the hummus incident.

My heart sinks as Mr. Lucas storms in, followed by some of the teachers—Mr. K conspicuously missing—and a man I don't recognize. Their footsteps stamp out all whispers in the room. I'm covered in goose bumps, a shiver drifting through my body.

"A serious matter has come to our attention tonight," Mr. Lucas says. "And I'm so angry about having to have these meetings that I kind of want to tell you all to call your parents, pack your bags, and leave my school."

Mr. Lucas is dead serious. This could be the beginning of the end.

38

Bette

"YOU NEED CASH?" MY MOTHER asks me for the fortieth time. She hands me a couple of twenties. We're sitting in the back of her car. She tells the driver to pull over to the right. We sit in silence for a few minutes. The rain makes a lovely beat on the car's roof. The school's lit windows cast a glow on the hood of her car. "And how's the new phone? Found the old one?"

She's being nice tonight. She had only one glass of wine during our dinner.

"It'll turn up. And if it doesn't, it was probably stolen and wiped clean already." I say the last part to myself, hopeful. It's been gone for weeks. It had important stuff on it, like those photos of El and Mr. K, and the camera app. I should've deleted them all ages ago.

"Don't worry about it. It's just a phone. And, Bette, you're doing great." She catches me off guard with that. "Really rising to the occasion, considering the mess that this has all been lately." She pauses for a second, wondering if that came out right. But with my mother, it never really comes out right. "Thank you for taking such good care of Adele. I know she needs your support right now."

"Of course." I actually kiss her cheek, then get out of the car, open my umbrella, and walk across the expansive Lincoln Center campus toward the Rose Abney Plaza. I'm about to go inside when Eleanor comes barreling out of the doors.

"Eleanor!" I call out. But she doesn't hear me. Or she's ignoring me. Again. She races away from the building, half running across the courtyard, full speed ahead, frantic.

"Eleanor, wait!" I chase her.

"El!" I catch her before she passes the fountain, grabbing her by the jacket, worrying it might fall apart in my hands. "Where are you going?"

She's upset.

"What's wrong?"

"It's everywhere!" She's breaking down, and I can't quite understand what she's talking about. "The photo you took at the hospital."

"What are you talking about?"

She flails her hands, the tears streaming now. "You were the only one from school who was there. How could you, Bette? How could you?" She's hiccupping through the words, her body shaking with anger or sadness or an ugly mix of both. "They think that's the reason that I got to dance at all." She's sinking to the ground, her knees hitting the wet concrete hard. I sink down with her, trying to get her to focus, to look at me.

"Breathe, Eleanor. Please. Tell me what happened. I can't help you if—"

The rain soaks us both as I struggle with my umbrella and helping her. She lifts her phone then, and I see the pictures I took of Mr. K and Eleanor at the hospital. The photos that were on my missing phone.

"They're calling me a slut, Bette."

"You're not—"

"Why am *I* the slut? He's done this a dozen times! Why am I the one to blame?" She's zipping through all the photos and the comments. They're on a bunch of different students' pages. "I'm not the first. I just wanted to—I thought, if I could just get his attention, I'd show him how good I was."

"Let's go to my house," I say. "We can hide out and figure out what to do."

She's shaking her head in a manic, determined way. "I don't want to be anywhere near you right now. This happened because of *you*. Because of the pictures you took."

I try to grab her hands, to lead her inside and out of the rain, but she takes off in the other direction. "Someone stole my phone!" I shout.

I chase after her, but lose track of her. The rain pours down in sheets. I can't even see the streetlamps in front of me. The plaza is so slick and the wind is so strong, I try not to fall, my umbrella nearly lifting me off the ground. I turn back to the school doors. I trip into the lobby, dripping with rain and guilt.

A male voice booms through the lobby, coming from one of the studios.

"What's going on?" I ask the front desk guard.

"Someone's in trouble, I guess."

One of the RAs spots me. She runs up to me and grabs me by the shoulder. "You're late." She's all pissy, as if it's going to reflect on her. "School-wide meeting. Studio D. Now."

I have a sick feeling that it's about those pictures from my phone. She pulls me into the studio.

"Someone is turning Mr. K's concern for a student into something reprehensible." Alec's dad stands in front of the crowd, as angry as I've ever seen him. "Something disgusting and inappropriate. They are posting the innuendos and lies all over social media. For something like this to come up at this turn—when we're finally about to set things right with the gala performance—well, it's simply unconscionable. There was nothing illicit about this picture." His face expressionless, as his eyes comb over every student in the room, looking for the dead giveaways. The clamminess, the smirks, the flushing or fear. But everyone is silent.

A bearded black man I've never seen before steps forward. "I'm Kevin McCafferty, the deputy VP of the conservatory board. Most of you do not recognize me because my role is largely behind-the-scenes—and that distance allows me to remain objective in these matters. As you know, the board of the American Ballet Company and Conservatory takes these charges very seriously. We cannot let this go without looking into the authenticity of these pictures and the veracity of the claims made online. Your parents have been notified of this situation." He looks around.

Whispers shoot through the room—the sound flinging itself up the studio's bare walls, bouncing off mirrors and from one student to the other, spreading like a brush fire raging out of control. I slip out and go looking for Eleanor.

I go back outside in the rain. No sign of her. I race to the coffee shop down the block. The barista says there haven't been any students here all day. I head back to the building.

"Any dancers come in late?" I ask the front desk man.

"Aside from you, there was one other." He barely looks up from his paper. I want to slam it down on the desk and make him pay attention to me.

"Was it Eleanor?"

"I don't know any of your names, miss. She was brown haired, sopping wet, and crying."

I race from the front desk to the elevators. I don't say thank you, even after he yells out "You're welcome" behind me. I fixate on the elevator numbers as it climbs from the first floor to the twelfth floor. I dart to my room and turn the doorknob. It's locked.

"Eleanor?" I knock again and say her name louder. I bang now and the door vibrates, but there's no answer. I dig my keys out of my bag, then push my way into the room.

The TV blasts a recording of one of Adele's old ballets. "Eleanor?"

Light pours out from under the bathroom door. I knock, but hear nothing. I turn the knob and it opens, just barely. There's a chair jammed against it. I slam into the door. The chair falls over. I push my way into the bathroom. My heart pounds.

Eleanor is passed out in the bathtub, arms dangling over the side, gashes across her wrists. Blood stains the water red, and my pills are scattered all over the fuzzy bath mat.

I scream for help and grab for Eleanor in the water. Her body feels too light, and sinks farther into the tub the more I pull. "Wake up, Eleanor. Open your eyes. C'mon." I manage to get her halfway out of the bathtub and cover her naked body with towels and a robe. I scream until I can't hear myself anymore.

After what feels like a lifetime, an RA rushes into the bathroom. She yanks me away from Eleanor. My hands are slick with her blood and my tights are soaked with bloodstained water. I fall back onto the plush blue bath mat my mother ordered. I feel the RA trying to lift me, but I am a thousand pounds and can't get my limbs to work or my legs to stop giving out from under me as I try to stand.

Another RA rushes in and behind her are paramedics. I'm taken from the room and into the hall where a crowd has gathered. People ask me questions. I see lips moving. I feel hands on my arms and shoulders. But I can't hear anything other than my heartbeat and the memory of my screams. My head fills with images of Eleanor.

The oozing gashes on her wrists.

The paleness of her skin.

The blood in the water.

They tell everyone to go back to their rooms, but I can't move. As soon as Eleanor is on a gurney and headed down in the elevator, I shoot for the stairs. I leap down them two at a time. I burst through the stairwell door and into the lobby. Mr. K is

SONA CHARAIPOTRA & DHONIELLE CLAYTON

there with all the teachers. They hover near the school entrance. Mr. McCafferty is outside, shooing away cameras with the help of police officers.

Eleanor's gurney clicks loudly against the marble floors of the lobby. It's the only thing I can hear. *Thump. Thump. Thump.*

She's strapped down, and an oxygen mask covers half her face. An EMT holds a bag of fluids over her and shouts something to his partner. Mr. K seems frozen as Eleanor passes, his eyes wet, his hand over his mouth, his pale skin white as paper. The night guard puts a hand on his shoulder, but he doesn't move.

Camera flashes pulse through the school windows and the red and blue lights of the ambulance mix with them until I can't see anything anymore.

All I can hear is a voice inside that says: *I just killed my best friend.*

39.

June

AS THEY WHEEL ELEANOR OUT the front doors of the American Ballet Conservatory on a gurney, the lobby is quieter than it's been in the six years I've lived in this building. So quiet, it almost feels like a funeral. It's not, I tell myself. I press my face to the glass, watching them load Eleanor's gurney into the ambulance. Others swarm around doing the same. A sheet covers most of her body, except for one leg that keeps slipping off the side, bare and bloody.

She's going to be fine, I keep telling myself. She has to be. I don't know Eleanor that well, despite being in school with her for a decade now. She's always been Bette's sidekick, but with roles like Arabian Coffee and the Swans, she was starting to come into her own finally. I'd heard the rumors, about a teacher and a student. But there have been rumors about Mr. K before, too. There have been rumors about Adele, rumors about Gigi, and others before them. *Mr. K takes liberties. He seduces students. Mr. K is a predator. Mr. K prefers blondes.* I remember overhearing Sei-Jin and her friends talking about Mr. K and Adele, about what she did to get to the top—and what Bette would have to do to beat that. "Wonder if he's into sisters?" one of them had said at the time. Seems they had the wrong girl all along.

Just as the ambulance pulls away, a horrible sound breaks the quiet.

I walk away from the windows, where the crowd is still gathered, and over to Bette, who's got a hand on the glass door. They won't let her out, but she refuses to step away. She's crying, mascara running, snot dripping, and she doesn't even care. I put an arm around her shaking shoulders, and it feels strange and familiar all at once, like new toe shoes that will be perfect once they're broken in. She doesn't stop sobbing, and an RA comes and guides her into the administration office, probably hoping to prevent other breakdowns.

The other Level 8s swarm around the elevator bank, unsure of what to do with themselves.

Mr. Lucas appears, taking charge, his voice droning as he's shouting commands. "Upstairs now. There's no reason for you to be down here. You can get your evening meals, but we will be instituting an eight thirty curfew tonight. No sign-outs, unless a parent or guardian comes to get you."

The old me would hope for a glance, a glimmer of warmth or recognition. But now I know not to have expectations, and I realize I don't care anymore. If anything, I feel disgusted by him and his presence.

As the next elevator opens, I follow the crowd into it. I head straight for my room, which is empty, thankfully. My first instinct is to head toward the bathroom—but I stop myself, my hand resting on the doorknob. I turn around and press my back to the door. If I give in to that, how am I any different from Eleanor?

I'm killing myself, too, just at a slower pace.

I climb into bed and pull the covers over my head, blocking out everyone and everything. I've always loved this place, longed for it when I was away for the summers, considered it home. But today, I feel done with it, ready to move on. It's all too much. I've never been able to relax here, not really. The competition, the anxiety, the sheer meanness that sets in gets to even me. Exhausted, I let myself go, give myself over to sleep.

It's just past midnight when I wake, my phone buzzing incessantly. My mom. I answer, my voice heavy with sleep. "I'm okay," I tell her.

"Thank God!" She sounds wide awake, frantic. "Want me to come get you?"

I shake my head, realizing she can't see me. "No, I'm okay. I'm in bed. I'll call you tomorrow."

"Okay, E-Jun. Stay safe. Love you."

She hangs up, and I look around the room by the light of the streetlamp. Cassie's not in her bed or the room. She's with her company friends, I guess. Or maybe with Henri.

Alone in the dark, I feel haunted. Butterflies, bloodstains, broken bones. They're all crashing in on me. I want to text Jayhe, to let him fold his arms around me or, better, take me away from this place. But I can't. Not after all that's happened. I look at the phone, willing myself to do it. Knowing I won't.

The cold call of the bathroom beckons, like death with its skeletal fingers gesturing me forward. I climb out of bed and follow the call blindly, not even stopping to turn on the lights. The sound of the swirling water from the toilet rushes my ears, bringing up that familiar instinct. Crouching there, I almost give in. Almost let all that hurt take over. I feel the warmth that always comes before the releases.

But then, faintly, I hear chatter in the hall. First quiet, then louder, closer. I push myself away from the toilet, propel myself up and out of the bathroom. I nearly gave in, gave up. I take deep breaths until the contents of my stomach settle.

I rush to the door and pull it open, hoping for Gigi or Bette or even Riho. I practically spill out into the hallway, where Sei-Jin and her friends are gathered, standing in their pajamas, headed toward the common room, no doubt.

"June." Sei-Jin looks surprised but not unhappy to see me. "We were just coming to get you." She gestures to the others, and Riho grins at me. "We're going to watch some K-dramas on the big screen. The RAs said it was cool, you know, to get our mind off things. Want to come?" If she notices how shocked I am, she doesn't let on. "Oh, come on. It'll be fun."

She offers her arm. For a moment, I look for an excuse. But she looks so hopeful, I just nod and take the hand she's extended. As the other girls walk ahead, she pauses for a second. "I'm glad you're coming." Then more quietly, she adds, "and don't worry. We'll put on the subtitles."

I smirk as she laughs, but I'm glowing with warmth inside.

It's a nice Saturday, so I sign myself out at the front desk. It takes me an hour and a half to get to Queens on the train. I have to switch from F to the E, and there's a big wait in between trains, and I should have brought a heavier coat, because it's still chilly for late April.

One week since Eleanor's incident, things have settled down in an eerie way—kind of like nothing has happened at all. Eleanor's recovering, but they don't know when—or if—she will be back. Mr. K has returned because the situation remains "under investigation." And I finally, weirdly, have friends again. I've tried knocking on Bette's door a few times, but she never answers. She hasn't been in class all week.

Riding the train, I look at the NYU acceptance letter I received. I try to picture myself at NYU, imagining myself in purple polka dots and a plum lipstick, in acting class or maybe creative writing, on a stage or maybe behind the scenes. I imagine myself at parties and studying in the library. I try to picture Jayhe's face when I share my news. It warms me up, and I must look like an idiot, standing there in pink tights and my little spring jacket, beaming. But for once, I don't care what anyone else thinks.

I get off the train in Elmhurst and realize I'm not quite sure which direction to walk in, because we always drove over in Jayhe's van when we went to the restaurant. I don't even know if this is the branch Jayhe will be at, or if he's full-time now at the new place in Brooklyn.

There are so many things I don't know anymore, and it makes

me want to just turn around and get right back on the train. What was I thinking? I'm already missing afternoon ballet, and by the time I get back, I'll miss my pre-calc tutoring session, too. I look around. This New York is so different from mine: the bustle of the street, people of all different shapes and colors and sizes. English, Hindi, and Korean and who knows what else mingle into a pulsating backbeat. This place is a different New York, teeming with life. Not all glass and metal and sheltered like the conservatory. Not so easy to shatter.

I can hear the sizzle of meat from the Indian restaurant across the street, and the pizza guy is tossing pies in the window behind me. I don't see Jayhe's dad's place. But there's something familiar about the street names, the shops around here. I don't think I'm far. The light changes and I go to cross the street and suddenly there's a whole lot of honking and I leap back.

The walk signal is still flashing and I should be okay. As I start again, there's more honking, and I finally look to where it's coming from.

But it's Jayhe, leaning hard on the horn in that junky old black van, the one we made out in countless times. He looks completely confused, but he's waving me over. I run back to the other side, and open the passenger door and climb in.

He pulls over, and just stares at me for a second. "Took you long enough" is the first thing that comes out of his mouth. He's not smiling or frowning or doing much of anything. I guess this is all on me.

"I didn't realize you were waiting." I have the envelope in my lap, and it's taking everything in my power not to shove it at him, to let it do the talking. "I thought that you didn't want to see me again. But I decided not to give you a choice."

He doesn't say anything. Anger simmers below the surface, hot to the touch, even in the silence between us.

I hand him the envelope. "I'm sorry. I'm sorry I disappeared. I'm sorry I kept pushing you away. I'm sorry you had to see me—like you did." I know he's seen it now, sized up the familiar emblem in the corner, the shape and thickness of the packet, the fact that I'm here at all. But he doesn't say a word. I wonder if it might be too late for us. But I have to say what I came to say. "I'm working on it. I'm trying. Really."

I pull my tablet out of my bag. I push it toward him. "Look. It's part of my treatment, a food diary, therapy sessions, scheduled workouts, and PT. I'm busier than ever. I mean, you'd think I'd barely have a minute to miss you." He's looking at me now, waiting. "But I did."

He's quiet then, focused on the little tablet, pushing keys. I realize then that he's looking at the menus and my notes. He sees when I felt good and when I was miserable, and when I wanted to throw up and didn't. And when I wanted to throw up and did. I want to snatch them away, all my secrets.

I know I have to let him in, trust him, if this is going to work. "I'm trying. I'm not perfect. I'll never be perfect, or fixed. It will always be an effort, maybe not like it is now, but—"

"Do. Or do not," he says. "There is no try."

"You sound like your dad."

He laughs. "It's a *Star Wars* reference."

We both laugh, but then he's looking at me, all serious and

intense. He pulls me in, closing the small space between us. The gearshift sits in the middle of the front seat, and it's the only thing keeping us apart right now. "It's too painful to watch you do that to yourself. And you can't promise me—"

I don't know quite what to say to that. I applied to NYU because he wanted me to. I came all the way here. I tried to fix things. And he can't give me an inch.

"There are no promises, Jayhe. Because those are always broken. But I mean this when I say it: I'm working on it." I pick up my bag, reach for the door, and leap out of the van. He doesn't stop me.

But when I climb down and hit the street, he's standing there, waiting. His strong arms surround me, and I can smell that familiar scent—dusty and rich, like charcoal pencils. He looks at me and smiles, waiting for the words. *"Kiss-jwo!"* I say, and he laughs and leans down.

We kiss for what feels like forever, as the cars honk down Union Street, and people climb on and off lumbering buses. We kiss until the words become unnecessary. We kiss until Jayhe's uncle shouts from inside the restaurant. *"Joka!* You gonna make those deliveries or what?" Then he sees me, tucked under a blushing Jayhe's arm. "Oh, hey, E-Jun. Didn't see you there."

Jayhe grins and heads around the other side of the van to get back in. I climb into the passenger seat, and I just look at him as we drive away. It feels like I will smile for the rest of the night. Even for the rest of my life, maybe.

40.

Gigi

I HOVER IN THE STAGE wings. It's the night of our performance, and the energy at Lincoln Center is electric—I keep wanting to sneak to the stage and stare out into the audience, to see each face lit with delight and expectation, but it would be too distracting to the other dancers, who are already out there making magic.

Still, I can sort of feel the audience there, even though they're all shadows and the lights are blinding and the big curtain hides the stage from their view. The noise of their movements, the squeak of the seats, and their energy pushes back to us.

"Curtain in fifteen," the stage manager calls out backstage.

I slip back to the dressing room. One of the stage moms waves me over to her chair. I wonder which *petit rat* belongs to her.

"Your forehead is all sweaty. Let me add more powder."

"Thank you."

She smiles down at me. "You look beautiful."

The tiny word fills me up. Tonight I have to dance beautifully. I have to make sure Damien sees that.

"Curtain in ten," someone shouts.

I take one last look at myself in the mirror. White swan feathers frame my face, strings of jewels interlock over my head and into a crown, and a diamond sits in the center of my forehead. I inhale, calming my too-quick heart. Stagehands with microphones move in and out, giving people directions.

Riho, Isabela, and the other new girls are hovering by the door, itching to go out toward the stage, to watch from the wings until it's their turn. I wonder if it's their first time here on the Lincoln Center stage, and try to remember what that was like when I danced here for the first time last year in *The Nutcracker*. I remember the power and the hugeness of it—both in real life, and in your head. Next year I'll call this stage home. I have to.

June dresses in the corner, putting on her first costume of the night—the Baroness—and looking at herself in the mirror. She takes a wig and slips it on. The tumble of dark curls transforms her into eighteenth-century royalty. Our eyes catch in the mirror. She gives me a little nod.

"You look great," I say.

"And so do you."

"Five minutes!" the stage manager tells me as the others go on.

I turn back to the vanity and I practice my stage grin in the mirror, flashing teeth and then closing my mouth into a soft smile.

I step out into the hall and warm up my feet again. I listen for the crunch of the pointe shoe shanks and know they're broken

343

in perfectly to support my movements tonight. I point, flex, and bounce until my feet feel warm and ready to be used.

Arms circle around my waist, strong and familiar.

Alec.

His hands linger in all those secret places. "You ready for this?" he whispers, his breath hot on my ear, sending shivers up my spine.

I turn around in his arms, letting him press his body up against mine, the heat seeping right through the glitter, tulle, and gossamer of my costume. I can't wait to be onstage with him again. I can't wait to see if this means we're back together. I can't wait for this part of my life to settle back into place. I answer him with a kiss, long and lingering. Even though it takes off some of my lipstick.

"Act two!" the stage manager shouts in our direction. "You're on!"

Alec takes my hand. "Come on." He pulls me toward the stage.

This is it.

I take a deep breath and follow.

It feels like the first time. The lights, the rose of my cheeks, the scratchy tights and tulle—the magic. It's all there, it's all back. The warmth of the stage lights at Lincoln Center hit my shoulders.

Thirty seconds till my solo in the coda. Two lines of swans edge both sides of the stage. It's just me in the middle. I lift my legs and stretch them into long, sharp lines. I present soft delicate hands. I fold into the slow melodies.

I finish. The audience claps, and I bask in every second of it, knowing how fleeting this joy might be. I bow and slip to the wings to catch my breath before my next entrance. I drink a little water. A stage mom helps towel me off and blot my face. I'm so out of breath I can't thank them.

The scene backdrop changes to the ballroom. Henri, as Rothbart, presents Bette. The music shifts, and the light turns to dark as Bette takes the stage. She smiles all teeth. Each lift of her leg and every *piqué* turn is perfect. The audience applause is thunderous.

All this time they've been calling me the comeback kid, but in that moment, I know that title should really belong to her. She was gone half the year, but it doesn't show.

Alec dances his solo. He leaps high in the air. I hear gasping from the crowd. His motions and his smile all show his love for Odile. Alec finishes his turns, and Bette spins forward, beginning those thirty-two *fouettés en tournant*.

I hold my breath, not realizing I'm counting until she hits the very last one and the audience bursts. From the wings, I spot some people in the front row up on their feet—a standing ovation. One that's well deserved. She's perfect, flawless, the black swan with an edge.

The one, in the end, who makes the story worth reading, the ballet worth watching.

It's inching toward midnight, but the evening is far from over. Tonight, fresh off the Lincoln Center stage, one more female

American Ballet Conservatory dancer will become the company's newest apprentice, alongside the two male picks. I stand before the panel in the upstairs studio, holding my breath, praying she might be me.

I knit my fingers and nibble at my bottom lip as I wait for Damien Leger to give me his decision. I feel transported back to the very first cast list at the conservatory when we were all huddled together in the lobby and waiting for Mr. K to dole out our fates. I feel like I should be back in that space and with him in front of me. I can't process the words coming out of the mouths of Morkie, Mr. Leger, and Mr. K. I catch bits and pieces of them in the fuzzy haze over my brain.

"Flawless."

"Strong technique."

"Nearly back to your old self."

"You have a flame."

But. But. But.

"Do you still love it?" Madame Dorokhova asks. Her deep Russian voice cuts through the cloud in my head, booming like thunder.

"Excuse me?"

"Do you love ballet?" she says.

I think back to that argument with my mother, of telling her I'll be dancing, with or without her support. "I don't know how to do anything else," I say, not sure if that answers her question. "I don't want to do anything else. This is my dream."

"You've come back from a very dark place," Mr. K says. "You've almost got it all back, but you're missing something." He pauses for effect. "The thing I loved about seeing you dance the most in that very first audition."

I'm speechless. The thing he saw in me—the thing he said set me apart. Probably the only thing that's really keeping me here.

"Gigi, while we think you are a talented and charismatic young woman, the talent pool this year was so stellar—beyond all our expectations," Madame Dorokhova says. "We do see something in you, but you've suffered a rough patch. Maybe with some time—" She must see my shattered expression and her face softens. "You remind me so much of myself when I was dancing at the Bolshoi. Yes, that's it. You dance like the old me used to."

Damien speaks then, and his face is pained. "Gigi, we see something grand in you. But I feel that you need more time to focus on your recovery—physically and mentally." He scribbles something on a paper. "That said, I'd love to follow your progress—and for you to check in with us before you accept any other offers."

His words don't quite register. I don't have any other offers. I didn't audition anywhere else. All I'm hearing is that I failed.

"Can you do that for me?" he's saying, quiet, concerned.

"So does this mean I didn't make it?"

"Not at this time, I'm afraid." Damien adds a sad smile.

I nod, and walk out, without looking at any of them again.

I failed. They don't want me. The weight of it is crushing, and I nearly stagger as I slip through the door. I press my back against the wall and slide down it. My head finds my knees. My heart races to the sound of Damien's words: *Not at this time, I'm afraid.*

41.

Bette

I STAND OUTSIDE THE LINCOLN Center studio where Damien, Madame Dorokhova, and Mr. K are having their meetings. Everyone else has gone through, the boys celebrating, the girls weeping. First there was June, Sei-Jin, and then the rest of that crew. They're long gone, all pink faces and lots of tears. But Gigi hasn't returned yet.

I whisper to one of the crying girls. "Is Gigi still in there?" She's sprawled out on the floor, her head tucked into her knees, and she looks up at me. Tears run like rivers through the powder on her cheeks, hot and fresh and humiliating. Her mascara is spiderwebbing in intricate patterns, making her look edgy.

"No, she left already." She sniffles out the words. I want to ask her if Gigi was happy or crying. But she transforms into another puddle, gets up, and darts out.

I press my hands against the door. A mix of English and Russian voices slip from behind it. I can't make out anything.

I start to pace and think through my performance. The whole time I was up there, I heard Adele's voice in my head. I spun for every wrong thing I did, every accusation used against me. I spun for every snub—from Will, from Alec, from Mr. K even. I spun for every triumph missed, for Adele, for Eleanor, for Gigi, for June—and for myself.

Whatever else happens tonight, I'll have that. A moment of perfection I can go back to over and over again, a memory that will stay with me. That I was more than good enough. That I was perfect.

The door opens. The sound makes me jump. Damien's assistant steps outside. "Bette Abney," she says, her voice sweet. "They're ready to see you now."

All in a row, behind a table, sit Damien, Mr. K, Morkie, and Dorokhova. It feels just like when I was six and first audition-ing for the conservatory, a *petit rat* in scratchy pink tights and a leotard. Back then, it didn't matter. I already had a spot before walking into the studio. I was an Abney. But now, that might not be enough.

It feels like there are a thousand steps to take before I reach them. As I walk behind Mr. K's assistant, I watch her move-ments, flowery, elegant. I wonder if she's a failed dancer. Some-one who had high hopes and big dreams, just like me, and didn't quite make the cut.

I wonder if that will be me, a year or two from now, desper-ately clinging to this world, whatever part of it I can hold on to. It all makes me think of Eleanor and our little girl dream. The one we used to stay up at night discussing. I'd like to see her happy, dancing somewhere, somehow. I imagine Eleanor, maybe five years from now, somewhere not too far from New York. She'll have a little dance school full of handpicked *petit rats*, she'll be the old Eleanor again. She'll swing around with the children and teach them all the good things she took from this place—the magic of performance and the grace of applause, the swish and the sparkle of the tulle and the makeup and the powdery scent of resin. All the things I've forgotten in the heat of the competition to be the best. All the things that I'll have to keep reminding myself about if I have a chance to continue this journey.

The assistant ushers me into the lone empty chair, facing the panel. I sit, ready to meet my fate.

Every fiber in my being wants to call out to Mr. K, to tell him I know exactly what he did and that I won't let him get away with it. But this is not the time or the place. First I need to know my fate.

Mr. K opens his mouth to speak, but Damien beats him to it. "Bette Abney, your performance in the American Ballet Conservatory's rendition of *Swan Lake* tonight was the best I've seen you dance," he says. "But we're hoping it's not all you can do."

His words thunder inside me.

"I told you once, Bette," he continues, "that you have something in you that echoes Adele. And just that would be useless to me. I already have an Adele."

A flush climbs up from my stomach to my chest and face. I gulp and wait for him to say, *No, Bette, you didn't earn an apprenticeship at ABC.*

"But you also bring something very different." He rubs his chin and pauses.

I count my heartbeats in the silence.

"That edge, Bette, that's what makes you stand out. At American Ballet Company, we are *only* looking for the standouts." He presses a finger to his mouth, and turns to Madame Dorokhova.

Her stern mouth breaks into what could be considered her form of a smile. "Bette Abney, we'd like to offer you a spot as an apprentice at American Ballet Company."

She waits for me to say something, anything. The words are caught in my throat. I look from Mr. K to Madame Dorokhova and back to Damien.

Damien clears his throat. "We're presuming you'd like the spot, Bette?"

I nod, finally finding my voice. "More than anything in the world, Mr. Leger."

"Great. We'll see you in company classes after graduation," Madame Dorokhova says.

I curtsy and bow my head, then blast through the door.

I know that Adele and my mother will be waiting outside, expecting the worst, for Bette to disappoint them once more. Not this time. This time, I'm the one who'll get the final word.

42.

June

IT'S MY LAST DAY AS student at the American Ballet Conservatory. After more than ten years, I'm saying good-bye to the only place I've really called home.

I'm in my room, boxing up the last of my stuff. Jayhe's been taking it down to the van in shifts, but it's double-parked and he's worried about a ticket. With NYU looming, he can't afford one. I think back to the night after the gala last week, when Damien Leger told me that while I was a beautiful dancer with flawless technique, my time at the American Ballet was over. *With so much talent in the pool this year, E-Jun,* he'd said, *I'm afraid we can't offer you a spot.*

That was it. My final rejection. My dance career finished in the span of a few small moments, with a whimper, not a bang. I cried that night. I did. But I won't now. I refuse to.

I put the teakettle and my box full of teas into the last cardboard box, and think back to the first day of this year—to finding

Cassie here in my room and how I let that moment define my year. I'm disappointed in myself, I am. I know things could have gone differently if I had taken the reins then and redirected. *But I'm in a good place*, I remind myself. I'm with Jayhe, I'm going to one of the best universities in the country, my mom and I are finally getting along. And I'm getting healthier every day.

I seal up the last box with tape, and take one last glance around the room, making sure I haven't forgotten anything. Cassie's side has been bare for days—she moved into the company apartments last week. Good riddance. It let me live my last few days here in peace, at least. Even if it was a little too quiet. I take one last glimpse, pick up the box, and head to the elevator to go down to the third floor to return my keys. It's hard to say good-bye to the American Ballet Conservatory. But it's time to move on, to move forward.

I'm in the elevator when my phone starts buzzing. It's an 801 number I don't recognize, so I send it to voice mail. I return my keys at the front office, and as I'm walking out, it rings again. The same number. Annoyed, I answer it, ready to yell.

"E-Jun Kim?" The voice is smooth and male. I don't quite recognize it.

"Yes." I set the box down and pause by the front door. I can see Jayhe in the van, sketching in his pad.

"Glad I caught you." Maybe it's about my NYU dorm situation. I asked for a single, which is unusual for a freshman. "Alan Willis. Salt Lake City Ballet. You auditioned for us in New York back in February."

"Yes, of course. It was lovely to meet you all."

"Lovely to meet you, too, E-Jun. In fact, I know we may be a little late in reaching out—and that you may have already accepted another offer—but we've been delayed in our casting confirmations for the upcoming year. We're hoping that you might consider joining us here in the corps de ballet at Salt Lake City."

I'm so stunned, I can't speak.

"Your audition performance of Odile was spectacular—fiery yet understated. It really stuck with me, and I certainly meant to connect with you sooner. Anyway, I wanted to extend the offer, but I do understand if you're already committed. In any case, I thank you for taking the time to audition. Good luck—"

"Wait, Mr. Willis, hold on." The words come out in a rush, frantic, and I hope not desperate. "I'd love to consider your offer. I've got some things to think about, though. Is it okay if I get back to you?"

"Oh, by all means. I'll email you all the details. Take as much time as you need. I'm hopeful here, E-Jun. I'd be so pleased to hear you'll join us. But definitely think about it and get back to me."

"Thank you, Mr. Willis."

He hangs up, and I'm left standing there in the hall, not quite sure what my next step should be.

Just as I'm about to walk out, I hear my name. "E-Jun. E-Jun. I'm glad I caught you."

Mr. Lucas. My father. "I thought I was too late."

Always too late, I want to say. *Or not there at all.*

"I know you had high hopes. But I've heard you're on your

way to NYU, and I'm so pleased."

I nod and pick up my box, ready to walk away for good.

"Listen, E-Jun. I heard about the dorm situation. I want you to know that's taken care of. Your mother—" He pauses, as if he's lost his train of thought. He pulls a set of keys out of his pocket. "She said you're waiting for a spot. But I don't think that's necessary."

He holds up a set of keys, waiting for something. A smile, a hug? But it's too late for that. "It's just a studio, like four hundred and fifty square feet. But it's right there on Waverly, in a safe, doorman building, and it's newly renovated. I saw it and I thought of you."

"Oh," I say. "You thought of me? For the first time maybe ever?"

He looks startled for a second—that definitely wasn't the reaction he was expecting. "I've thought of you a lot, E-Jun. Even if I haven't been able to show it." He puts the keys into my empty hand, closes my fingers around them. It feels awkward, the intimacy. Foreign and formal. "I know you won't be able to begin to understand that until you're much older. The apartment is yours if you want it—and it's paid for, all of it. So you don't have to worry about that, and neither will your mother. You don't have to say yes today. Or at all. I won't hold it against you. I know it doesn't begin to undo all those years—" He looks at my face, intently. "NYU is a great school. And you can maybe learn some Korean—I wish I had, back in the day. I wish I'd done a lot of things."

I nod again. He nods, too. He leans close for just a second, as if he's about to hug me, but stops just short. He heads off toward his office. I walk in a stupor out the building's main door. Alec is standing in front of it. He's been watching this whole time. He's seen everything. But he doesn't look surprised, just relieved.

"You knew, didn't you?" I say. He doesn't have to nod or say yes. "You let me think I was alone this whole time."

"I couldn't—" His ears are red already. "I was just so mad at you. Even though none of it is really your fault. It's been him all along. It took me a long time to figure that out."

He doesn't hug me or offer a hand. Nothing's changed. He won't suddenly turn into a real brother just because the truth is out there. But it's a relief, just to know that he knows, that someone else besides me bears this burden. "I have to say, it took you a lot less time to figure out that our dad's an asshole than it did me."

I grin back at him. "I got in to the Salt Lake City Ballet." I don't know why I blurt it out. I guess that I just had to share.

"June, that's amazing!" This time he does hug me. It's awkward and stiff, but the intent is there. "Are you going to go? What about NYU? You have to dance."

He's taken my thoughts and laid them bare. I do. I have to dance. Right?

"Whatever you decide, good luck with it." He grins at me again and heads inside the building.

For ten minutes or ten hours, I'm not sure exactly, I stand steps away from the van, watching Jayhe sitting in the driver's seat. His sketchbook leans on the steering wheel in front of him, the cityscape of the Lincoln Center area scrawled in pen and ink. Commemorating the moment, he's drawn a small figure in the front, wistful and hopeful and happy. It really reflects what my life has been for the last decade—the American Ballet Conservatory and its insular little world. A world I'm about to leave behind.

In a moment, I'll go over there, and he'll smile at me and call me beautiful and we'll drive away. I'll start the rest of my life.

Two versions of my life play out in front of me. In one, I'm in Salt Lake with new people, doing exactly what I've always wanted to do—what I know I'm *meant* to do. Dancing is in my veins, in my pores, in my soul. I can't imagine a life without it. I imagine telling him the news, his face falling, for our amazing future to turn to dust and distrust. I hear the false words of hope he'll say then. *We'll make it work.*

But I could stay here. I could go to NYU and be with Jayhe. After all, for a month now, I've been plotting what it will be like: new classes and new people with him by my side. Late-night study sessions that turn into make-out sessions. Maybe even finding a whole new passion. And, yes, ballet, but not the same way. It'll be a hobby, a faded dream, one that I'll someday share as a story. *I used to dance*, I'll say, wistful. *It was amazing.*

I know now what I have to do. I just have to find the strength to do it.

43.

Gigi

ALL MY THINGS FIT NEATLY into the three new suit-cases Mama sent me. They stare up at me. Tights, leotards, bal-let slippers, ribbons, hairnets, pins. The pieces of my life at the conservatory headed back to California with no real purpose anymore. I fold the rest of my tights and bag up pointe shoes that still have life in them, thinking I'll take a class or two in San Francisco. I squeeze the last few things inside.

I gaze around the room. It's naked, unfamiliar. The linens are stripped from the beds. The walls are bare. The closet is full of lonely wire hangers. No terrarium sits on the windowsill. There's no trace that I ever lived here.

Mama never said I told you so. She never looked pleased or even mentioned being happy that I'm headed home. I think she gets it now, finally, what I've lost. What I'm mourning.

What's next? I flush with worries and unanswered questions.

Mr. K's question replays in my head: *Do you still love ballet?*

The answer booms straight through me: *Yes!*

Disappointment sets in again. I didn't audition anywhere else. I fixated on the American Ballet Company. Now I have no place to go but home, jobless. My truce with Mama will only last so long before she starts in with the college talk.

A knock interrupts my pity party. "Come in."

The door creaks open. I see a white hand and in it a tiny origami airplane. Alec's buzzed blond head peeks in.

I slip the origami plane from his hands. The edges are perfectly creased and the plane's wings so light when I bounce it, they flap up and down.

"You ready?" he says.

"No."

He tucks my hair behind my ear. We haven't talked about what's going to happen to us, or if there's even an us left. He's moving into the company apartments. He's got an apprentice spot at ABC, along with Henri. He's starting his life as a professional dancer. A life we were supposed to have together.

"You think this whole thing is karma?"

"For what? You're a good person." His blue eyes flicker with confusion.

"I wasn't myself this year."

"I don't think any of us were, really."

"I let all of it turn me into someone I wasn't." I think about soaking Sei-Jin's shoes in vinegar, about sending Bette magazines, about cutting June's hair, about giving Eleanor peanuts, about trying to put those pictures of June up. I think about how good I felt doing it. I think about Cassie, about all the times we sat and plotted and said horrible things about people. I think about how different I was last year. "I feel like—maybe—if I had just forgiven Bette, and even Will, things might've turned out differently."

"I can't ever forgive Will." His eyes narrow and his jaw clenches. "I still can't believe he did that. There's nothing that can explain it."

"I'm just tired of being so angry. I feel like it defined me this year. I feel like I let it distract me. That's why they didn't pick me."

He shakes his head, taking my hands. "You can start over now."

I want to tell him that I don't want to start over. I want to be right here with him. He lifts me up into his arms. I tuck my face into the nook between his shoulder and his neck. I take in a breath and try to hold the smell of him inside me. I don't know when I'll see him again. I don't know if I'll ever see him.

"I wish we didn't have that fight." The words land against his skin. "I wish we hadn't wasted that time, now that I'm leaving."

"Me, too." He kisses my neck, then finds my mouth. His tongue parts my teeth. I taste the slice of pineapple he must've just had. His hands hold me just like we're beginning a *pas de deux*. Their warmth find its way through my clothes and into my skin. I wonder what life would've been like if I had gotten chosen as one of the apprentices. Would we be back together?

He traces his fingers along the curves of my face. He counts the freckles.

"What are you doing?"

"Memorizing your face."

A smile bubbles up inside me.

"I don't want you to leave." His fingers find my mouth and chin.

"I don't want to leave New York. I don't want to leave you."

An RA yells from the hall that the airport shuttle is out front. My stomach does a flip. Alec squeezes me one more time.

"You can always come back. There are other companies here. The American Ballet Theatre. The Dance Theatre of Harlem."

"I just thought I'd be—"

"I know. I did, too."

He moves my suitcases into the hall. The RAs load them onto a cart to bring downstairs for the shuttle to the airport.

"Gigi, let's go," the RA calls out.

I linger in the room and take it in one last time. I slip my phone from my pocket and group text Mama, Dad, and Aunt Leah that I'm leaving the school for the airport. My finger scrolls past Will's name in my contact list.

"Gigi!" Alec calls from the hall. "We gotta go."

I type three words to Will: *I forgive you.*

I hit Send, then delete and block the contact.

I close the door, and walk away from the American Ballet Conservatory for the very last time.

44.

Bette

ELEANOR IS TUCKED INTO HER childhood canopy bed, her cheeks rosy, and I feel like we're six again. Her room still has the buttercup yellow wallpaper, a dollhouse, and a collection of plastic horses peeking out from her bookshelf. It's so weird to see her here. This room doesn't feel like she belongs in it anymore after all our years at the conservatory.

I thought she wouldn't want to see me after everything that happened. But when I called her mother, she invited me right over, said Eleanor had been waiting for me to call.

"How are you?" I'm lying on the pillow beside her, and we're face-to-face. I try to sink into the bed, not let the anxiety of everything that happened this year linger between us.

"Better."

I don't know if I believe her. Bandages cover her wrists, and her eyes are rimmed with purple and black half-moons. Her skin is translucent and little tremors make her hands shake a little.

"I'm sorry about everything getting out," I say to just rip the Band-Aid off. "The pictures, all of it."

"It wasn't your fault."

"Someone took my phone."

"I know." She smiles at me for the first time in what feels like forever, and in this moment I feel like nothing has changed, even though everything has shifted into unrecognizable shapes. "I'm glad you got the spot," she says. "You worked really hard."

"So did you."

"I just don't have it in me. Not like you do." She sighs. "Not the talent, not the stamina, not the charisma. That's why I felt like I had to—" She stops there, afraid to say too much.

"You're stronger than you think, El."

"Just not strong enough." She lies flat on her back, staring up at the ceiling. It feels like I'm losing her again, like she'll shut me out for good this time. But then I feel the tremor move through her and right into me, and I know what she's thinking. About him. About them. About things I might never understand. I always felt like the grown-up, worldly one of us, but she's so far out of my reach now, I'll never catch up.

"It's not your fault, Eleanor. No one blames you."

"But they should. I knew what I was doing. It started out as a tease, just to see what would happen. But I got caught up in the glamour of it. The attention, the adoration. The way he looked at me. It was all about the power. It had nothing to do with dancing at all."

I inch closer to her. "This wasn't your fault." I say it again, because she needs to hear it. "Everything got all messed up. You didn't do this all on your own."

"Bette, I can't blame him."

"Why not? I do." I force her to turn over and face me. Her eyes brim with tears, which cause mine to do the same. "He's the grown-up here, Eleanor, and what they say is true. He's power mad, a predator. You weren't the first, and you likely won't be the last. But not if I get my way, Eleanor. Because I'm going to make him pay."

"Don't you dare, Bette Abney. I made my choices." She blinks away falling tears and takes a deep breath. "I decided that I would allow that whole thing to happen. I touched him first."

"But—"

"I want to let it all go. Ballet hasn't made me really happy in a long time. It's sort of messed me up."

"I hope you know, you're a beautiful dancer. Even if I didn't tell you enough." The truth is I should've told her all the time. I should've made sure she knew I thought she was great. I should've been a better friend. A best friend, like she was always to me. Maybe she wouldn't have done this. Maybe she would've relied on me and the strength of her feet and the beauty of her movements to get what she wanted. Maybe this thing with Mr. K would've never happened.

"I don't know what I'm going to do without ballet, but I'm excited to find out. I'm excited to learn what will actually make me happy."

I slip my hand in hers. "You'll find something. I'll help you."

"And you'll dance for the both of us," she says.

"Always."

❧

I walk into the American Ballet Company building for the first time as a company apprentice, as a professional ballerina. It's my first ballet class after graduation. I stand in the lobby and look straight up. Pictures of the great ballet dancers seem to float down from the ceiling, held by string I can't see.

"You're a little Adele," someone says.

I whip around.

It's Alina Rozanova, one of the soloists. She doesn't stop to chat, just smiles at me as she heads to the elevator. I want to tell her that I'm Bette, that I'm my own person, but she's already long gone.

"Hey."

I turn, and see Alec. He's already dressed for rehearsal, in tights and a slim-fitting white T-shirt. It's only been a few weeks since I've seen him, but he looks different somehow. Bigger, more grown-up. Like the shift from student to apprentice has changed him already.

"Hey." I kind of want to run up and jump him, to snuggle in close and inhale the clean, woodsy scent that's always Alec. But he's keeping a safe distance, his eyes on me but wary, his ears pinkening as I watch him. He rubs the back of his neck with a palm, as if he's exhausted or uncomfortable.

I take a step closer, wishing I could ease it all away, close the distance between us. But he moves back, nearly ending up against the wall, and it tells me all I need to know. We're not the same, Alec and me. We're not a we at all anymore.

He smirks, sheepish. "You excited to get started?" I nod. "So weird, isn't it? The same, but not. Like we're tiny guppies."

"Yeah, among the sharks. When we used to be them." Well, me anyway. I almost have to grin at my silly joke. And it gets a smile from Alec finally. But he doesn't come closer, doesn't offer the hug I realize I've been hoping for.

"I should get moving," he says. "I need to warm up."

I almost ask him if he wants to stretch together. It feels so natural, so us. But he's already headed off toward Studio 3, where male soloists congregate. They shake his hand and jab at him, welcoming him to the fold like he belongs there. He's Alec Lucas, legacy, conservatory star.

So do I, I remind myself.

I go to the ABC finance office and fill out paperwork, which I should have done last week. But as excited as I was, I didn't want to come here before it was official. I fill out a tax form and an emergency card—I put down Adele and my mom. I get paperwork about my salary and health insurance. Signing my name makes me feel like an adult. I'll be paid. This is a job now, not just my passion. After I finish filling out the paperwork, they tell me to go ahead and get ready.

I take the elevator into the empty locker room near Studio 10. I slip out of the clothes that make me just a regular girl, and into my brand-new leotard, tights, leg warmers, and a ballet sweater for this big day. I make the most perfect and important bun in my hair, and dust my face with makeup. I open a brand-new tube of Chanel pink lipstick and glide it across my mouth. I look in the mirror. I definitely look the part of the music box ballerina.

There's humming in the hall outside the locker room. I peek

out. Mr. K walks toward the elevators. The back of his head bobs up and down, and there's a smug rhythm to his steps. My breath catches in my chest. Heat rushes just beneath my skin. I might fall over from the weight of it.

I step forward. "Mr. K."

He turns around. A smile overtakes his face. "Great to see you here at the company. I always knew that you'd make it far, Bette. You have what it takes."

"Which is what, exactly?"

"Willingness to devote your life to this. To do whatever you have to." He pats my shoulder like I'm a poodle in need of reaffirmation.

"Eleanor had the same passion."

Her name makes him recoil. He shifts his weight back and forth, and looks like he wants to scurry off somewhere. A company member walks down the hall. He bows to Mr. K, then slips into a nearby studio.

"Have a good rehearsal, Bette. I wish you well. Make us all proud."

I step in front of him. He tries to move left, then right. I block his path.

"You ruined her life," I whisper.

"Ballet can ruin many people—if you're not tough. But you don't have to worry about that." He looks me straight in the eyes. "You will be fine here. You will make yourself important because that is what this world is about. Those who aren't important don't stay. Those that are can stay no matter what they do. You will learn this. As I have."

He slips past me and into the elevator. I think about his words for a second, feeling defeated. Is what he said true? Is it all about legacies and bloodlines and paying for spots? Or can talent raise you up, as we've always been led to believe? Would I be here if my last name wasn't Abney? If that's true, then I have nothing to lose. But he definitely does. And eventually, he's going to have to pay. I'll make sure of that.

I'm the first one in the studio. It already feels like home. I sink into a stretch on the floor. I focus on making sure this is the best first ballet class I've ever had, better than my very first ballet class with Morkie. I hear feet and sit up, thinking company dancers will come in soon.

But it's Cassie, staring down at me. "Don't get too comfortable, Bette," Cassie says. "You won't be here for long."

I choose to ignore her, bending back down into a deep V.

"It should've been Gigi."

I don't get up, focusing on the floor and my breathing. "Well, you know what they say about karma." I pause. "Which means you'll be gone soon enough."

"I think it's you they'll be replacing."

I rise, nearly knocking her over in the process, and start to walk away. "I'm not going anywhere, so you can drop those fantasies."

She smiles, following right on my heels. "Did you find your phone?"

"How did you know I lost my phone?" My heart thumps. My fists ball up. I turn to face her, and she's grinning like a cat on a mouse.

"I told you that I'd never forget or forgive you for what you did to me." Her eyes flash with rage. "That I was willing to do whatever it took."

"You posted those pictures of Eleanor." I step close to her. "You're the reason my best friend tried to kill herself. You." I want to hit her in the mouth, to tear that smug grin off her face. I'm shaking.

"It's nothing worse than what you did to me." She shoves me back. "You weren't supposed to come back. You weren't supposed to still be here." Her face is bright red from the tip of her nose to the lobes on her ears. Like Alec's. "You should be banned from ballet and every company. I'll make sure of it."

"There you go again, ranting and raving like a crazy person. Someone should take care of that. Lock you up again." I look around innocently. "Where's your keeper, anyway? Did you finally scare Henri off?"

"You leave Henri out of this. He told me everything you did while I was away. How you tortured Gigi and the others. You're evil, Bette, truly."

"I'm evil? Why don't you worry about your boyfriend? He nearly got that poor girl killed, and he messed with Will's head. He's disgusting, you know? And while you were gone, he was all over me."

"Don't flatter yourself. I told him to get close to you." She laughs.

"Did you tell him to kiss me?" Her face falls, her eyes wild. "Because, let me tell you, he really enjoyed his mission. Couldn't keep his hands off me. Wonder if he was up to the same antics with Will. Maybe I'll call and—"

"You're lying."

"You and I both know I'm not." We're face-to-face now, so close I know she can smell my Chanel perfume and almost taste the lipstick I'm wearing. "Ask him about the mole on my rib. He'll know exactly where it is. Now, if you're done, I need to finish warming up."

She grabs my arm. "You didn't win! Adele and Eleanor suffered because of you—everything that happened to them is your fault. You took those pictures. I did Eleanor a favor by posting them. And you were supposed to fall through the trapdoor. Not Adele. It was all for you. How can you live with yourself?" She's scratching so hard, bloody red welts have come up on my arm. "If you think I'm anywhere near done, well, you're even stupider than—"

"Cassandra, hands off Bette this instant."

Cassie's eyes dart to the studio doorway.

Madame Dorokhova stands there, her hand to her throat, worried but composed. She's got a phone in her hand, and she dials a number quickly. "Damien. We need you in the girls' studio now."

45.

Gigi

"WHAT'S NEXT?" AUNT LEAH ASKS. We're sprawled out on Mama's couch, legs intertwined, watching a bunch of old movies. Mama's in the kitchen. I smell the smoky scent of barbecue wafting in from the patio. I spot my dad's shoulders through the window, leaning over the grill.

"I don't know. Maybe I'll wait for audition season for the San Francisco Ballet, or go up to Portland." I pull the blanket over my legs. "I don't want to think about it."

"Your mom wanted me to try to talk to you about it. Talk you into putting in some applications. Maybe community college, then apply in the fall for a university."

"I don't want to go to college yet."

"What is it about ballet?" She pushes her foot against mine.

I love to dance now more than ever, but there are moments when, if I'm honest with myself, I regretted going to the American Ballet Conservatory, and all that's happened. There are days since graduation where I still feel broken, and the whole thing feels pointless, not having earned an apprenticeship.

But then I think of the accident and what I went through to get it all back. It makes me want it that much more.

"You never danced," I say.

"Yes, but I do understand art." She goes off on a tangent about the art world.

I don't tell her that I feel like ballet is like a drug. A rush that always goes to my head—the zip of excitement and thrill that comes with every casting, every performance. I always want to bask in it, and when the rehearsal period is over or the performance curtain comes down for the last time, I want it all back again.

But ballet hurts sometimes. I wonder if the high is worth all the lows—all the criticisms, the chewed-up feet, the bloody blisters, the aches that never seem to go away. All the time wasted in front of the mirror, watching every bite that goes into your mouth and wondering where it might end up on your body, the thoughts that you aren't good enough.

I cut into Aunt Leah's story about museum curation. "I know you all don't understand it. I just need you—and especially Mama—to trust me. Can you tell her that for me? Work on her? I've only been home a week."

"Okay," she says, smiling.

I play on my phone to avoid talking about this anymore. A picture of June appears in my feed. She's at the barre at Salt Lake City Ballet. There are a string of congratulations. I take a large breath and type in a bunch of smiley faces. I'm happy for her. I am.

Mama comes in from the patio with trays of food. She hands both of us bowls of fresh summer corn, cut from the cob and cooked with tomatoes and okra. I smile up at her. The phone rings, and she scurries to answer it.

Aunt Leah and I turn back to the movie.

"Gigi," Mama calls from the kitchen. "It's for you."

"Tell Ella I'll call her later." She's been trying to get me to come out with her new friends, plotting another bonfire. But I haven't been up to it. Not just yet.

"It's not Ella," Mama says, waving the phone at me.

I grab the receiver. "Hello?"

"Gigi, it's Damien Leger from the American Ballet Company."

I hold my breath and pray that my heart slows, beats out a rhythm I know is safe. But it's not listening, thumping hard and fast in my chest. I'm instantly flushed and sweating.

"Gigi? You there?" he says.

"Yes, I'm here," I manage to squeak out.

"Well, I'm calling because we have another opening at the company. We lost an apprentice. We'd love to have you. You still interested?"

An excited panic rushes through me. My heart goes into overdrive, triggering my monitor, and I can already feel Mama panicking. I want to scream.

"Yes," I shout.

Mama rushes out of the kitchen. Aunt Leah pauses the movie. I feel frozen as Damien explains the process for me moving into the apprentice apartments and the paperwork I need to send to him. "Everything clear?" he asks.

"Yes. Yes." It's the only word I can seem to form. After he hangs up, I still stand there gripping the phone and waiting for my heart to slow down, waiting till I can breathe again, to tell them the good news.

A week later, I'm back in New York, back at Lincoln Center, back home. At the company building, the skylight windows let so much light into the locker rooms, I sit and bask in it for a minute, letting the sun warm my shoulders. I'm early for my first ballet class at the company. I run my fingers across principal and soloist members' lockers and trace over those important names: Becca Thomas, Samantha Haan, Svetlana Barkova, Angela Liao, Michelle Feldman. The space is three times larger than the one at the conservatory. Vanities are well stocked with bobby pins and hair spray.

The doors open. One of the corps de ballet members enters. I think her name is Maria. She smiles at me as she heads to the back to the showers. Other girls start to pour in. Ballet class will start in two hours. I pretend to keep getting dressed just to linger here and see who comes in. I don't know what to do with myself. The excitement bubbles up in me.

"Gigi!" Bette is right behind me.

"What are you doing here?" Her words echo around us, getting tangled in the warm lights and the hanging practice tutus and the clouds of hair spray of the dressing room. Her beautiful blue eyes flash with shock.

I smile. "I'm back."

"It's good to see you," she says, as other company members watch.

"I'm sure it is, Bette. I'm sure it is."

Acknowledgments

WE'VE LEARNED FROM OUR TIME in the trenches that publishing is all about family—the family you're born into, which helps you get to *The End* in the first place, and the family you make. We're so grateful to be surrounded by both kinds. To keep it short and sweet, we want to thank our own families, for all their love and support along the way, always.

To our pint-size powerhouse of an agent, Victoria Marini. Thank you for always taking the risk and making the leap with us. We couldn't do it without you.

We want to thank our HarperTeen family: our editors, publicist, the library and marketing team, and all the people behind the scenes who make this magic happen.

We can't forget the lovely early readers who helped us vet the manuscript through edits: Alla Plotkin, Ellen Oh, Kathryn Holmes, and Renee Ahdieh. Thank you so much for giving us your time to make sure we got things right.

We're also forever grateful for our publishing tribe: the We Need Diverse Books team, our cheerleaders, our confidantes, our safety net, and our shoulders to cry on. We're so proud to be a part of this very important mission.

And finally, last but certainly not least, our readers, who stuck around despite the cliffhangers and crazy antics. Thank you so much for reading.

BEING A PRIMA BALLERINA ISN'T ALL SATIN AND LACE. . . .

Don't miss the start of this drama-packed series!